WOMEN, WORK AND THE
EVERYDAY POLITICS OF WELFARE

Civil Society and Social Change

Series Editors: **Ian Rees Jones** and
Paul Chaney, Cardiff University,
Mike Woods, Aberystwyth University

This series provides interdisciplinary and comparative perspectives on the rapidly changing nature of civil society at local, regional, national and global scales.

Also available in the series:

Commons, Citizenship and Power
edited by **Filippo Barbera** and **Emma Bell**

Civil Society in an Age of Uncertainty
edited by **Paul Chaney** and **Ian Rees Jones**

Analysing the Trust–Transparency Nexus
by **Ian Stafford, Alistair Cole** and **Dominic Heinz**

Local Civil Society
by **Robin Mann, David Dallimore, Howard Davis, Graham Day** and **Marta Eichsteller**

City Regions and Devolution in the UK
by **David Beel, Martin Jones** and **Ian Rees Jones**

Civil Society and the Family
by **Esther Muddiman, Sally Power** and **Chris Taylor**

Civil Society through the Lifecourse
edited by **Sally Power**

The Foundational Economy and Citizenship
edited by **Filippo Barbera** and **Ian Rees Jones**

Putting Civil Society in Its Place
by **Bob Jessop**

Find out more about the new and forthcoming titles in the series:

policy.bristoluniversitypress.co.uk/
civil-society-and-social-change

WOMEN, WORK AND THE EVERYDAY POLITICS OF WELFARE
Work, care and civil society

Helen Blakely

First published in Great Britain in 2025 by

Policy Press, an imprint of
Bristol University Press
University of Bristol
1–9 Old Park Hill
Bristol
BS2 8BB
UK
t: +44 (0)117 374 6645
e: bup-info@bristol.ac.uk

Details of international sales and distribution partners are available at policy.bristoluniversitypress.co.uk

© Helen Blakely 2025

The digital PDF and ePub versions of this title are available open access and distributed under the terms of the Creative Commons Attribution-NonCommercial-NoDerivatives 4.0 International licence (https://creativecommons.org/licenses/by-nc-nd/4.0/) which permits reproduction and distribution for non-commercial use without further permission provided the original work is attributed.

British Library Cataloguing in Publication Data
A catalogue record for this book is available from the British Library

ISBN 978-1-4473-5364-5 paperback
ISBN 978-1-4473-5366-9 ePUB
ISBN 978-1-4473-5365-2 OA PDF

The right of Helen Blakely to be identified as author of this work has been asserted by her in accordance with the Copyright, Designs and Patents Act 1988.

All rights reserved: no part of this publication may be reproduced, stored in a retrieval system, or transmitted in any form or by any means, electronic, mechanical, photocopying, recording, or otherwise without the prior permission of Bristol University Press.

Every reasonable effort has been made to obtain permission to reproduce copyrighted material. If, however, anyone knows of an oversight, please contact the publisher.

The statements and opinions contained within this publication are solely those of the author and not of the University of Bristol or Bristol University Press. The University of Bristol and Bristol University Press disclaim responsibility for any injury to persons or property resulting from any material published in this publication.

Bristol University Press and Policy Press work to counter discrimination on grounds of gender, race, disability, age and sexuality.

Cover design: Clifford Hayes
Front cover image: Freepik/rawpixel

Contents

Acknowledgements vi

1	Introduction	1
2	The policy story	11
3	The Valleys	25
4	A space of activism	40
5	The girls	52
6	The interview	65
7	The working activists	79
8	Solidarities	93
9	Trajectories	104
10	Conclusion	118

Notes 127
References 129
Index 165

Acknowledgements

Above all, I am grateful to the people who shared a little of their lives over the course of the research, including the community and union organisers I met and spoke with, but most especially women who took the time to discuss their life stories with me. I owe a great deal to their generosity and insight. I am lucky to be part of the WISERD collective and to work with the support of the Economic and Social Research Council. Special thanks are owed to Huw Beynon for getting this work off the ground and to Ian Rees Jones for keeping it going. Also to Rhys Davies, Jean Jenkins and Kate Moles for their consistency, kindness and wisdom. I am in debt to the anonymous reviewer and to Paul Chaney for reading a draft of this manuscript; their suggestions and comments made the final manuscript much better. Thank you also to Policy Press and especially Jay Allan, Zoe Forbes, Laura Vickers-Rendall, Rupert Spurrier, Rich Kemp and Lee-Ann Ashcroft for their help and patience. And finally to Lorna, Andy, Mari and Ted for the quiet support over the years.

1

Introduction

> I've always said that they've saved me.
>
> Lifeline girl, 2021

A reunion, 2021

On a drizzly autumn morning on a housing estate in the upper reaches of the South Wales Valleys, a group of women gather to reminisce about an experience they share that dates back well over a decade. Each of them belonged to Lifeline, a community education project that ran on the estate between 2007 and 2014.[1] Referring to each other simply as 'the girls', their conversation is lively, and it is with remarkable consistency that their engagement with the project appears as a profound turning point in their lives. Lifeline came along at a time when they found themselves in conflict with a politics intent on limiting their lives, as successive governments attempted to coerce them into the 'crap at the bottom' of a chronically weak local labour market. In response, they sought the power to change their lives before they would be compelled to do so. On the shared ground of acute hardship and stigma, this small circle of women knitted together to change their circumstances. As they pushed themselves and each other towards a new life beyond just 'existing', a fruitful set of relationships grew through practices of mutual aid and support; taking a path towards a greater measure of security and advancement was daunting, only possible in the company of others. With the help of the project workers the women reshaped who they wanted to be and learnt how they might get there. For those with the strongest connection, Lifeline became a refuge of sorts, a space beyond the gaze of a punitive welfare state and the confines of domesticity where they could think and act a little more freely.

At this reunion, years after their involvement with the project, the women speak candidly about how their lives might otherwise have unfolded. Their sense of place in the world – their orientations to education, paid work and unpaid care – has altered. For them, the impression made by Lifeline runs long and deep.

The study

The social relations of everyday life – how paid work and unpaid care are distributed, organised and valued economically and culturally – are produced through welfare state settlements. Any settlement provides material support by redistributing wealth, but also constructs historically contingent interpretations and representations of who is eligible for that support and how best to regulate them. People who draw on social security to meet some or all of their needs must yield to the judgements of others regarding how they have lived so far and how they will live in the future (Young, 1995). For decades in the UK, a patriarchal logic shaped the post-war approach to social security, institutionalising the role of male breadwinner and anchoring women in the home as wives and mothers whose own rights to assistance derived from their marital status (Lister, 1990; Lewis, 2005). While social assistance for widows provided lifelong support, lone mothers were reliant on less generous, means-tested benefits, which were paid without condition for as long as their youngest child remained in education (Knijn et al, 2007). For the most part, these women were faced with a choice between full-time paid work or full-time unpaid care. An ideological emphasis on the importance of the latter meant most chose to remain at home.

This social contract between state and citizen has been radically reimagined and reconfigured in the contemporary era, as being a 'good' citizen has become increasingly synonymous with being in employment (King, 1999; Dwyer, 2004; 2016; Lewis and Giullari, 2005; Paz-Fuchs, 2008; Lister et al, 2011; Wright, 2011; 2023; Dwyer and Wright, 2014; Griggs et al, 2014; Reeves and Loopstra, 2017; Andersen, 2023). Since the late 20th century, the category of people deemed capable of and available for paid work has expanded; choices over whether, when and how to work and care were limited as securing benefits was made increasingly contingent on the fulfilment of a set of work-related requirements and conditions. In this social sorting, caregiving was recategorised as 'worklessness', and many women – including carers and those with long-term health conditions or disability – were incrementally repositioned as part of a wider cohort of 'workless' people required to either actively seek or be in work to be eligible for benefits (Andersen, 2023). Lone mothers were among the first categories of claimants targeted in an approach that devalued unpaid care, positioning it as a barrier to paid work that could be fully commodified (Lynch and Walsh, 2009; Deacon and Patrick, 2011; Whitworth and Griggs, 2013; Davies, 2015; Andersen, 2023; Wright, 2023). The long-standing legitimacy of the 'citizenship right to time to care' was curtailed and unpaid caring commitments were further hidden as more people were restricted in making the decision to engage with the labour market (Knijn and Kremer, 1997: 332; Rafferty and Wiggan, 2011; Davies, 2012; 2015; Whitworth and

Griggs, 2013; Johnsen and Blenkinsopp, 2018; Millar, 2019; Andersen, 2023; Wright, 2023). The normative assumption that all adults, including lone mothers, should work even if that work is of poor quality also sedimented with time (Crompton, 1999; 2002; 2008; Himmelweit and Sigala, 2004; Braun et al, 2008; Mahon, 2009; England, 2010; Park et al, 2010; Hall and O'Shea, 2013; Roantree and Vira, 2018). This reconfiguration gave new meaning to the 'obligations of citizenship', emphasising 'duties over rights' and 'sanction over support' (Wacquant, 2010: 201), as new mechanisms of welfare conditionality were introduced 'not to determine entitlement or to establish need, but to change behaviour' (Deacon, 2004: 912; Tyler, 2020).

These measures meant the 'austerity' project of the last decade neatly aligned with an already well-established neoliberal ideological platform that involved extending 'pro-capital' processes and dismantling social protections (Grimshaw and Rubery, 2012: 107; Farnsworth and Irving, 2018). The disciplinary apparatus of the state incorporated new forms of economic and cultural coercion that intensified over time and both hardship and stigma were cultivated with the intention of moving people off benefits (Tyler, 2020). Public consensus for reform was secured through the crafting of a political and cultural imaginary that positioned many more people as undeserving of social protection (Taylor, 1998; Rodger, 2003; Mau, 2004; Munch, 2012; Morris, 2019). These developments culminated in the most extensive application of welfare conditionality to date, directed at those in and out of paid work and underscored by the prospect of privation and shame (Dwyer and Wright, 2014; Wright and Dwyer, 2022; Wright, 2023).

The profoundly detrimental impacts of broader welfare retrenchment – accomplished through a multitude of cuts, squeezes and caps to social provisioning – were not evenly distributed, but concentrated in demographic and geographic clusters, including minoritised ethnic groups, families with children, lone parent families and post-industrial localities (Rabindrakumar, 2013; Rubery and Rafferty, 2013; Greer Murphy, 2017; McDowell, 2017; Millar and Bennett, 2017; De Henau, 2018; Emejulu and Bassel, 2018; Jensen, 2018; Reed and Portes, 2018; Reis, 2018; Watts and Fitzpatrick, 2018; Richards-Gray, 2020). That there are huge variations in the prosperity of places continues to be obvious and these spatialised expressions of inequality add complexity to analyses of formations of class, gender and race (Rees and Rees, 1980). The UK is 'one of the most regionally imbalanced countries in the industrialised world', with stark inequalities between and within localities (McCann, 2020: 256). Financial hardship increased because benefits provided less income and more limited income security (Bennett and Daly, 2014; Reis, 2018; Bennett, 2019), and food and warmth banks were being used by rising numbers of people as a 'last resort' to meet their most basic needs (Lambie-Mumford, 2017: 16). Women were hit hard because they were more likely to use public services and receive social security benefits related to caring roles (MacLeavy, 2011; Rubery and Rafferty, 2013; Durbin et al, 2017; De Henau, 2018; Reis, 2018). Commentators, grappling with how to describe the foreseeable and avoidable damage inflicted, have revived Engels' concept of 'social murder' (Grover, 2019; Medvedyuk et al, 2021). For Imogen Tyler, the process amounted to a 'planned social catastrophe' produced through the enclosure of our welfare commons, an effective 'fracking' of our public goods and forms of collective provisioning (2020: 4, 170).

Employment can be a route out for some, but not reliably for the most disadvantaged (Shildrick et al, 2010; McCollum, 2011; Newman, 2011; Shildrick et al, 2012; Orton, 2015; Thompson, 2015; D'Arcy and Finch, 2017; Hick and Lanau, 2018; Reis, 2018; Shildrick, 2018; Judge and Slaughter, 2020; Nightingale, 2020). Rates of in-work poverty have increased, and there is an association between recurrent poverty and poor-quality work (Shildrick et al, 2010; Davies, 2012). Women are more likely to be in non-standard forms of employment: short-term, low-wage, low-status, part-time, non-unionised jobs (Grant, 2009; Bowlby et al, 2010; Jensen and Møberg, 2017; Rafferty and Wiggan, 2017; Reis, 2018; Nicolaisen et al, 2019; Francis-Devine and Foley, 2024). Women are also more likely to need to take on multiple jobs and follow complex employment trajectories, remaining in poor-quality work but moving in and out of jobs or moving back and forth between benefits and wages, and enduring periods of unemployment and underemployment (McCollum, 2011; Rafferty and Wiggan, 2017; Shildrick, 2018; Smith and McBride, 2021) – part of a 'coerced flexible workforce continually in fear of losing their income' (Wright and Dwyer, 2022: 35). These forms of paid work are not so much 'a first rung on the ladder' as 'the only rung' (D'Arcy and Finch, 2017: 5; Millar and Ridge, 2020). Any economic gains tend to be 'very thin' (Millar, 2019: 96) and extremely 'hard won' (Millar and Ridge, 2017: 28). For women the challenge of sustaining caring commitments alongside paid work can be considerable, not least because formal provision, where available, is typically prohibitively expensive (Sidel, 2006; Orloff, 2009; MacLeavy, 2011; Wright, 2011; Ingold and Etherington, 2013; Bennett and Daly, 2014; Boyer et al, 2017; Greer-Murphy, 2017; Miller and Ridge, 2017; 2020; Power and Hall, 2018; Jupp et al, 2019; Hall, 2020). All of this makes embedding security challenging, and particularly so for lone mothers, who are 'vulnerable to even quite small shocks' to their circumstances (Ridge and Millar, 2011: 95; Millar and Ridge, 2017; 2020).

Still, any welfare resettlement is textured by fluidity, instability and ambiguity, subject to resistance and contestation. Alongside and through these developments, the geographies of the welfare state were also being remade: various processes of 'decentralisation, devolution, contracting and partnership' involved the dispersal of welfare governance to alternative spaces beyond the sites of traditonal street-level state bureaucracy (Clarke, 2004: 10; Haylett, 2003; Staeheli, 2003; Barnes and Prior, 2009; Clarke and Newman, 2009; Newman, 2012a; Beck, 2018). This activity encompassed a range of settings often not understood to be part of the welfare system, including those sponsored by the state and found within civil society – spaces in 'which emergent practices and alternative rationalities encounter dominant ruling relations' (Newman, 2012a: 15). Lifeline (2007–14) was one such space, an alternative site of street-level provisioning that emerged in a post-industrial community, partly in response to the expansion of the work imperative to lone parents under the New Labour government (1997–2010). This project can perhaps be best summed up as an experiment in pragmatic mitigation, an attempt to stave off the worst excesses of a restructuring welfare settlement by attempting to offer local people the chance to pursue their education and secure a 'good' job. I first met some of the women who took part in Lifeline in 2008, just as they were finding that 'getting by' on benefits was becoming a less tenable possibility and they were looking to secure a 'better' future for themselves. They went on to live through the further intensification of welfare conditionality driven by Conservative-led governments (2010–24) in the era of austerity before we spoke again in any great depth during 2021 and 2022. The account offered here spans this period of radical remodelling, charting welfare resettlement as it unfolded through the biographies of this small circle of women in the South Wales Valleys.

The approach draws on scholarship concerning the everyday politics of welfare, paid work, unpaid care and activism from a range of different fields, including sociology and social policy but also human geography and political theory. There are several conceptual touchstones that ground the account. Perhaps most fundamentally, it follows Carole Hanisch (2006) in the understanding that 'personal problems are political problems' and attempts to foreground the intimacies of everyday life with the understanding that '[s]mall facts speak to large issues' (Geertz, 1973: 23). C. Wright Mills' (1959: 14) assertion that the promise of sociology lies in exploring the interconnections between 'personal troubles' and 'public issues' is also helpful here. While personal troubles are concerned with our biography and the local environments that we are directly aware of, public issues involve those matters that transcend our immediate milieu, produced through the interconnections and entanglements that form the structures of historical society. Our interest lies at the intersections between these personal and public domains, in making linkages between biography and history to explore 'the public issue or problem contained in the private trouble' (Gane and Back, 2012: 405; Massey, 1984; Tyler, 2020). This involves tracing the flows of contemporary welfare restructuring – its logics of economic redistribution and cultural recognition – through the specificities and complexities of personal life. Of concern are the everyday politics of welfare, those interactions, practices and narratives that are grounded in the social fabric of place (Massey, 1991; 2005; Dyck, 2005; Compton-Lilly, 2017; Neale, 2021). Here, we draw on a body of literature that contributes direct, personal perspectives to these debates and discussions, from authors including Lynsey Hanley (2012), Linda Tirado (2014) and Lisa McKenzie (2015). Carol Smart's (2007) analysis of 'personal life' is also useful in its suggestion that our biographies are produced relationally, through our interactions and encounters with others. We are encouraged to understand biographical trajectories as interconnected and entwined through the connections and spaces we share (Hall, 2019a). Bren Neale (2021) makes the case for longitudinal, qualitative approaches that enable the granularity of personal biography to be explored as it intersects with wider dynamics of social-historical change and continuity. Referring to analyses that bring to light these processes, she suggests they can generate insights into the stasis and flux of unfolding lives shaped by the consistency of recurrent and steady conditions but also the instability of more volatile or disruptive forces (Flowerdew and Neale, 2003; Corden and Millar, 2007; Crow and Lyon, 2011; Goodwin and O'Conner, 2015; Neale and Davis, 2016; Millar and Ridge, 2017; 2020).

The research developed through traditional ethnographic work within the Lifeline setting itself and, by extension, the wider community, as well as biographical interviews with the women who took part in the project and its workers. The first wave of fieldwork took place between 2007 and 2010, and this was followed by a second wave during 2021 and 2022.[2] At first, ethnographic work involved spending time with the residents, engaging with the rhythms of daily life, mostly through the community development work on the estate. This included participating in a range of activities: walking in the nearby National Park; potting plants in the local, public greenhouses; frying onions for hotdogs at a community 'funday'; playing basketball, football, rounders and bingo; volunteering with the cinema club, an after-school club and a life skills class; attending biology and cookery classes; and organising a seminar series with contributions from academics from a local university. This was complemented by 30 interviews with people who either worked or lived on the estate and a further 8 interviews with policy makers responsible for community development in Wales. A more intensive phase of ethnographic work with Lifeline itself followed, with regular and frequent visits to the project for a sustained period of six months during the academic year of one cohort of learners. At that time, the study's core participants reliably consisted of 10 of the Lifeline 'girls' and two project workers.

Opportunities for spontaneous ethnographic conversations were numerous and conducted in a variety of situations, most often during tea and lunch breaks at the community centre within which the project was based. But moments opened up at other times as well, including various celebrations, like the 'graduation ceremony' at the end of the project's academic year, family days out as part of the project's 'summer school', and there were also occasional invitations to spend time with the women at home. This ethnographic work laid the ground for biographical interviews as the first wave of research drew to a close (Hemmerman, 2010). These interactions were extensions of our earlier ethnographic conversations, intended to be open to what mattered to the women and to draw out accounts of their lives that looked to the past and present but also to the future. How this collective made sense of the world through various 'styles of telling', 'stories of experience' and 'ways of knowing' was of interest here (Hatch and Wisniewski, 1995; McAdams, 2008; Riessman, 2008a; 2008b; Plummer, 2019).

A further wave of biographical interviewing took place over a decade later in a series of visits to the Valleys during 2021 and 2022. The revisit provided an opportunity to boost the numbers a little with women from different Lifeline cohorts (between 2007 and 2012), and a total of 18 learners and 5 workers took part. The approach allows us to attend to the everyday politics of welfare through more extensive biographical trajectories and historical processes (Millar, 2020; Neale, 2021). These later conversations allow us to consider the ways in which their lives unfolded over time, but also how biographical narrations of the past, present and future are told and retold, refined and overwritten with different suppressions and emphases, with the passing of time (Neale and Flowerdew, 2003; Halbwachs, 2020).

Tracing some of the women was straightforward, possible either through the reunions that were organised periodically or via word of mouth. Both avenues spoke to the sustained, closely bonded relationships between many of them. The workers, for their part, remained extremely protective of the women they cared for even in the years following their engagement through the project. On more than one occasion a worker took the time to advise me of 'how troubled their lives were' and 'how far the girls had come'. These were gentle reminders to take care, a variation of the 'ethical talk' that tends to circulate during fieldwork and suggestive of the need to reflect on the women's participation in the research and its limits (Birch and Miller, 2002: 99). For some, taking part did involve sharing the accumulations of injury and harm they had endured. The passage of time appears to have made some difference here. Our more recent conversations seemed to invite greater intimacy; the disclosures of deeply concerning and harrowing experiences were more common and more detailed. Perhaps with a sense of distance, some experiences could be more firmly relegated to the past and spoken of more freely (Burton et al, 2015). Over the course of the study, the project workers acted as mentors for each of these interactions. The quality of the research relationship can be attributed to the store of trust the women placed in them, which I was able to borrow from a little. They had taken the time to build solid connections, listening and responding to the women with kindness and compassion. I attempted to offer the same (Hall, 2017; 2020).

For clarity it is also worth noting that the descriptors in circulation among those who took part in the study are consciously adopted. The women who took part in the project are on occasion referred to as 'the girls' because that's how they referred to themselves and each other; they also tended to use the term 'single parent' or 'single mother' rather than 'lone parent'. Similarly, the place where they lived is referred to as the 'estate' here because that's how residents commonly referred to the place when they weren't using its name, even though the term can be felt as 'a bruise in the form of a word' (Hanley, 2012: 7). The words 'poverty' and 'poor' are used only rarely because the women didn't tend to use this terminology. Only once, and years later when her substantive circumstances had changed, did one woman remember 'feeling poor' when she was 'getting by' on benefits. The popular descriptions of social assistance have changed over time and notably since the Department of Social Security was supplanted by the Department for Work and Pensions in 2001. On the estate 'the Social' slowly came to be referred to as 'the Jobcentre' (though both terms were in use). Similarly the term 'welfare' displaced 'social security', especially among policy makers and local officials (and so each of these terms is used at various times here). The women tended to refer simply to 'benefits' when describing the cash income provided by the state, and while the term 'social security' can jar given the lack of support the contemporary system provides, the tendency here is to make reference to social security benefits (Shildrick, 2018). Finally, the South Wales Valleys is referred to as it is colloquially known: 'the Valleys'.

The next chapter sketches the 'causal story' (Stone, 1989) of contemporary welfare resettlement – its rhetorical apparatus – exploring how a public issue was narrated, collectives blamed and the means of solving the 'problems' established. In Chapter 3, attention turns to the Valleys and the estate itself. Here the people who took part in the study are situated more firmly, through those 'shared meanings' that help 'shape who they are by virtue of where they are' (Beynon et al, 1994: 5). Of interest here are the specificities of place, the distinctive patternings of continuity and change that have unfolded over time in the Valleys and on the estate, and their linkages to wider social forces (Massey, 1994; 2004). Then, in Chapter 4, Lifeline is introduced as a 'site of contestation' (Newman, 2001: 138), an experiment in pragmatic mitigation, textured by both acquiescence and dissent to prevailing welfare policy narratives, frameworks and practices (Clarke, 2004). This is followed in Chapter 5 by an account of the women's lives prior to and during their participation in Lifeline. Conversations at the time they were directly engaged with the project and those of more than a decade later are drawn on to attend to how these women understood their place in the world. Chapter 6 attempts to cast light on the ways in which political discourses are embedded in 'social practices, codes of behaviour, institutions and constructed environments' (Sayer, 2000a: 44; 2000b; Wright, 2012; Morris, 2019; 2020). The focus here is on the Jobcentre's welfare eligibility interview, exploring the ways in which the Lifeline women and local activists managed and narrated these interactions. Discussion in Chapter 7 turns to the activity of Lifeline's 'support workers', who are understood as worker-activists here, moving 'within and against the state' to resist the worst excesses of intensifying welfare conditionality (Craig and Mayo, 1995: 105; Newman, 2012a; 2012b).

Later chapters return to looking more closely at the girls themselves. In Chapter 8, we consider the extent to which their activity – their practices of care and commoning – can be understood as quietly political and how Lifeline itself can be understood as a space of a 'less obvious', 'quiet activism' (Horton, 2016: 352; Martin et al, 2007; Horton and Kraftl, 2009; Hall, 2020). We then explore their longer, more extensive biographical trajectories in some depth in Chapter 9, again returning to how this small group of women saw themselves, and their changing orientations to education, paid work and unpaid care. The final chapter draws the threads of the account together to offer some reflections relating to the future development of the welfare state.

In conclusion here, and mindful of the opportunities and constraints presented by my own good fortune, my biography bears some scrutiny (England, 1994; Williams, 2021). At the very least, it seems important to share something of how I came to meet and work with the women of Lifeline. I think the impetus for this work lies in the stories told and retold by the women in my family: a great-grandmother's hatred of Churchill for sending police and troops to tackle striking miners in Rhondda in South Wales in the 1910s; a grandmother's hopes for an apprenticeship as a hairdresser dashed when the money put down had to be picked up again the next week, as the depression hit South Wales mining communities in the 1930s; and a mother's path to teaching the children of Windrush in 1960s London, the free school lunches she ate in return for playground duty and the free milk the children drank each day. These stories and others, stretching back over a century, tell of struggle and hardship, limit and constraint, but also the advancements and expansions of a welfare state that even despite its recent retreat continues to reach far deeper into our lives than most imagine (Hills, 2017). My motivation, intent and privilege are a product of these experiences of struggle, hardship, limit and constraint, advancement and expansion, and the symbolic and material gains generations of working-class people secured over the course of the 20th century. This account of contemporary resettlement explores the politics of welfare through the encounters, practices and narratives of everyday life (Smith, 2005; Wacquant, 2008; Wacquant et al, 2014). The contribution shares insights into the importance of the personal, the fabric of place and the entwinement of material and cultural processes for analyses of class and gender formations (Fraser, 1995; 1999; Skeggs, 1997; O'Brien and Penna, 1998; Williams, 2021). Elements of ethnography, biography and history are combined in an attempt to draw the lives of the women together as a collective living in the post-industrial landscape of the South Wales Valleys. This is not to suggest their personal circumstances and experiences were congruent or uniform; rather, it is an expression of how this circle of women saw themselves, through ideas of solidarity and mutual aid.

2

The policy story

> Aspirations cannot be raised in the abstract.
> Community development worker, 2009

A welfare regime is created in part through its discursive apparatus. The circulation of persuasive narratives is key to policy making, and any policy begins with the framing of a social development as a societal concern (Stone, 1989; Stevens, 2011). This is accomplished through the narration of 'a causal story', which defines a public issue by attributing blame and assigning responsibility to individuals or collectives and claiming the right to remediate by imposing burdens or sanctions to 'stop the harm' (Stone, 1989: 282). In this way, civic virtue is defined, institutionally circumscribed and embedded in a broad framework of public norms (Morris, 2019; 2020). Any welfare resettlement is produced through and productive of our changing commitments to or investments in paid work and unpaid care, with a clear moral dimension defining what it means to be a 'good' citizen and who should work and who should care, as well as how and why this should happen. The story of the contemporary welfare state is, in a sense, an old one; an imaginary seeded in earlier iterations, revised and retold over the course of decades if not centuries and produced through a set of deeply embedded orientations towards inequalities and poverty (Ferge, 1997; Davies, 2012; Walker and Chase, 2013; Hall, 2021). One traceable thread involves the strategic narration of a symbolically charged 'common sense', constructed through representations of deservingness that describe a set of apparently well-established facts and enrol a definition of the 'undeserving' that is tied to ideas of voluntary idleness (Hall and O'Shea, 2013; Jensen and Tyler, 2015; Jensen, 2018). Government through the production of stigma – its cultivation to draw distinctions between the decent and dutiful and the 'undeserving' – plays a pivotal role in rationing social security. Imogen Tyler (2020) convincingly argues that stigma is put to work as a technology to build consent and consensus in the process of welfare state resettlement (Scambler, 2018). Societal divisions are made through cultural representations, which in turn justify any associated economic implications; in other words, a series of value judgements classify people and places and make them subject to particular policies and associated forms of social control and discipline.

The story of the post-war settlement positioned the experience of unemployment as a societal disservice and understood social security benefits as a form of compensation to replace the earnings of those out of, or unable to, work (Titmuss, 1967/2000). For those able to work, the receipt of social security benefits was conditional on their involuntary unemployment; that is, their incapacity to seek, be available for and accept paid work (Trickey and Walker, 2001; Griggs and Evans, 2010; Watts et al, 2014; Dwyer, 2016; Fletcher and Wright, 2018; Andersen, 2023; Wright, 2023). A cornerstone of this system presupposed that men would earn a 'family wage', on which women and children should and could depend. The National Insurance Act 1946 meant husbands made contributions to insurance-based unemployment benefits on behalf of their wives through their paid employment. Any associated benefits were paid to husbands on behalf of wives when their husbands were unemployed. Women were written into the settlement through their caring roles in the domestic sphere, principally in terms of their roles as wives and mothers, reinforcing their economic dependence on men (Pascall, 2002; Andersen, 2023; Wright, 2023). (The additional Family Allowance payments that mothers received directly for homemaking and child-rearing fell far short of securing their economic independence.) In the case of lone mothers, social security eligibility did not rest on the expectation that they would actively seek and secure work; rather, they were entitled to benefits by virtue of their parental status. With the exception of widows, the National Assistance Act 1948 provided lone mothers with less generous, means-tested benefits until the youngest child reached 16, or 18 if still in full-time education (Knijn et al, 2007; Haux, 2013; Johnsen, 2014). This settlement positioned lone mothers as an 'underclass of women ... directly connected to the state as claimants rather than indirectly as men's dependents' (Pateman, 1989: 196; Lewis, 1997). Still, the social contract at least partially recognised the societal contribution made by mothers, including lone mothers, as caregivers (Daly and Rake, 2003; Pateman, 2004; Orloff, 2009; Davies, 2015). A measure of unconditional social security was granted (Lister, 1990; Orloff, 2009; Daly, 2011; Davies, 2015), even if the value of social reproduction – the care beyond the market that sustains households and communities and on which economic production 'free rides' – was hidden (Fraser, 2016: 101; Pateman, 1989; Skeggs, 2014).

Over the course of the 20th century, as women entered the labour market in growing numbers and the role of the male breadwinner diminished (Crompton, 1999), the paradox at the heart of women's claim to citizenship became increasingly apparent. Women were presented with a choice Carole Pateman (1989) describes as either becoming a 'lesser citizen' and assuming domestic and care duties within the home or becoming a 'lesser man' and accepting relatively poor-quality paid work in the labour market. It was also increasingly evident that a welfare settlement built on the premise that marriage would provide women with sustained economic protection over the life course was not borne out by experience (Andersen, 2023; Wright, 2023). The historical prevalence of lone motherhood is difficult to discern accurately, but in the last decades of the 20th century, with the collection of more robust national statistics, lone mother families appeared to be growing 'faster than at any time in history' (Thane and Evans, 2012: 3). And many of these women were choosing to become 'lesser citizens'; their employment rate was falling in comparison to partnered mothers, lower in the 1990s than it had been in the 1970s (Gregg and Harkness, 2003). In response, successive governments intent on 'rectifying' this 'public issue' expanded and intensified welfare conditionality, linking eligibility for social security benefits to various work-related behavioural requirements.[1]

Towards the end of the 20th century, the Conservative government (1979–97) reformed the criteria for claiming unemployment benefits to ensure that fewer people were eligible. A new set of work-related requirements for unemployed claimants was introduced, notably through the eligibility criteria for Jobseeker's Allowance (Trickey and Walker, 2001; Watts et al, 2014; Dwyer, 2016; Wright, 2023), which was widely regarded as 'a watershed moment in the history of UK benefits system' (Andersen, 2023: 39). Securing entitlement to this benefit involved attendance at fortnightly interviews at the Jobcentre and demonstrations of availability for and amenability to paid work (Freedland and King, 2003; Watts et al, 2014; Fletcher and Wright, 2018). The approach established the framework for the reforms of the subsequent New Labour government (1997–2010) (Trickey and Walker, 2001; Griggs et al, 2014; Fletcher and Wright, 2018; Andersen, 2023; Wright, 2023), with the New Deal for Lone Parents, introduced in 1997, one early indicator of a changing policy landscape characterised by 'creeping conditionality' (Dwyer, 2004; Dwyer and Ellison, 2009). This development repositioned lone parents as 'workless', signalling the end of their special status as carers, cutting back their social rights and drawing them into a disciplinary regime (Trickey and Walker, 2001; Griggs et al, 2014; Dwyer, 2018; Andersen, 2023; Wright, 2023). At first, their engagement was voluntary, with support consisting of employment advice and information provided through specialist personal advisors. In time, these 'work-focused interviews' became mandatory, rolled out nationally in 2002 for new claimants with older children. Framed as helping lone parents to understand that paid work was the best route for them, ostensibly these interactions were intended to encourage people to lead more fulfilling lives, of which paid employment was the decisive feature (Wright, 2011; 2023; Whitworth and Griggs, 2013; Johnsen, 2014). This was 'targeted support for those who need it most', 'those traditionally assumed to be outside the labour market' (Department for Work and Pensions, 2006a: 20), and 'employment action plans' were formulated to educate people 'about the opportunities available to them and the benefits of work' (Department for Work and Pensions, 2006b: 54). The suggestion was that some people were simply not aware of the financial rewards that the labour market offered, had become content with their 'dependency' on the state and did not understand their responsibility as citizens to contribute to wider society.

Then, two independent reports (Freud, 2007; Gregg, 2008) gave rise to a further phase of reform, and welfare conditionality measures expanded and intensified (Etherington and Daguerre, 2015). By 2008, a lone parent's entitlement to social security remained in place until the youngest child was 12 years of age, and in 2009 the threshold was reduced again to the age of 10 (Millar and Ridge, 2020). At this point, people were recategorised as 'jobseekers' and were required to 'sign on' every fortnight and demonstrate they were available for and actively seeking paid work (Petrongolo, 2009; Haux, 2013). Those with younger children were required to participate in work preparation activities (Wright, 2011). Measures addressing low pay, childcare shortages and child poverty, particularly in deprived localities, were introduced alongside these measures. Best understood as social investments 'grafted' onto the pursuit of an already well-established neoliberal agenda (Grimshaw and Rubery, 2012: 105), these reforms are often cited as examples of New Labour's intention to use a combination of enabling and disciplinary measures to support those who did want to work but struggled in the face of low wages and poor childcare provision (Millar, 2008; Ridge and Millar, 2011; Wright, 2023).[2]

The Coalition government's (2010–15) Work Programme launched in 2011, and the Welfare Reform Act 2012 and the later Conservative government's (2015–24) Welfare Reform and Work Act 2016 saw conditionality expanding ubiquitously (Dwyer and Wright, 2014).[3] Of far greater intensity and scope, these developments went further in abolishing the traditional distinctions between those classified as exempt from and those subject to work-related welfare conditionality requirements irrespective of personal circumstance (Dwyer, 2016; Beck, 2018; Morris, 2019; 2020; Andersen, 2023; Wright, 2023). This involved the introduction of a form of workfare, Universal Credit, a household means-tested benefit for people in and out of paid work, intended to mirror an employment contract and so manufacture overt displays of employability (Friedli and Stearn, 2015; Wright, 2016; Millar and Bennett, 2017; Beck, 2018). Tightening conditionality included compulsory full-time job search as a matter of default, compulsory training and (unpaid) work placements, as well as emotional, cognitive and psychometric testing and psychological referrals (Friedli and Stearn, 2015; Wright, 2023). All of this was managed through intrusive forms of surveillance and financial sanctions for non-compliance, which were embedded in the design of the programme (Rafferty and Wiggan, 2011; Friedli and Stearn, 2015; Wright, 2016; Millar and Bennett, 2017; Beck, 2018). The aggressive application of conditionality involved sanctioning of unprecedented severity; any perception of non-compliance with the established requirements of a claim could result in the reduction or complete withdrawal of benefits (Dwyer and Wright, 2014; Wright and Dwyer, 2022; Andersen, 2023; Wright, 2023).

Over this period, a lone parent's entitlement to social security by virtue of their parental status was curtailed further through changes to the point at which they were subject to full-time job search requirements without protection from sanctions – in 2010 it was when their youngest child turned seven, in 2012 it was age five, and in 2016 it was age three (Johnsen and Blenkinsopp, 2018; Millar and Ridge, 2020; Andersen, 2023; Wright, 2023).[4] Even those lone parents claiming benefits while in paid work were subject to forms of conditionality and could be required to seek and secure better wages, additional hours or more than one job. The system produced a new kind of 'coerced worker-claimant' (Wright and Dwyer, 2022). In the absence of specialist support, lone parents had to demonstrate they were actively seeking and available for work through a set of basic and generic tools and standard interventions (Graham and McQuaid, 2014; Andersen, 2023; Wright, 2023). Measures tailoring requirements to personal circumstances and any right to an easement of requirements due to their status as caregiver – for example, the possibility of a reduction in the number of hours dedicated to seeking work in response to a lack of childcare, or the possibility of an alternative payment arrangement in response to personal experience of domestic abuse, ill health or housing precarity – were also eroded (Cain, 2016; Andersen, 2020; 2023; Wright, 2023).[5]

This radical resettlement was accomplished in part by leveraging stigmatising misrepresentations of the 'workless' to create social division (Tyler, 2020). A set of interconnected ideas – a new conventional wisdom coalescing around the work imperative – displaced the principle of providing social security to meet need (Shildrick et al, 2010; Wright, 2011; 2012; 2016; Shildrick and MacDonald, 2012; Tyler, 2013; Dean, 2014; Gill and Orgad, 2018). Most fundamentally, the causal story crafted to narrate (and legitimate) these developments tied claiming benefits to a morally corrupt set of personal values and behaviours, rather than any sense of personal misfortune or structurally embedded societal inequality. A too generous post-war settlement had generated moral decay. Those entitled to benefits were culpable failures in moral self-governance, and poverty was a matter of personal deficit; taking paid work was an act of redemptive citizenship. These claims were embedded in a broader myth of meritocracy, whereby the public issue at hand – some sense of some kind of pathological 'dependency' – was emphatically framed as a matter of individual responsibility, motivation and choice (Littler, 2017). A cast of unambiguously blameworthy characters were integral to the storyline, a foil to the 'good' and the 'normal' people who were working hard enough. The working-class single mother was among those positioned as morally bankrupt, and, to be specific, the 'unemployed teenager who became pregnant just to qualify for a council home and live on benefits' (Thane and Evans, 2012: 4; Tyler, 2008; Jensen, 2018). While she might have been hard to find, the circulation of this representation of a contemptible 'grotesque and comic figure' was pernicious and pervasive in both the cultural and the political economies (Tyler, 2013: 154; Jensen and Tyler, 2015). Languishing on benefits, she was part of the unproductive residuum, a deficient and self-interested 'underclass', a 'feckless' threat to our collective morality and a material drain on our resources, someone intent on 'playing' and 'milking' the system (Kiernan, 1998; Haylett, 2003; Phoenix, 2013; Shildrick, 2018). While changing social norms saw an increase in the numbers of lone mother families and a broader acceptance of a variety of family forms, deeply scored gender, sexuality and family ideologies meant that these families continued to be positioned as a 'social risk', marginalised as an exceptional category in the 'moral panic' of our welfare imaginary (Roseneil and Mann, 1996; Kiernan et al, 1998; Knijn et al, 2007; May, 2008; 2010; Phoenix, 2013). Through these mythic distortions, lone motherhood became a 'taxonomic category' with causal explanatory power, as with little interrogation of the category's structure or substance, a process of homogenisation hid the variety of social positions that lone mothers occupied (Duncan and Edwards, 1999; May, 2010). Alongside these developments, the moralising tones of a gendered discourse of disgust and revulsion (Tyler, 2013; Zartler, 2014) spilled over into working-class family life when parenting itself became a public issue (Jensen, 2018). While state surveillance and regulation of working-class family life has a long history, by the end of the 20th century the social policy apparatus mobilising ideas of 'good' parenting went into overdrive (see Crossley, 2017; Jensen, 2018).[6] Representations of somehow intrinsically dysfunctional, 'broken' families saturated social policy as the hallmarks of 'a deficit understanding of what poor families offer their children' (Treanor, 2020: 199; Gillies, 2005; Jensen, 2018). Professionals were enrolled in large number to help 'make good' the deficiencies and damages of 'poor' parents (Lawler, 2017; Jensen, 2018).

These kinds of narratives – the positioning of those drawing on social security as feckless and shiftless – were key pillars of the causal story of austerity politics, and its ideologically 'cost-cutting' justifications for the wholesale contraction of collective social provision (Grimshaw and Rubery, 2012; Wright, 2016; 2023; Farnsworth and Irving, 2018; Morris, 2019; 2020). Deep cuts to public spending, including targeted measures of taxing, capping and freezing social security benefits, were anchored to increasingly antagonistic representations of claimants. Our perceptions of the activity of the welfare state were narrowed to the allocation of cash benefits, to the omission of its broader public service offering, which encompasses systems of social care, health, education, housing and more (Hills, 2017). Not only were those eligible for social security benefits a threat to our collective morality, but the costs of 'dependency' were related to global economic instability, financial crisis and recession (MacLeavy, 2011: 355; Wiggan, 2012; 2024; Jensen and Tyler, 2015; Tyler, 2020).

The accomplishment of welfare restructuring through representations of dysfunction and deviance was not confined to particular types of people during this period. A process of spatialising difference was also prevalent in an entwined story that consisted of representations of disadvantaged and marginalised neighbourhoods as containers of problematic populations (Hanley, 2012; McKenzie, 2012; 2015; Skeggs, 2014; Crossley, 2017). The circulation of phantasmal projections of particular housing estates as 'dreadful enclosures' of 'moral inferiority' and 'social pathology' denoted that some places were in desperate need of fixing (Walter, 1977: 155; Hanley, 2012; McKenzie, 2012; 2015; Tyler, 2013). Policy produced through and productive of these developments involved place-oriented approaches to social provisioning, which extended to the establishment of street-level employment services. This included interventions contracted out to organisations in the private sector, like Working Links, which ran a programme on the estate that forms the setting for this research, and in communities across the Valleys. Working Links (Employment) Limited was an outsourcing subcontractor established in 2000 that specialised in the provision of employability services on behalf of successive governments, including various New Deal initiatives and the later Work Programme. By 2012, the company's turnover had grown to £123 million (Peacock, 2012), and it had gained some notoriety following a report that it had referred more cases for financial sanctions against welfare recipients than any other supplier (Boffey, 2012). Despite its status as a subcontractor, Working Links itself outsourced its own contracts, including to a company that reportedly referred to benefits recipients as 'LTBs', or 'lying thieving bastards' (Williams, 2013).

Scholars have pointed to the dispersal of welfare governance to various spaces through contracting to the private sector, but also through processes of decentralisation, partnership and devolution (Newman, 2001; Clarke, 2004; Beck, 2018). Beyond entities like Working Links, the flow of governance was evident in the often less visible geographies of local provisioning found within civil society (Staeheli, 2003). In the UK, state-sponsored, community-oriented interventions of this kind date back to 1969, when the Community Development Projects became the 'largest ever government funded social action experiment', created to address the persistence of deep inequalities (Loney, 1983: 1).

These projects were intended to improve local and central government support of deprived communities in the Valleys and elsewhere, and were conceived 'as a means of creating more responsive local services and of encouraging self help' (Loney, 1983: 3; Loney and Banting, 1979). The teams on the ground analysed local issues in terms of 'structural inequalities and the uneven distribution of power, wealth and resources inherent in capitalist societies', refuting assessments that claimed 'deprivation was attributable ... [to] a prevailing "culture of poverty" ' (Day, 2015: 67). The experiments concluded in 1976 and the approach went into abeyance until the mid-1990s, when its revival across the devolved nations of the UK, Europe and elsewhere was at the forefront of policies designed to address inequalities (Popple, 1996; Barnes et al, 2004; Grimshaw, 2011; Nicholls et al, 2025). At that time, as in its earlier iteration, policy was narrated through the premise that local communities were well placed to devise the solutions to local issues, in recognition of the contribution that might be made by day-to-day, experiential expertise. Within new spaces and structures of participatory policy making and delivery, residents could act collectively to remedy the deficiencies of mainstream policy interventions (Craig and Mayo, 1995; Cornwall and Gaventa, 2000; Mayo, 2004; Adamson, 2010). 'Community' and its adjuncts are nebulous terms in popular usage and tend to be undertheorised in academic analyses (Studdert and Walkerdine, 2016). Still, the 'community' was an integral, albeit ambiguous, actor in approaches that stressed the importance of 'community capacity building', 'community empowerment', 'community regeneration' and more; concepts subject to a multiplicity of definitions and interpretations, practical applications and implications (Craig and Mayo, 1995; Bennett et al, 2000). The connotations of these concepts are benign, suggestive of democratic renewal (Grimshaw, 2011) and a kind of folk politics characterised by small-scale and authentic responses to public issues (Srnicek and Williams, 2015), and for politicians, this charming imprecision can be useful. Regardless, the resurgence of this place-oriented model of intervention proved critical for the inception and longevity of the Lifeline project, which was supported by the European Social Fund's EQUAL Community Initiative and by the Welsh Government's Communities First programme.

The EQUAL Community Initiative was launched in 2001 with the aim of promoting innovative solutions to a range of issues, including the perceived deficits of economically inactive groups. Under the auspices of the European Employment Strategy,[7] EQUAL sought to identify experimental approaches to labour market policy through new forms of cooperation between local stakeholders, including local and regional authorities, education bodies, employers and civil society organisations. Housing estates in the Valleys and elsewhere became 'laboratories' or 'testing grounds' for new ways of working

(European Commission, 2000: 2–3). In the UK, the implementation of EQUAL focused squarely on employability. This meant the qualities of individuals – their capabilities, behaviours and attitudes relating to paid work and skills, but also their expectations regarding working conditions and likely rewards – were of primary concern. In the case of Lifeline, the pilot phase of the project was funded to examine the personal development and support necessary for local people to progress from unemployment or unskilled work to skilled jobs in health and social care.

The revitalisation of the community development tradition in Wales was seen by policy makers as part of this wider turn, as 'a kind of spirit of the age sort of thing' (policy maker, 2009). The Welsh variant, Communities First, was a community-led regeneration programme rolled out in 2001 to target the most disadvantaged and marginalised localities:

> We weren't inventing new stuff here. We were very much picking up on a very broad literature and quite dominant themes emerging within social policy theory itself and ... it was a very dominant paradigm. I think there was a paradigm shift somewhere in the early nineties that said community empowerment is of critical importance. (Policy maker, 2008)

Its aim was to provide an opportunity for residents and those delivering services in localities 'to examine the realities of poverty and to learn and work together to address it' (Welsh Assembly Government, 2007: 1). Again, the 'voice' of the community would be heard through forms of partnership working between local people, public bodies, civil society organisations and the private sector – structures that were expected to materialise from and strengthen existing community development traditions (Adamson, 2010). Early policy statements emphasised that the programme 'does not prescribe a solution but sets out a vision for the future' (Welsh Assembly Government, 2001: 2). As elsewhere, this involved drawing 'the community' into taking responsibility for developing and implementing solutions emphasising innovation, experimentation and evaluation, and a broader reshaping of civil society (Newman, 2001).

Many working in the community development field in Wales at the time felt the signature lack of prescription and precision inherent to the programme dogged Communities First throughout its implementation, especially as its articulation suggested that community-based solutions could be found for structurally grounded issues (Corkey and Craig, 1978; Craig, 2007). Interrogating this argument, and given the scale of the issues facing the Valleys, one policy maker explained: 'The phrase 'communities identify their priorities', it was like a mantra. ... If you think through the implications of that ... it has some inbuilt contradictions ... the logic of that is to imply something well beyond what Communities First is able to deliver' (policy maker, 2008). They went on to explain 'you can only think outside the box as far as the state will or maybe can allow'. In this environment, and as entitlements to social security were curtailed and welfare conditionality intensified across the UK, the principles of community regeneration and empowerment became entangled with the representations of the wider workfare imaginary. In lieu of structural models of intervention, which would require a far more extensive commitment from the state, policy makers working in the community development sphere in Wales drew the conclusion that 'help[ing] people to be job-ready' was one clear and 'measurable' way Communities First could 'actually add value'; the programme could 'reawaken … that thirst for work, which has traditionally characterised these communities'. Policy makers advocated for employability initiatives that would lead to behavioural change, often through often psychologised interventions that associated unemployment with personal deficit and dependency; the lack of 'that thirst for work'. Here, some clearly felt there was little discursive room to manoeuvre; that you couldn't 'argue for getting people back into work without seeming to be in the camp of people who want to take their benefits off them'. It was widely felt that they had 'to live in that world of welfare to work to a large extent'.

As the 'spirit of the age' shifted, the focus on 'community' fell away from the governing agenda across the UK, as the Conservative-led governments' (2010–2024) austerity project stripped out and down spaces of local, community-based provisioning (Nicholls et al, 2025). Over time, the aims of the Communities First programme also became more circumscribed; its contribution lay in building human capital for economic activity, with the implication that the Valleys' communities were increasingly positioned as pools of untapped labour. Later iterations of the programme, in 2009 and 2011, each ceded ground to delivering concrete 'outcomes' relating to employability and enrolled a weakened concept of 'community involvement'. Development workers' roles were redefined and outcome indicators reset in another example of policy creep that focused on measuring the extent to which peopled were moved closer to the labour market (Friedli and Stearn, 2015; Pearce et al, 2021). Policy makers, some of whom lived and worked in the Valleys, acknowledged that these arguments were uncomfortable to make in that context; that there was 'something very sad about this job-ready thing' and the paucity of the intervention in place to help individuals adapt and adjust to structural processes of the magnitude of de-industrialisation. Along with many of the programme's development workers and the community residents, they perceived these efforts as merely 'a drop in the ocean' for a place that needed 'post-industrial rescue'. Nonetheless, when the programme concluded, learning the 'lessons' of Communities First (Equality, Local Government and Communities Committee, 2017) involved establishing that its strengths had lain in enhancing employability. The European Social Fund and Welsh Government continued to fund Communities for Work and Communities for Work Plus (Davies, 2024a), which can be understood as the legacy of Communities First – a too thin set of offerings that tend to be limited to boosting an individual's employability.[8]

Given how the Communities First programme unfolded it is difficult to refute the suggestion that policy built on forms of geographical referencing inevitably reinvigorates or reinforces spatialised constructions of 'an underclass' (Harrison, 2013: 103). There is certainly a paradox at the heart of interventions that require 'ordinary', local people to draw on their own latent qualities and take responsibility for their communities in lieu of external remedies for structurally embedded inequalities: communities become 'both the problem *and* solution' (Fremeaux, 2005: 271, emphasis in original; Shaw, 2011). It can be difficult to discern if and when the invocation of 'community' to anchor a policy means the state apparatus is redistributing its power and renewing democracy (Uphoff and Krishna, 2004), extending its control by managing social conflict or dissent through a 'manufactured civil society' (Hodgson, 2004: 157) or hollowing out and retreating from its responsibilities and providing cover for the fractures of economic decline and social decimation (Shaw and Martin, 2000; Delanty, 2002; 2009; Muir, 2004; Taylor, 2011; Rogaly and Taylor, 2016). These kinds of arguments – around 'how seemingly radical initiatives may be appropriated by government regimes' – are now well rehearsed (Nicholls et al, 2025: 2; Newman, 2012). In a helpful contribution to these debates and discussions, David Adamson (2010: 116) concludes that arguments that these approaches are merely 'a mechanism for extending state power ... and a means of controlling civil society ... suggest a complete lack of agency on the part of community actors and a hegemonic project so successful that they do not see their incorporation and domination by the state'.

This analysis suggests welfare resettlements are actively produced within civil society through community oriented interventions; created (and contested) through competing pressures and forces and, so, generative of divergent spaces that retain a degree of autonomy and are textured by resistant narratives and practices (Clarke, 2004; Newman, 2001). This is a process of 'proposing new social ends as well as different means for arriving at them' as local people 'draw upon—and sometimes extend, rearrange, and transform—the master frames' of the broader political culture (Emirbayer and Mische, 1998: 993). There were, then, possibilities; contesting hegemonic ideologies involves finding some room to manoeuvre and carving out space for alternative forms of welfare provisioning.

Reflection

The radical restructuring of the welfare state sketched here spanned two decades. It cohered around a neoliberal impetus: the assumption that becoming a 'good' citizen is synonymous with seeking and securing paid work (Wright, 2016; 2023; Monaghan and Ingold, 2019). Labour (1997–2010) and subsequent Conservative-led governments (2010–24) repeatedly endorsed the work imperative for groups with traditionally low employment rates. And while various forms of conditionality were attached to the earlier system, as 'creeping conditionality' (Dwyer, 2004) yielded to 'ubiquitous conditionality' (Dwyer and Wright, 2014), the scale of reform dwarfed previous attempts to persuade or encourage people to enter the labour market. Interventions were tethered more securely to explicitly individualised, psychosocial explanations of personal deficiency. Lone parents, alongside the long-term unemployed, carers, those with ill health and disability, were reframed as 'workless' by default (Knjin et al, 2007), creating new fault-lines of social conformity that made those who fell short visible targets for scrutiny. The welfare state can be understood as a site of 'social sorting', through which 'inequalities are inscribed and materialised' (Tyler, 2020: 90). There were gendered impacts of restructuring of this type, which further marginalised the value of social reproduction; the consequences for women, and lone mother families in particular, proved hugely significant, not least because neither the personal and societal significance of their unpaid care nor their relatively weak labour market position were sufficiently recognised (Conaghan, 2009; Ingold and Etherington, 2013; Holloway and Pimlott-Wilson, 2016). The assertion that a job, any job, was almost always 'good' for almost everyone emerged alongside a blinkered understanding of care as easily commodifiable that was incongruent with many people's day-to-day experience (Grover, 2007; Millar, 2008; 2019; Dean, 2014; Beck, 2018; Wright, 2023). Here, 'the right to work had become the requirement to work without a complementary right to care' (Rubery and Rafferty, 2013: 429). Increasingly punitive and coercive measures were designed to reconcile people to a precarious and deregulated labour market and a state divested of social protections (Wacquant, 2009; Guetzkow, 2020). The idea that harsh sanctions should underwrite the obligations of citizenship was normalised, as was singling out paid work as paramount among these obligations, regardless of its quality or personal circumstance (Dean, 2014). The 2024 *Get Britain Working White Paper* (Department for Work and Pensions, 2024) describes 'transforming a department for welfare into a genuine department for work' suggesting that resetting this course under the current Labour government is unlikely.

The social contract between state and citizen was rewritten in a reconfiguration accomplished through a state machinery deeply embedded in an altered public imaginary of the 'common sense' of meritocracy, whereby paid work is 'an individual's moral meritocratic task' (Littler, 2017: 89). Societies neatly stylised as meritocratic absorb the logic that, regardless of social location, each of us is in a position to combine aspiration, effort and talent to secure advancement; opportunities for social mobility are distributed with an even hand and we are free to fashion our destinies as we wish. These ideas have sedimented despite an abundance of critical analysis suggesting they are best understood as mythological, a powerful cultural trope put to work to legitimate decades of deepening inequalities within capitalist democratic societies (Marmot, 2004; Wilkinson and Pickett, 2010; Dorling, 2011; Littler, 2017; Bloodworth, 2018; Bukodi et al, 2015; Bukodi and Goldthorpe, 2018). This body of work documents the entrenched nature of inequalities to unpick an argument that obscures the specificities and complexities of personal life and detaches biographical trajectories from the wider social and economic formations of dispossession and disenfranchisement in which they are embedded (Bottrell, 2013; Gill and Orgad, 2018).

A damaging corollary of a discourse that understands our fates as purely a matter of personal responsibility and aspiration is the corrosive framing of some of us as society's 'skivers', 'shirkers' and 'scroungers'; this manoeuvre entwines economic position with cultural status (Goodhart, 2020; Sandel, 2020; Bukodi and Goldthorpe, 2022), dimensions of the everyday politics of welfare that are experienced mutually and concurrently (Haney, 2000; Clarke, 2004). Populations were reimagined as unwilling to work and, so, undeserving of protection and censured and controlled as such (Tyler, 2020), a casting that predated but intensified with the era of austerity politics. While the cultivation of stigma as a device for rationing welfare has strong historical roots, its role in legitimating rising inequality and poverty has expanded (Jensen, 2018; Tyler, 2020). Despite evidence that people on out-of-work benefits do want to work (Shildrick, 2018), a 'pervasive toxic narrative that shames and blames the poor has secured a stranglehold on our collective understanding of poverty' (O'Hara, 2020: 1). Poverty ceased to be framed as societal injustice, citizens were no longer 'legitimate claimants of entitlements' so much as morally suspect 'beneficiaries of government largesse' (United Nations Development Programme, 1997: 96; Morris, 2019) and social security eligibility was no longer bound tightly to immediate need (Dean, 2014). Successive governments reified misrepresentations to justify and legitimate behaviourally coercive strategies built on individualised and increasingly psychologised conceptions of responsibility, culpability and accountability (Wright, 2012; Whitworth and Griggs, 2013; Etherington and Daguerre, 2015; Friedli and Stearn, 2015), the logics of which extended beyond particular groups of people to particular kinds of places.

Lydia Morris convincingly argues that these policy frameworks have offered only a thin discussion of everyday life based on 'a diminished view of agency' (2020: 287; Morris, 2019). Here, policy that privileged an abstract theory of agency with scant regard for little beyond our economic value as workers amounted to a 'narrow institutional framing of who has value and what is valued, whether in relation to individual hopes and plans, accommodation of varied and variable capabilities, patterns of care and concern for others, or the whole complex fabric of claimants' lives' (Morris, 2020: 287). Driven by a focus on changing beliefs and behaviours, the model framed our motivations, intentions and choices as a straightforward question of free-floating, calculable, instrumental self-interest as opposed to a product of our embedded personal interdependencies, attachments and commitments and their linkages with wider social processes and formations (Wright, 2012; Morris, 2019; 2020). This 'illusion of choice' (Morris, 2020: 288) displaced the nuanced interpretation of the situated complexities of everyday personal life; poverty became an individual responsibility as opposed to a collective concern of societal injustice. The fallout of this policy story would hit some places far harder than others, and we would be hard-pressed to find a place hit harder than the old coalfield of the Valleys (Beatty and Fothergill, 2014a; 2014b; 2017a; 2017b). For their part, the residents and those working on the estate had long felt the retreat of the state; the fallout of a protracted process of de-industrialisation a lesson that welfare retrenchment only confirmed. They also knew that even if a strangulated community development approach was a 'drop in the ocean', the support for grass-roots activism it provided was something.

3

The Valleys

> The common people have been exploited and it is still happening … nothing ever changes.
>
> Estate resident, 2008

Y Dic Penderyn, 2021

In 2021, across the Valleys, the pandemic lockdowns are easing and the pubs are opening up. The national news is peppered with accounts of the high rate of COVID-19 deaths in the region, and local public health officials stand out for the surety of their explanations. Among them is Cwm Taf Morgannwg's director for public health: 'the rate had been predictable'; it 'is fundamentally about poverty and health inequalities' – issues 'we've known about for years' (Glyn Jones, 2021). Y Dic Penderyn[1] is one of a handful of Wetherspoon pubs in the Valleys, an area that covers some five hundred square miles of old coalfield and is home to roughly one million people. It's mid-morning, mid-week. The pub is warm and quiet aside from a group of mothers with pushchairs settled into one corner. They like it because the Wi-Fi is free, the baby-changing facilities are clean, and the coffee is refillable. It's a good place to catch up and exchange gossip.

The young woman sitting across the table has been a domiciliary care worker for almost a year. She describes her day-to-day routine in some detail. It's packed with tasks accomplished on rotation as she moves from home to home – bathing the person, changing their pads, creaming them, emptying their bag, feeding them, giving them medication, a drink, sometimes putting a load of washing on, sometimes doing a shopping call. She says: 'we leave them, we move along to the next one'; most 'clients' get 'four calls a day – morning, noon, tea and night'; most days, she will 'deal' with around 30 clients, and on a 'really bad day', well over 40. Some days, she will not have time to 'eat tidy'; there will be no break and no chance to go to the toilet. They get told by management to use the toilet in the client's home, but it's not always as easy as that. She 'pissed' herself once. They are 'constantly on the go'. We are meeting between shifts, as she just picked up another for later in the day. She left her house at ten past six this morning and is now not likely to make it back home much before ten o'clock tonight. She explains that if the call is scheduled for 15 minutes, she gets paid for 15 minutes.

Anything more than 'a couple of minutes over' is difficult because she won't be paid for that time. Besides, running over time with one client means time taken away from another, as she would be 'trying to catch back up' later in the day. Stealing 10 minutes here to give it back there. Cutting a call short or cutting one altogether can mean they 'get dissed' by clients and their families, who have 'their angry heads on', even though 'we provide the best care we can'. It's a judgement call about how fast to care when there are not enough carers.

She believes that providing the 'best care' involves making 'a little connection' even though the employer says 'don't form a bond, don't get too close'. She cares for people the way she would like her own family to be cared for, and while she knows the people she cares for 'are going to die', it is hard when it happens. The first time this happened, she remembers 'sobbing' her 'heart out over the bed'. She was allowed a 20-minute break before 'getting told stiffen up, move along ... move on to your next client'. It's 'draining', and she cut down her hours because 'taking the full force' of a broken system was 'killing' her. Still, she can't live on part-time wages, so she is being 'pushed back' into picking up shifts, full days instead of half days, and it is starting to feel like she is working every day. She is proud of what she does, but the desirable features of caring for a living are offset by the sheer volume of the care work there is. 'It is a lot of work', especially for her basic wage of £8.91 an hour. She has applied for a job in the National Health Service (NHS) – similar work on the 'bank', where she could just work a Saturday and Sunday and earn what she does now.

A set of mounted prints hangs on the walls around us. 'Spoons is known for its deliberate engagement with local history and each frame contains a piece – you can learn a lot in Y Dic Penderyn (Smith, 2024; Wetherspoon, 2024).[2] In this pub, the curators have given wall space to the qualities of the local natural resources and the industrialists and engineers who drew on them: by 1803, Richard Crawshay's Cyfarthfa Ironworks was the largest in the world, and its significance for the production of cannonballs merited a visit by Lord Horatio Nelson; in 1804, Richard Trevithick ran the world's first successful steam locomotive, which carried 10 tons of iron nearly 10 miles, from the Penydarren Ironworks to the Glamorganshire Canal; in 1821, Josiah John Guest was master of the Dowlais Ironworks, which made the rails for the pioneering Stockton and Darlington Railway. These are the broad brush strokes of a kind of public history. The area emerged as a powerhouse of the Industrial Revolution: the proximity to iron ore, coal, timber and limestone and the plentiful water supply created ideal conditions for production. The region is synonymous with old industry: the story of the Valleys is of the rise and protracted decline of the extractive heavy industries of iron and coal and the associated industries of rail and steel. Its communities sit in ribboned terraces along the deep north–south valleys that cut through the landscape, still clustered around what were the pitheads of old works, often in isolated, rural locations. During the 18th and 19th centuries, people moved to the Valleys in their thousands for work. Over time, as the inland location became disadvantageous for iron production, the advent and expansion of coal mining and steel manufacturing gave renewed impetus to the local economy and people were drawn to several large employers.

The spatially differentiated capitalist development across the UK led to variations in the ways in which capitalism and patriarchy accommodated each other and to the formation of distinctive hierarchies of work roles and home duties (McDowell and Massey, 1984). The industrial structure of the Valleys settled women firmly in the domestic sphere, and there were comparatively low levels of paid work for women compared to elsewhere, notably the English potteries and the textile belt, where women were employed on a significant scale (Bradley, 1986; Gordon, 1987; Glucksmann, 2000; Todd, 2004; 2005; Jenkins, 2017; Beynon, 2019). Still, while the relatively small proportion of women in paid work remained one of the region's outstanding features well into the 20th century, characterisations of women's contributions in the Valleys have also been textured by myth (Rees, 1988; Jenkins, 2017). Throughout the 19th and 20th centuries, the collection of labour force statistics 'grossly' underestimated and undervalued women's paid work in the region (Rees, 1988: 120). For a time, the paid work of married women was excluded altogether, and any part-time, irregular, seasonal, casual or home-based employment was under-recorded. More broadly, women were vital to the functioning of these communities, even if the value of social reproduction was not recognised (Rees, 1988; 1999; Jenkins, 2017); the glorification of the 'Welsh mam' as an archetype of domesticity, self-sacrifice and respectability was a cultural device that rendered the contribution of women less visible (O'Neill, 2011; Jenkins, 2017). At the core of this society was the reconciliation of heavy, hazardous and precarious paid work by men for a family wage and a deeply felt masculine pride in labouring (Jimenez and Walkerdine, 2011; 2012; Walkerdine and Jimenez, 2012).

The extraordinariness of the coalfields was created through this dense set of distinctive, deeply gendered social relations (Bennett et al, 2000). The narrow industrial base – single-industry settlements organised around and through places of work – sustained a sense of shared experience (Bennett et al, 2000). The relatively homogeneous, geographically isolated communities were characterised by a set of widely recognised features: a strong working class steeped in forms of collective solidarity, dominated by industrial labour and manifest in the creative activity of institutions of civil and political society, including the nonconformist chapels, cooperative stores, the Labour Party and the trade union (Francis and Smith, 1980; Bennett et al, 2000). Collective bonds extending through tight networks of comradeship and kinship meant work, home and community intertwined in everyday life.

The industrial Valleys harboured significant pockets of socialist influence, the legacy of which persists: the villages and towns once dominated by coal mining remain among the strongest and most durable bases for the labour movement in the UK (Beynon et al, 2021). Accounts providing a sense of what it meant to belong to mining communities emphasise values and practices of solidarity and collectivism (Dennis et al, 1969; Bulmer, 1975; Warwick and Littlejohn, 1992) to the extent that they attain almost 'mythical status' in the post-industrial era (Walker, 2021: 3; Day, 2006; Linkon, 2018).

The reliance on the globalised demand for raw materials proved critical to the fortunes of the Valleys. Most communities were completely dependent on the coal mining industry and their collieries as a source of paid employment for men (Bennett et al, 2000). In the 1920s and 1930s, the vagaries of the market and collapse of this economy, along with the failure to secure significant manufacturing or commercial activity, led to a drop in wages, unemployment, severe poverty and mass outward migration (Jenkins, 2017), with hunger marches from South Wales to London taking place in 1927, 1934 and 1936 (Ward, 2016). In the immediate post-war period, nationalisation saw improvements in both wages and working conditions, but over time the demand for coal declined and pits deemed uneconomic were closed (Curtis, 2013). The impact of the contraction of the coal and steel industries in the middle of the century was partially mitigated by the advent of mass manufacturing (Bennett et al, 2000). Contemporary accounts shared by local people of this era refer to a small number of paternalistic employers for whom 'everyone used to work' and the factories that made all sorts of things: buttons, bras, lamps, chocolate bars, prams and vacuum cleaners. Perhaps the best-known was Hoovers, which is remembered fondly in the region. These kinds of workplace were understood as extensions of family life (Jenkins, 2017). As one local woman explained:

> These jobs were on your doorstep. You didn't need to travel for work. The big companies, too, were very good companies to work for. Fantastic pensions, you know, and when you worked for places like that ... it was a family affair. There was only my grandfather working down there from our family, but you had fathers and sons working there, and then their grandson would go to work there as an apprentice. You had the whole family. (Estate resident, 2021)

Being on Hoovers' payroll was seen as 'more than just a job'; the workplace was widely understood as a 'community' of personal ties and connections that extended well beyond the production line. While heavy industry contracted, there were some new opportunities for women in low-skilled and semi-skilled employment at the point of production as well as clerical work in light industry, the utilities and public sector (Jenkins, 2017). But traditional attitudes tended to prevail. Local family histories were replete with examples of mothers and grandmothers either taking on 'little' jobs to bring in a 'bit extra' or dropping paid work altogether. Hostility towards working motherhood was commonplace, as one local resident recalled with reference to her grandmother:

> They wanted my nan to go on and do more and my grandfather was like 'No, you've got a small family to think of. You need to be at home.' And she never did. She never went any further. And I said to him, 'You stopped her from going where she could've been.' I said, 'I understand the culture of the way things were then, you know, women needed to be at home … but you really, like, pushed her.' (Estate resident, 2021)

Towards the end of the century in the Valleys, it was increasingly apparent that there were deeply entrenched, structural economic weaknesses. A manufacturing sector of any significant scale had failed to develop, and the accelerated loss of the newer forms of employment that had surfaced, combined with a crisis of traditional industry, was closely associated with rising levels of economic inactivity, particularly among men (Bennett et al, 2000). The whole country was affected by recession, but the situation in the Valleys was dire. In 1981, during a speech to the Conservative Party Conference in response to the Brixton uprising of that year, Norman Tebbit, Secretary of State for Employment, reflected: 'I grew up in the thirties with an unemployed father. He didn't riot. He got on his bike and looked for work, and he kept looking till he found it' (Tebbit, 1981). Years later, one resident of the Valleys recollected both this speech and the local labour market conditions at the time: 'The month Tebbit made his famous 'get on your bike' speech, we actually went to the Jobcentre … where there were 3,500 people registered unemployed and there were seven vacancies. We said, "That is some bike you are gonna need!"'.

The struggle for jobs in the Valleys would flare and fade with the miners' strike of 1984–85. Widely understood as a watershed moment in industrial relations history, the dispute played out on an epic scale. Collective memory coheres through recollections of the injustice meted by the state in its various forms – by government, police and courts – but memories of 'the camaraderie', 'unity and community spirit' also circulate, and the activism of women during the strike has emerged in accounts that document their contribution in building 'an alternative welfare system' to support mining families (Massey and Wainwright, 1985: 166; Spence and Stephenson, 2007). In the years following the strike, the intensity of economic decline was marked with profound repercussions for the social fabric of the coalfield (Beynon, 1985; Curtis, 2013). As one local labour movement activist explained:

It absolutely devastated the Valleys. ... I lived in the street where there was numerous colliers there and in different collieries around the place. And whereas you couldn't say they were rich, because they weren't, but they became very, very poor afterwards. You know, they could not afford any ... because through the whole strike they sold furniture and things. Well, even after the strike finished and they went back to work, they weren't there long. ... I remember it happening. (Valleys resident, 2015)

The historically large reserves of women's labour also had major implications for a changing local labour market, where men might be overlooked in favour of women or might resist 'feminine' jobs far removed from the archetype of industrial masculinity (Jimenez and Walkerdine, 2011; 2012; McDowell, 2011; 2012). As one resident explained: 'them boys couldn't work anywhere' because the 'new work' is for 'for women'. Changing patterns of employment – the emergence of paid work demanding the traits of care, deference and docility – meant the 'traditional ways of becoming a man' all but disappeared (McDowell, 2011: 4; Sennett, 2003; Skeggs and Wood, 2009; Jenkins, 2017). These developments meant women in the Valleys became 'a numerically substantial but distinctly disadvantaged section of the workforce' (Rees, 1988: 127). As one resident explained, more local women often 'left school ... did a bit of training, then into a factory maybe ... then got married, children and sort of just had part-time jobs really, nothing much'. Still, traditional, deeply entrenched gender relations were disrupted: working-class women taking paid work secured a degree of emancipation by becoming wage earners, even if the work was of poor quality and with employment patterns that tended to accommodate the rhythms of their domestic, home-making and caring commitments (Rees, 1988; Jenkins, 2017). By the turn of the century, it was the increasing numbers of working mothers that was notable (Jenkins, 2017).

In time, women would face more competition for employment. While 'the men made redundant a generation ago from industries like coal, steel and heavy engineering may have shunned what they saw as "women's work", their sons have rarely had the same luxury' (Beatty, 2014: 831). Jimenez and Walkerdine's (2011; 2012) study of a former steel town in the Valleys identified the acute shame older men felt in relation to the employment of their sons in poor-quality service jobs, which were often the only source of work in the locality. This account included descriptions of the former steelworkers refusing to acknowledge their sons when they were wearing their pizza delivery uniforms. The young men themselves also understood these jobs as being shameful. They retained an 'attraction to manual work and an inability or unwillingness to engage in emotional labour' (Gater, 2022: 123). For some, unemployment was preferable if it meant salvaging pride in their masculinity, but as the benefits system tightened, new forms of conditionality intensified the requirement to seek and secure paid work and more young men took on roles in the kinds of jobs that traditionally might have been occupied by women. This intertwinement of the labour markets of men and women was 'all the more remarkable given the historic and overwhelming domination of coal jobs by men and the sharp differentiation of gender roles in the wider coalfield' (Beatty, 2014: 832).

The Valleys became a 'hyphenated economy', a place where work was more likely to be low-paid, part-time, unskilled, short term and non-unionised (Beynon et al, 2002) and formal childcare provision, especially in the most disadvantaged communities, was poor (Symonds and Kelly, 2005). There is also evidence of an acute shortage of jobs – in 2017 there were just 42 jobs for every 100 residents of working age – with many travelling out of the region for work (Beatty et al, 2019; Beatty and Fothergill, 2020). As an older industrial region with a weak local economy, the Valleys has also shown stubbornly high levels of 'hidden unemployment', which persist with a 'near-permanent' rise in claims relating to poor health among men and women (Beatty and Fothergill, 2017a: 166; Beatty and Fothergill, 2023). During the first wave of fieldwork, headlines consistently described the Valleys as home to the 'sick note' capital of Britain and one of Britain's least desirable places to live (see, for example, Fagge, 2010). And because the distinctive geographical patternings of de-industrialisation were replicated in welfare spending, the Valleys were among those places 'worst-hit' by austerity politics, which substantially reduced direct benefit payments to a wide range of low-income and out-of-work households (Beatty and Fothergill, 2014a: 77). Beyond cuts to benefits and rising in-work poverty, social investments in the Valleys – including for housing, schools, social services and social care – were decimated in the 'deepest and most precipitate cuts ever made in social provision' (Taylor Gooby, 2013: viii; Hills, 2017; Farnsworth and Irving, 2018; Bennett, 2019). The spatialised impacts of reforms to the benefits system were consistent with the geographically uneven distribution of cuts to the local investments in social provisioning across the UK (Gray and Barford, 2018). Both sets of measures 'should be understood first and foremost as about reducing public spending in the poorest places' (Beatty and Fothergill, 2018: 950; Beatty and Fothergill, 2023). Access to public services has become 'increasingly conditional upon the health of the local tax base – where poorer places provide fewer public services and less basic infrastructure' (Gray and Barford, 2018: 559). The local capacity to help people targeted by measures that cut into social security benefits was curtailed in those places hit hardest, places also characterised by higher levels of in-work poverty (Beatty and Fothergill, 2014a; 2014b; 2018). Women in the Valleys and elsewhere were hit hard by protracted economic crisis and a state in retreat because they are more likely to use public services, draw on benefits and have 'crap' jobs (MacLeavy, 2011; Pearson and Elson, 2015; Hills, 2017; Hall, 2020).

The community

The estate itself sits distinct and separate in the upper reaches of the Valleys. Constructed in stages, beginning in the 1930s and lasting well into the 1970s, it was a piece of state social engineering mirrored across the country to rehome those displaced by slum clearances. The estate provided better-quality housing for working families, with indoor plumbing, hot and cold running water and electricity. Those living in the old industrial terraces were moved street by street as entire communities were uprooted and pieced back together on a new landscape. One resident, drawing attention to a map of the area, recalled:

> They knocked the whole street down and half the street opposite when they sent us up to new housing. They lifted that street of the community and they put us in that street there. So, my mother's mother and father just lived round the corner and my aunties too. ... Communities were picked up and dropped in ... so we brought our sense of family, community with us to a large degree. (Estate resident, 2009)

The early development created semi-detached two-storey houses with fair-sized front and back gardens. The original plans included open green spaces and public amenities, including a cinema and a library, but after World War II 'they just couldn't afford all the add-ons, so they just built the houses really', along with a small cluster of shops. Later development was designed at higher densities through a model of social housing that incorporated small, close-set maisonettes with lanes as common entries and exits to homes, with less clearly private space for residents and the more uniform look of municipal housing (Hanley, 2012). Despite these disappointments, many residents with experience of relocation attested that, for a time at least, the estate represented a better quality of life and the possibility of a better future – it was described as 'a wonderland' with a 'fresh, optimistic horizon'. Recollections of this kind were often yoked to accounts of relative prosperity because for a time there was an abundance of paid work: 'most families were working back then' and 'you could literally walk out of one factory and walk into another'. The place had what Lynsey Hanley describes as a 'settled quality' – 'people had jobs, people had families' in this time before the estate became a 'dream gone sour' (Hanley, 2012: 2, 10). Older residents' accounts were at times inflected with a longing for 'the ways things were' and representations of the estate often juxtaposed the industriousness and security of the past with a more recent sense of obsolescence and precarity. The myth of a population consisting of 'never worked families' was easily debunked (MacDonald et al, 2014: 199; MacMillan, 2014; Shildrick, 2018).

In recent decades, the quality of life on the estate has been ranked by governments across a range of indicators, including the numbers of people in receipt of social security benefits, living with chronic illness, progressing to higher education and offending, plus a standardised all-cause death rate. A series of 'basic capabilities' (Sen, 1992; 1999) are measured and recorded, including those relating to housing, heating, food and other essential goods, social engagement and access to local public spaces and services, transport, employment and education (Power, 2007; Hick, 2016; Bramley, 2018). The estate consistently ranks 'highly' against each of these measures. But for most of the people I met and spoke with, the dominant thread of its contemporary narrative was high unemployment or underemployment and residents trying to make the most of the 'hand they had been dealt'. Levels of male employment were relatively low, and while in recent years women have entered the workforce in growing numbers, women's employment also remained less extensive than elsewhere. The numbers of residents working in lower paid, lower skilled, elementary occupations, including care, retail and hospitality sectors, were high in comparison to both surrounding areas and further afield. And a lot of people 'have got to have two jobs to keep a roof over their head'.

When discussing work, residents often pointed to the high prevalence of care work in the area, and some care companies were known by their 'honestly, not good' reputation as employers. It was widely felt that 'the caring job is shown as a lesser job, isn't it?' One woman took the time to explain that you could earn 'more at Tesco, with wages at £9.55', and another that 'everyone says you can go to McDonalds and flip a burger for £10.50'. Much of the community's workforce was trying to claw something out of the most basic wages and protections. But in response to questions about local employment, residents, particularly women, tended to dwell on health and social care work because 'there is a lot of care work about' but also because there were some good local jobs for women in the sector. Several conversations drifted into how to get 'onto the bank' of NHS healthcare workers in the local hospital: 'everyone wants to get onto that' because it's more money than working for a private care home or going to someone's home, 'where you've got 15 minutes to do everything for the person you're going to see'. If mothers can get on 'the bank', one resident explained, they 'can just work one or two nights and they're there for the kids, but the pay is really good'. It was a good opportunity for those 'who haven't really got any qualifications' as 'you can go into it without anything', even if 'it can be quite hard to get in'; they only 'take people on the training course every so often and there's a big demand'. In the short term, for people without transport, it can be difficult because the shift work is unpredictable; work might come up for the next day, down the valley or the next valley over. But 'if you can … do banking quite regularly on the same ward, if any shifts come up with the hospital', 'you've got a good chance of getting like a permanent role there then'. It's 'the way in … a job for life really, then, when you're in the NHS'. The paucity of choice was such that often this was presented as *the* good opportunity for many women on the estate.

In contrast, it was widely understood that there was 'not a lot for men, not much for men': some worked away on the 'rails', others were tradesmen, some travelled for warehouse jobs. Conversations around work for men often moved on, tellingly, to the 'job clubs' on the estate: 'You've got Bridges into Work and you've got Communities for Work, or Communities for Work Plus … and you've got Working Skills for Adults.' Some can help if you are already in paid work, some if you are not, some if you have no qualifications, some if you have a few: 'they've all got different criteria' but 'there's always some criteria'. In the words of one resident: 'it's obviously, it's not brilliant is it, round here, for work?'; 'there's a lot of people out of work, on benefits'. Back in 2010, a time when enlisting meant deployment to a war zone was likely, one mother thought it would be good for her son to join the Army, as an alternative to unemployment or a 'dead-end', local job. The Valleys is targeted by recruitment campaigns (not least within the school system) and has seen a resurgence of military presence in recent decades – part of the wider 'common sense in Britain today, that there is and should be an organic link between areas of economic deprivation in the country and participation in the military force' (Tannock et al, 2013: 5).

Discussion of these shifting orientations to, and patterns of, paid work and unpaid care on the estate was morally freighted. At times, women's entry into the labour market was framed as a break from 'old-fashioned' values and as an opportunity for emancipation and independence. But more frequently their efforts were cast as an attempt to hold a family together. Several residents leant into the dominant political and cultural stereotypes that circulated to offer scathing descriptions of a generation of men who had 'gone AWOL', leaving women to 'make a fist of it'. Yet despite the disintegration of the economic structure and the erosion of an ideology that fixed women in the domestic sphere (Rees, 1988; 1999), the advantages men retained over women were a common point of discussion. Many believed that 'a very macho culture' persisted on the estate – one thread of continuity with the industrial past – not least in the context of family life, where there were few claims of gender neutrality or equivalency in the roles of women and men (Duncan and Smith, 2002). Some framed the community as insular and out of step with a more progressive outside world, and there was a sense that patriarchal structures remained largely intact, possessing an enduring, if residual, meaning (Williams, 1965; 1989). Another recurring motif was the recognition of local women for their contributions to the estate's 'social infrastructure', through caring for family, friends, neighbours and their efforts in the community more widely (Grimshaw, 2011; Pearson and Elson, 2015). Reflections of this kind positioned these practices as critical to the sustenance of everyday life on the estate, indicative of a set of deeply ingrained, gendered commitments and responsibilities (Hennessy, 2009).

In the public imaginary, the 'housing estate' had become synonymous with working-class life caricatured by deviance and dependency (Hanley, 2012; Rogaly and Taylor, 2016). Estates emerged as enclosures of pathology, containers of collective disintegration; and poverty became a deserved consequence of being unwilling to work at all or being unwilling to work hard enough. Some estates have become shorthand markers for descriptions of 'undeserving' populations in a particular town or region, sometimes generating national and even global renown (Skeggs, 2004). In this case, residents were well aware of the community's reputation as a place of relegation and for a particular type of endemic, self-inflicted poverty – as a home to society's 'down and outs' and 'dole bums'. They often acknowledged 'that stigma of living where you live' and the sense of segregation it conferred. For some, this sense was woven into the material fabric of the estate, something residents themselves pointed out at times: 'it looks rough and ready and whatever, that's the first thing you see'; 'we've only got to take a look around there to see it'. On occasion television programmes made in and about the estate were also cited:

> They did a few of the estate, the deprivation, but what they didn't show was the community spirit. People ignore that. I've always loved [the estate] … but they didn't show that. They just … they depicted them as down and outs, dole bums, drunks. They picked the drunks to talk to and you didn't talk to anybody who was working 12-hour shifts, you didn't choose anybody like that. You chose the most down and out people you could to make it look worse. (Estate resident, 2021)

The circulation of 'poverty porn' or 'poverty propaganda' (Jensen, 2014; Shildrick, 2018), produced through pseudo-journalistic accounts and reality television, was integral to the restructuring of the welfare state. A new 'commonsense' would 'congeal' through a 'highly editorialized "debate" between fast media and fast policy' (Jensen, 2014: 4; Jensen and Tyler, 2015). Accounts reproducing the 'myths and misrepresentations about poverty and those who experience the condition' proliferated (Shildrick, 2018: 2; Tyler, 2013; Jensen, 2014; 2020; Jensen and Tyler, 2015; O'Hara, 2020). All of this meant that awareness of the stigma attached to the estate was acutely felt when residents ventured further afield:

> You can go round the world and people have heard of [the estate]. I went to Las Vegas, for my 50th, first time I had been to America, and the first person I bump into, I tell 'em where I am from – it's a Yank, like – went to the bar, chap came in, heard me ordering a drink ... got talking, 'Where you from?' 'Wales.' 'You from anywhere near that ... place?' (Estate resident, 2009)

> We was known from here to Bangkok, I think. Everybody knew about [the estate]. 'Where you from?', 'Oh, I'll check my watch first, see if it is still there on my wrist.' Terrible, terrible, wherever you went. (Estate resident, 2009)

The cultivation of stigma textured residents' relationships with a myriad of different kinds of people, including, journalists, policy makers and academics (Wacquant, 2008; Crossley, 2017). Local public officials even considered changing the name of the estate, with one politician commenting that, 'it was laughed off ... but it was something we probably should have done'. One of the implications of these developments was the estate's relative popularity as a site for social scientific and journalistic inquiry, to the extent that one community worker described it as a 'human zoo' experiencing 'research fatigue'. Another concern related to residents' interactions with public officials, like housing and social services departments but also the police, which were primary sources of frustration and resentment, cast as 'a battle' pervaded by anxiety and a sense of powerlessness. Reflecting on residents' sense of respect and dignity, one community development worker commented of this dynamic: 'There is a hostility to the establishment and the experiences people have had from the establishment. ... There is a strong sense of what is right and what is wrong as far as the way to be and the way people deal with people from the estate.'

The 'spatialising of difference' (Skeggs, 2004: 89) through representations of dysfunction – the 'dreadful enclosures' and 'phantasms' of myth – binds and fixes people in and to their place (Walter, 1977). While conscious to avoid reifying these narratives by restating them here (Hall, 2020), they remain profoundly consequential, impoverishing everyday life (Tyler, 2013; Crossley, 2017). Years of debasement were immensely damaging (Hanley, 2012; McKenzie, 2015). For those living on the estate, it was understood 'that stigma will stick with you, no matter what you do, whether you work or not'. Residents negotiated these representations with complex accounts that cut 'symbolic boundaries' around and through a place that they described as home to both the 'salt of the earth' and 'the roughest of the rough' (Lamont and Molnár, 2002). Descriptions served as signifiers of residents' awareness of spatialised class tension, and in each case, and across instances, they adopted a strategy to manage these representations – positions and points of acquiescence, evasion, resignation, recalcitrance and resistance (Wacquant, 2008; Ravn, 2021). Some argued these representations were homogenising, with issues and concerns acknowledged with resigned acceptance but attributed to the proverbial 'bad apples' of the estate (the neighbour who was 'trouble', the 'drug dealer in the house opposite' or someone 'fiddling benefits over the road'). Some playfully leant into representations that suggested the estate should be feared by outsiders – for example, during one early fieldwork visit, one resident laughed and asked: 'Aren't you scared? You are [on the estate] now!' Some, self-consciously disengaged with the wider world, ameliorating and resisting harm by drawing on the protections available to them (Peacock et al, 2014; McKenzie, 2015). The strongest narrative thread, however, was one of strident resistance – a quiet outrage in defence of the estate and its residents.

There was a common emphasis on the 'sense of community', descriptions of a set of valuable practices and relationships put to work to suggest that the estate was not a place that simply needed to be fixed (Power, 2007; McKenzie, 2012). These accounts were suggestive of a great deal of harmony, security, familiarity and mutual aid: often neatly summed up as 'community spirit' or just 'the community'. It was the vibrancy of solidarity that lingered, a sense of belonging that both deflected stigma and provided critical forms of material aid, care and concern (McKenzie, 2015). One small but typical example arose in 2021 when pink ribbons could be found on many of the estate's front doors to denote support and raise donations for the family of a very poorly little girl. This kind of activity was not at all unusual, and it's hard to overstate its central importance. It pointed to a set of taken-for-granted beliefs and practices: the ordinary and often overlooked acts of kindness that unfolded in and beyond times of crisis. It was perhaps one thread of continuity with the past and the 'old community', reconfigured and reoriented. These interdependencies and interconnections – ties of belonging established in part through the sense of segregation, abandonment and marginalisation – are felt and expressed in similar places elsewhere. Much as Lisa McKenzie (2015: 149) describes of St Ann's in Nottingham, the estate was 'a tight-knit community, which has been built on pride, a sense of belonging, humour, and sharing, but also fear, instability, and stigmatisation'.

Reflection

The approach here attempts to move beyond a thin reading of place as backdrop to gain an understanding of the ways in which the fabric of a place shapes everyday life (Kearns and Parkinson, 2001; CRESR Research Team, 2011). The work of geographer Doreen Massey (1984; 1994; 2004) is a useful touchstone here. Of interest are the social interactions, practices and narratives that make a place and their linkages to wider social forces, contexts and scales. The 'specificity of a place' is understood to be 'continually reproduced', resulting not from a 'long internalized history' but through particular constellations of social relations, that weave 'together at a particular locus' (Massey, 1994: 155–6). In the Valleys, the cycles of the economy were tightly bound to extractive industry – rapid growth followed by severe contraction, then resurgence followed by protracted, irreversible decline and collapse – and mirrored in the fortunes and prospects of the people living in the locality. The region consists of communities made for and by industry that are now far removed from sites of wealth production: a region opened up, dominated and then deserted by capital (McDowell and Massey, 1984). Concepts such as 'social haunting' (Gordon, 2008) and 'half-life' (Linkon, 2018) have been developed and applied to grasp the ways in which people experiencing these processes are shaped by their industrial past, with the conclusion that even as living memory fades, the landscape, but also the social values and practices, are textured by this history (Linkon, 2018). Residents offered compelling narratives of how the Valleys have changed, with cracks opening up all over – a place where they continued to live under the shadow cast by the loss of traditional industry and its associated dislocations (Beynon and Hudson, 2021). The decline of the economy so prolonged, its fragility so persistent, that more recent crises and state retrenchment only overlaid preexisting deprivations. A process of territorial marginalisation has transformed the area through the corrosive loss of employment, the degradation of what employment there was and the erosion of the right to social assistance and protection (Wacquant, 2008). Concepts like 'job for life' or 'family wage' bear little relevance when a flexible, casualised and insecure workforce is considered part of a normal, functioning labour market (Jenkins, 2017; Beynon, 2019).

The old institutions of working-class life placed great value on principles of equality and communality in often dangerous and difficult circumstances. While we are urged to guard against romantic or nostalgic representations of the industrial past (Cowie and Heathcott, 2003), these were values and practices produced through and productive of a protective sense of pride (Peacock et al, 2014). As the old institutions disintegrated, the estate, like other working-class communities, was repositioned through stigmatising frames; ideas like the 'underclass' thrived in part because 'alternative value systems' were in scant supply (Skeggs, 2004: 90; Lamont, 2009; Jones, 2020). People bound up in these developments offer insights into the value of good quality, paid work and the associated sense of loss, erasure, abandonment and injury that persists into the contemporary period (Bennett et al, 2000; Dicks, 2008). The collective memory of the Valleys coheres around historical events textured by extreme, often violent, injustice – stories of working-class struggle and adversity in the face of a hostile and negligent state. Notable cited examples included Churchill's decision to tackle the coal miners by mobilising troops and the Metropolitan Police in the Rhondda in 1910–1911 and the miners' strike of 1984–85. Tragic events are discussed too, including the collapse of the coal spoil tip in Aberfan in 1966 with the loss of 116 children and 28 adults. The framing of the state as 'common enemy' in these narratives appears in relief against the 'sense of community', the dense set of local social bonds and practices of reciprocity, which residents explained had 'absolutely never changed'. Raymond Williams (1965; 1989) referred to these kinds of threads of continuity as a 'structure of feeling' – a culture's collective beliefs and shared behaviours, which endure across periods of transformation. Here, residents' accounts pointed to the importance of a sense of place, of belonging, for our ontological security, perhaps especially so when material realities and cultural status are limited and likely to remain so. Families were dug in together, closely knit and appreciated, and deeply woven into imagined futures (Jamieson, 2000; Ravn, 2021). Some laughed at any suggestion that perhaps they move out and move on; even if it was possible, leaving would mean separation from a place and people they knew well and 'loved', and in a world where, for many, much else was in scarce supply, these relationships were centrally important. This was well understood by activists with roots on the estate, and at the turn of the century, when the community was at its 'lowest ebb', they began to share their experience and knowledge, building on these interdependencies and interconnections in an attempt to invigorate communal life (Studdert and Walkerdine, 2016).

4

A space of activism

Battling against the tide.

Diana, Lifeline founder, 2009

The thing was about getting people together, because once you got people together around anything, that's when the magic happens, isn't it?

Diana, Lifeline founder, 2021

Contemporary social security reforms have been contested through various formal processes and channels, including parliamentary reviews, legal challenges and policy consultations (Morris, 2020). There are also 'small arenas of autonomy at the margins' of the welfare state (Burawoy et al, 2000: 31), including alternative or divergent sites of governance found within civil society, which are often positioned as more responsive to local and individual need, and noted for their work in supporting those termed the 'hardest to help' (Damm, 2012: 14; Irvine et al, 2024a). Analyses of these settings direct our focus away from procedural battles to counter-hegemonic, street-level practices, and cast light on the paucity of choice people encounter in navigating the labour market and the limitations of the supply-side, employability policy interventions (Wright, 2016; Beck, 2018). Lifeline was one such setting, a 'site of contestation' (Newman, 2001: 138) where a degree of 'conditional autonomy', textured by logics of acquiescence and dissent to prevailing policy narratives and frameworks (Clarke, 2004), was leveraged by those working 'within and against the state' (Craig and Mayo, 1995: 105). While the project was established in 2007, its origins lay in over a decade of community development activity on the estate. Residents and community development workers alike remembered the 1990s as a turning point in the history of the community. By then, the cumulative impacts of de-industrialisation meant people were coming under increasingly acute economic pressure, and the social fabric of the estate was rapidly unravelling. Residents 'weren't happy'. They felt they had been abandoned, left to manage the aftermath of economic restructuring in the absence of state intervention of any import and with a dearth of public service provision: 'at the time, the estate ... it was pretty grim; it was probably at its most troubled point in its history'. Accounts of this era, more than any other, tended to refer to the fractures and tensions within the community, the 'massive problems going on'. There were concerns for young people, who were framed by the common tropes of that time: they faced 'social exclusion' and exhibited 'anti-social behaviour'. One local authority official explained, the 'residents had really, really had enough' and so the estate began 'to help itself'. A community activist described how the estate's tenants' and residents' board reformed to become 'a stronger force' and address the issues, the 'load of things that people wanted' to put in place with the hope of arresting decline. Community projects sprang up and with people 'coming together ... we'd built it up ... we started with little things'. Small pots of funding were syphoned off for various services in the community, including witness support services, citizens advice provision and youth outreach programmes, as well as a raft of small but important activities, like a film club, a cooking course, a basic skills class and a playgroup.

The local people who had been involved in these developments described the estate at that time as a seedbed of grass-roots activism and experimentation, with forms of social cooperation that emphasised and strengthened relationships between residents. As in other communities facing similar challenges, these initiatives were often organised and sustained through the (paid and unpaid) work of women with strong connections to the estate (Larner and Craig, 2005; Barnett and Land, 2007; England, 2010; Grimshaw, 2011; Askins, 2014; Pearson and Elson, 2015; Hall, 2020). Their efforts were widely framed as critical to everyday life on the estate, productive of the kinds of social bonds that help bolster a sense of belonging, stability and security (Atkinson and Kintrea, 2004; Power, 2007; Livingston et al, 2008; McKenzie, 2012; 2015; Daly and Kelly, 2015). This activity was intent on taking care, repairing and maintaining the community to better meet need, helping people to 'live in it as well as possible' (Fisher and Tronto, 1990: 40; Tronto, 2015; Fraser, 2016). In time, 'as it grew ... and the projects were successful', practices of 'strong informal organisation' – the residents' 'resilience for finding solutions for their problems' – established a more secure foothold (McKenzie, 2015: 16). By the turn of the century, the policy climate had also shifted. The European, UK and Welsh 'community' agenda galvanised local officials and activists into action, and they came together on the estate to draft 'a list of priorities, ... a whole plan', and to apply for funding.

It was in this environment that one community development worker, Diana, who went on to found Lifeline, made her name locally as a skilled organiser and advocate for local people. Born and raised on the estate, she was trained and employed by a local university to run a health inequalities action research project funded by the Welsh Assembly Government. Diana took the time to detail the approach she developed and sedimented through this work:

> I follow those principles of finding out what people want and then tweaking the action, so you are always guided by what people actually say they want, or what needs doing and their own opinions on things. It's assuming that people in communities are the experts on their own lives and the experts on their own issues, and they are. So, they live it, they breathe it every day, and we are just following their views on how things should be tackled. (Diana, 2009)

Drawing on these principles, she created a piece of work to engage local women with a healthy living programme for families. As part of this project, those taking part routinely cooked and ate together, and, as she explained, it was when they gathered together at the table that the 'magic' happened; it was then that talk would invariably turn to their worries and troubles, 'what was bothering them'. For Diana, these conversations provided the material she needed. As time went on, conversation turned, with increasing frequency and rising concern, to the personal impacts of prospective New Labour reforms to social security benefits. Many of the women were lone mothers living on benefits, and many were beginning to feel the pressure to search for and secure paid work, regardless of its quality or sustainability. One woman shared that she couldn't make the sums add up: she would be working for 'next to nothing' in terms of additional income. Another, that she couldn't manage the 'awkward' hours she was offered alongside caring for her children. More than one story circulating on the estate told of mothers reluctantly leaving children to wake themselves, dress and feed themselves and make their own way to school so that they could work graveyard shifts. The following example is typical of the challenges and pressures women faced and discussed together:

> I went for a job just before I found out I was pregnant ... hotel cleaning and working in the kitchen. And I went to a lone parent adviser and when she worked it out, I would have to find childcare for the weekends 'cos I had to work weekends as part of the job offer, and by the time we worked it out, I was working all week and all weekend for an extra £10 on top of the benefits, plus I would have had to have paid more or less, I think it was £6 less rent than what other people would have to pay. (Lifeline girl, 2009)

More generally, people responded to the prospect of a having 'shit job' with dismay and there was no guarantee they could get one. One of the women applied for cleaning work in a care home only to find that she didn't meet the criteria because she didn't have the necessary qualification.

These examples crystallised the experiences and concerns of many living on the estate who, alarmed by welfare reform, were grappling with the question of what the conditions and requirements of the new policies might mean for them. The collective sense of foreboding among the estate's community workers and activists was also plain, and they were beginning to cast their role as one of 'picking up the pieces': 'Welfare reform is coming. We have to gear up for this. We have to be able to react to it and to try and prepare people as much as possible. The fallout is going to be massive. We have to prepare them as much as possible.' The impulse to resist was strong, because, as Diana put it, there was a feeling that those public officials who were 'coming into' the estate were not just ineffective, but 'disrespectful':

> We knew that there was stuff coming into the [estate], projects coming in, especially from DWP [Department for Work and Pensions], that were saying we are coming to help people get back into work la-de-dah. And when people didn't turn up ... it was always because people couldn't be bothered or they're lazy up here, they'd rather be on benefits. Well, we knew that wasn't true. It was just the way they were delivering and the people who were delivering. It was awful. It was disrespectful. (Diana, 2008)

Still, the question of how best to respond was both preoccupying and frustrating. The turning point – a moment of serendipity – came when Diana happened to attend a seminar organised by a local charity:

> Obviously these people are skilled, they are bright ... but cannot access the jobs because of the lack of qualifications. ... You have got to have a qualification ... I was just in this quandary. ... I was half thinking to myself, well, I don't know if I can go on anymore. ... I have reached a point where I can't do anything more for these people 'cos we are hitting upon this and there doesn't seem to be any solution. Lucky for me ... I went to a seminar ... on a tranche of research around employability. ... I said: 'Look, what you are talking about here ... I know I have got a group of women who are ready for this now.' (Diana, 2008)

The approach was appealing. It presented an employability initiative explicitly designed to help people avoid 'shit jobs' through a holistic approach to education embedded in communities. Delivery involved constructing an argument to engage local people fashioned around ideas of resisting coercion, exercising autonomy and being a 'bit canny':

> With the sort of change in government policy now, seeing all the time that people are being encouraged to go back to work, what we say to people is: 'Well take your destiny into your own hands – do something

about it before you are forced into a situation where you are going to have to take that on. Be a bit canny. Come to us – we will help you so your destiny is going to be in your own hands, you are going to get a better job because you have used your time wisely.' And so that's ... what we are trying to do is to avoid the situation where people are being forced into minimum wage jobs ... the children won't be cared for so well. ... I don't know who would be looking after the children, because we have actually looked at the jobs that are available to people ... not that many are child-friendly hours – the figures just don't match. So I don't know what they are gonna do about that, especially with this change coming in, in October with single parents. (Diana, 2008)

The lack of affordable, good-quality child or social care, the paucity of social protections and the high prevalence of jobs with low pay and poor terms and conditions meant many women on the estate could not support themselves and their families easily. Convinced local people deserved more and inspired to act, Diana created Lifeline with the express purpose of providing them with a 'better' choice, a chance of 'a new life' for those seeking to make a change before they would be compelled to do so. The thinking was that 'if they are going to have to work, let's make this as positive an experience as possible for them'.

And while, with the onset of welfare reform, Diana did identify the precarity of single parents in the new policy environment, this group was not explicitly targeted, nor was intake restricted to women (although the project engaged very few men over the years):

We know there is a high percentage of single parents. We didn't have to actively target them. We knew. ... If you run something, we know a percentage of them are going to be that. We don't have to stigmatise people. You know they are here and that's it. (Diana, 2008)

Debunking the myth of the feckless single mother, the challenge was to secure good jobs for women who were among 'an awful lot of people here who have so much more potential'. Local labour shortages in the field of health and social care were identified, including some that offered 'careers', such as speech therapists, nurses and social workers, as well as 'good jobs' in allied sectors such as education, childcare and mental health. Targeting these types of work – entering the labour market in deeply gendered occupations (Hochschild, 1983; James, 1989) – was framed as making a great deal of sense. It was the path of least resistance, complying with broader cultural imperatives that construct caring as one of the few ways working-class women are able to demonstrate their respectability (Skeggs, 1997). After all, as one of the project workers explained, 'it's what they have been doing all their lives'.

Their personal biographies were positioned as an asset; their 'everyday caring roles' could be 'put to use'. The practices of unpaid care in the domestic sphere were reinterpreted as a valuable skill set to be honed and transposed, exchangeable in the labour market:

> When I sort of looked at the girls then, and they were sort of telling me, I could see from the way that they were living their lives with their families, the kind of support they were giving people, the drugs problems they were handling, children with special needs, behavioural difficulties, looking after elderly people in their own family as a matter of course. Caring took up a big chunk of their lives. (Diana, 2009)

These narratives drew on wider, collective constructions of emotion work, coded through gender and class relations, that lead us to understand that 'to care' for others is a 'natural' preserve and strength of a working-class woman (Oakley, 1974; James, 1989; Bolton, 2005). It might not have been the ideal or first choice for all of them, but it was thought to be realistic.

A bid for European funding was successful and a space was found in a community centre on the estate in 2007, tucked away in the middle of a row of homes high on the edges of the estate, with views across the community, the town, the valley and the mountains beyond. It was modest and functional; a kitchen, office, a small room filled with computers and a larger room, big enough to hold a group of 15 or so learners very comfortably around a pod of desks forming a horseshoe. While the workers would suggest that 'catching' people was not always easy, the initial draw for most 'joining up' was clear enough, as one learner succinctly explained at the time: 'She said, "we'll sort out childcare for you"; she said, "you will get qualifications at the end of it."' A good number could be reached on these grounds. Focusing on the 'needs of learners' meant introducing practical measures and incentives to ease their way, and the provision of good-quality, free childcare in particular was a deliberate and politically charged lure:

> One big thing ... is childcare ... how can these women access things on an equal basis when there is no childcare? It's alright for the government to say, but the reality is very different. ... There is no point in having this course unless we can get quality childcare, we have got to have quality childcare for people coming on the course. (Diana, 2009)

While childcare provision was often cited as a key tenet of government social policy, provision on the estate and the surrounding area was poor:

> Childcare is a nightmare, always, always a nightmare. ... Because it is a poor area, we have got Flying Start. ... But ... Flying Start doesn't

cater to us because it runs from like half past nine in the morning 'til half past eleven, which is no good to us, and then it runs from like one 'til three ... so what do you do with kids in the middle? (Lifeline activist-worker, 2009)

At the time in Wales, there were 3,600 registered childcare places for children under nine years old (this figure included childminders, day nurseries and holiday or after-school clubs). This meant there was one registered childcare place for every seven children. In the most disadvantaged communities, the reality was worse. In Merthyr Tydfil, for example, there was one place for every 12 children under the age of nine (Symonds and Kelly, 2005). The project was also run within school hours so that mothers could drop off older children and be back in time to pick them up from school, and free transport to and from the venue was provided to the few who needed it. Small, essential but prohibitively expensive items, like scientific calculators and stationery, which could easily have been overlooked, were also provided. It cost very little if anything to attend. As one of the workers explained, part of 'the beauty of Lifeline' was that they made 'sure coming to Lifeline costs nothing'. Unlike being at college or university, where you might 'look out of the way' if you haven't got any money, the women could go 'with no money all the time'.

During the first couple of years, the project engaged a core group of around 10 learners each year, with a workforce of one and then two 'support workers' (one of whom was always on hand, sitting with the learners during classes and taking breaks with them). While workers were keen to foster a 'sociable', 'relaxed' atmosphere, they also explained to the women what they 'were about', insisting that they 'would expect commitment ... expect them to achieve things ... so that they can move on'. The day-to-day routines of Lifeline were timetabled as you might expect: lessons led by tutors ran in blocks through the day, punctuated by breaks. One of the project workers explained this meant that 'the actual structure wasn't so different from college, you know – you've got your tutor, you've got your work'. But the same worker also made it clear that Lifeline was a highly managed space that was 'totally different' from the formality of a traditional classroom or lecture theatre. For their part, the women described the project as 'a nice place, a warm and cosy place', a 'homely' place where the rhythms of learning meant it 'wasn't going into anything too quick' and you could 'just rock up' a little late if you needed to and simply take the time to explain why.

The project worked in partnership with local organisations like the further education college and the Workers' Educational Association (WEA) to offer qualifications on the 'first rung of the ladder'. Diana described designing a bespoke course, which involved carefully curating a curriculum from a range of resources:

> With the WEA, we were really lucky. … They moved into our building, which we'd given them, so they were really friendly with us. I['d] just go to them and I'd say: 'Can I have a look at what courses you offer?' … So I would go in there and say: 'Oh, that's not good, that's not good. I like a bit of that one and a bit of that one and a bit of that one.' … I'd say: 'I don't want [it] accredited at that level. I only want it at this level', and I want the way the learning is, what do you call, certified or whatever. I said. 'I don't want it done that way. I think they could be able to do that by recording this or doing that.' And so I learned how to write the course as a sideline then, so I learned how to make the courses. (Diana, 2021)

The result was a set of materials designed to put the women on the path of 'learning how to learn', the creation of a year-long 'access to access' course that prepared them for college, perhaps university, and the world of work. In this setting, they would work towards a range of recognised qualifications in subjects including maths, English, information technology, sociology, criminology, psychology, counselling and women's history, as well as taking part in work experience placements with local employers, including the local hospital. At the end of the academic year, everyone 'graduated' with something, and the workers were careful in that they 'wouldn't put anyone forward' for a qualification who they 'didn't think could complete it'. The tutors were described as 'gentle' and 'non-threatening' in the classroom, and a 'summer school' was put in place to 'keep' the women and their children. This final component was framed through a process of action research, an example of how the workers could 'tweak the action':

> The people that we'd supported and got accepted to do access courses and other type things, like teaching assistants and that in [college], okay they finished with us by about July and then they were due to go to college early September. Well, I'd start hearing rumours then, because I'd work all summer, oh so and so is saying she's not going now. So I started to look into what was happening. People's confidence was dropping over the summer. So we said: 'Well, what can we do about this then?' We need to, the first thing is we need to keep in contact with everybody regularly, so we'll have the centre open for the staff. I said, 'We got to have the centre open and if that means we got to have the children here …'. We had Paula and the Cinema Club ladies running a crèche for me downstairs so I could have the things upstairs. (Diana, 2021)

Over the long school holidays, they started 'something educational' but also had 'some fun' (cooking, gardening, bushcraft, pond-dipping, crafting and taking day trips to local beauty spots or further afield to visit the Maritime Museum and play in the rock pools in Bracelet Bay in Swansea).

Critically, as one of the project workers would explain years later, while funders might have wanted measurable, concrete outputs against objective indicators of employability, among all this activity there was an understanding that this was 'not just about getting them through qualifications' and into college and paid work – this was 'about keeping them on track, [and] there are many tracks'. The intervention was finely calibrated, with 'support workers' on hand to provide practical action, advice and emotional support with any personal troubles the women had (perhaps with family relationships, housing concerns or financial insecurity). The worker 'was a constant who was going to be there through it all ... working on the estate, wasn't there once a week, was always there ... If they wanted to come and see me, they had my phone number' (Diana, 2021). The setting was framed as a space of care. For some, coming to Lifeline could 'just' be about 'taking time out' from overburdened lives.

One of the consistencies across the women's accounts, both when they were directly involved with the project and later, was the high regard they placed on the subjects and topics that leant towards the therapeutic. Most notably, the principles of counselling practice – how to be a counsellor – were studied through an element of group counselling, whereby the women were asked to share and reflect on aspects of their own lives. These kinds of interventions were framed by the workers through ideas of personal development, self-scrutiny and self-reflection, and the associated idea of building 'resilience' so that 'if they do fall, they can get back up'. The counselling course was well received among the women, a salve for the corrosive impacts of hardship and stigma. These kinds of interactions – in place to help women 'understand how they feel' – can be viewed as a kind of 'political therapy', far removed from any sense of self-blame and personal inadequacy, or expectation of a straightforward personal adjustment to a set of objective conditions (Hanisch, 2006). These practices were understood to bring 'about interconnection, interdependence and collectivity', creating the space for the reparative work of caring for each other (Hall, 2020: 247; Barnett and Land, 2007; Askins, 2014; Horton, 2016; Jupp, 2017).

Reflection

Weaving the threads of Lifeline together was a capacious and creative process. Its footings were precarious, and like other civil society organisations working in this field, the project lacked consistent, reliable funding (Damm, 2012; Beck, 2018; Irvine et al, 2024b). The founder, Diana, appeared tireless in her efforts to bring in money from funders and contributions in kind from a range of local organisations. Adept at forging partnerships, she pieced and then held together the project by bending with policy and programme streams, which required political savvy. Securing contributions meant forming and drawing on personal and professional connections across public and quasi-public bodies and voluntary organisations at local and national and supranational scales. This kind of activity – working the angles of these different sites of power in this way (Newman, 2012a; 2012b; Jupp, 2017) – involved leveraging networks in the hope that a well-placed sponsor might be receptive, and this required gentle persuasion on some occasions and conversations with a little heat on others. It was a patchwork of 'various pockets of money over the years', which meant salary costs for workers were paid for by one funder, the rent for the building by another and childcare by another again, and tutors were provided by various further education providers. Beyond 'tweaking the action' in response to the needs of the women, there was a need to account for public funds and demonstrate 'value for money', which meant that monitoring and evaluating the women's progress also textured everyday working practices. This was the kind of consuming hard work that was needed to generate and open up 'new spaces of possibility', 'new potential pathways' and 'new emergent practices' for social provisioning (Newman, 2012b: 473, 474). Most fundamentally, it involved working across scales and sites, building and sustaining relationships, using local knowledge 'in ways that enable traditionally "silent" voices to be heard' (Larner and Craig, 2005: 418).

The therapeutic frames the everyday life of contemporary institutional settings (Furedi, 2004). It is the subject of a great deal of scrutiny and debate. Here, commentators suggest emphasising an individual's emotional competence and regulation risks neglecting material or practical remedies to personal troubles, as practices of self-help or self-actualisation are repositioned as solutions to structurally embedded social issues (Gillies, 2005; Bottrell, 2013; Harrison, 2013; Evans and Reid, 2014; Gill and Orgad, 2018; Jensen, 2018). These arguments, suggesting 'individualised solutions have colonised debates about what were once considered to be collective social problems' require careful application here (Jensen, 2018: 97). The Lifeline approach to education and welfare moved well beyond narrow, individualising calculations that detach women from their biographies and the places where they lived (Rees et al, 1997). For those on the ground, the figure of the welfare subject as a self-governing, entirely autonomous, morally corrupt agent in need of 'activation' by officials was unrecognisable. Diana may have confronted the arguments more forcefully than others, but she was not alone on the estate in her scepticism and condemnation of the intensification of welfare conditionality. Many development workers were radically minded and took their activist commitments into their working lives (Newman, 2012a), believing that institutions needed to be torn down and rebuilt rather than merely modified. But they were also practically minded – neither revolutionary opponents nor unwitting managers, but pragmatic mitigators of welfare reform, intent on ameliorating its worst effects. Lifeline was not the product of softening beliefs, but an articulation of a set of demands – for good-quality, sustainable education and paid work with a feminist impetus – connected to the fights for women's equality, for workers' rights and for social protections. Repudiating the prevailing politics and policies of the time, the workers were attuned to the knowledge that 'there are those people who say these people do not deserve this opportunity, do not deserve to have money spent on them'. The project was an attempt to circumvent the benefits system, neutralise state levers and help women protect themselves. Its ethos was underscored by the idea that social provisioning should be attentive to need and responsive to personal circumstances, capacities and commitments as well as wider social-historical conditions (Newman, 2012a; 2012b; Wright, 2016). The therapeutic model was regarded as helpful, but it was also understood that the work of self-reflection and self-determination could not be severed from tight purse strings, caring commitments or the baked in realities of a local labour market.

Deep disillusionment with national politics and policies and, by association, local welfare officials, was scored deeply into the interactions and practices of the space. Working within and against the state – 'doing our own thing' – was challenging, and it wasn't only potential funders that needed to be persuaded, as one of the project workers explained:

> One was really concerned about how Lifeline was going to affect her benefits. She said, you know: 'I am really, really worried.' I said: 'Look, it isn't a problem. I've actually written letters for the girls to the Social, and they have never ever, you know, and they haven't.' I wouldn't lie. But ... 'cos we are not an official educational body ... so when they have gone to work-focused interviews ... the Social will say to them: 'Well, I will need proof that you are going, that you are attending that course.' ... So just a small letter – yes they are attending, they attend full days on blah blah and they will be subject to the offer and hopefully they will get a place, you know, send them on the right career path, education pattern in the end. So, I said, you know, 'It's not ....' She couldn't, she wouldn't have any of it at all. ... 'It's really quite daunting Hel', 'Cos it really opens your eyes to the fact, even though, you know, I reassured her ... the girls reassured ... the other girls from the year before. But somewhere in her mind, she was really worried that she was gonna end up committing some sort of a fraud. (Lifeline worker, 2009)

The state funding that the project secured both provided material resource and conferred some symbolic legitimacy, but clearly it was not enough to convince everyone. The workers were trying to offer women on the estate 'a way out', but some were understandably wary if not outright fearful of an intervention that wasn't quite 'official'. In this case and others, the reassurance was no match for the Social. But some were drawn in, and in the next chapter we consider their collective biography in some depth.

5

The girls

> The underclass.
>
> Lifeline girl, 2009
>
> All our own fault.
>
> Lifeline girl, 2021

The account of 'the girls' in this chapter looks back to their lives as children and young adults, prior to 2010, their engagement with the Lifeline project and the reforms that made 'getting by' with social security benefits a less tenable position, both materially and culturally. Drawing on conversations from the first wave of the study (2007–10) and those that took place more than a decade later (2021–22), the chapter shares something of their experiences, the rhythms of their day-to-day lives, the values they held and the commitments they pursued. Most of the women were drawn to Lifeline from the estate or just beyond, and many had long-standing connections through friendships, family, school or other channels. A far smaller number were relatively new to the estate when they first connected with the project, finding themselves slightly adrift having moved from further afield for a new home. At that time, all but one of the women were claiming benefits and all but three of those were in receipt of benefits by virtue of their lone parent status. All were White, all but one were in their teens or twenties, and all but two were mothers to young children (although of the remaining two, one described 'bringing up' a 'stepchild' and the other 'adopting' a grandchild). In the later wave of fieldwork, perhaps with a greater sense of security in their circumstances and the benefit of some distance, the women appeared more forthcoming. These later interactions often seemed to elicit fuller and franker accounts and, at times, involved the disclosure of intimate details of harrowing experiences – things that they were 'going to say now', but that they didn't 'really want … on paper'. Taking care to respect this kind of assertion, the approach taken here is in keeping with how the women tended to see themselves – as a tightly bound collective who held an awful lot in common and shared a great deal with each other. While each woman has a distinctive life story, a collective biography is sketched here to present the broad contours of their lives and draw together the threads that cohered, rather than detailing the intricacies and complexities of the personal lives that implicitly form such a narrative.

One summer evening in 2009, a graduation ceremony was held in a function room of a local pub to recognise and celebrate the achievements of the most recent cohort of Lifeline women, and the progress of the 'old girls'. The event was marked in calendars as a special occasion, weeks if not months in advance. Everyone was excited; it was going to be fun. New dresses were bought, make-up done, hair styled and nails painted. Each of the girls could invite close family and friends, and Lifeline's workers had invited some of the local 'great and good'. The girls were beaming as the ceremony got underway. Certificates were handed out – 'I can't believe I passed that – I never thought I would' – to a raucous reception from a small band of supporters. These were a hard copy of achievement, and no one left empty-handed. Giggling and bashful, a couple offered a few well-chosen words, thanking the workers for all they had done for them. Then the roll of honour was extended to the women from the previous year. Presented as mentors, their accomplishments were positioned as examples of what was possible (one had enrolled in nursing, another in social work, another …), the easy manner of these women was suggestive of a greater self-assurance that had come with time. After the ceremony, attention turned to the buffet, a few drinks and a disco. That night provided my first opportunity to talk with some of the old girls at length, and a spontaneous conversation with one of them in the pub toilets stood out. As we checked our make-up in the mirror, we spoke a little about how the research was going and how she was getting on in college. Talk turned to her interest in sociology and her reflections on her own life and the lives of the rest of the girls. Honing in on the term 'underclass', she said: 'Well, that's me at the end of the day – that's all of us.' The baldness of the statement was startling, unusual, and years later, in 2021, I raised this conversation with much the same response:

Helen:	You probably don't remember this … we were in the toilet looking in the mirror. I think my mascara … it had been raining and I was all over the shop with it. And you said, if you're in, if you're receiving benefits, you're part of the underclass.
Lifeline girl:	Yeah, that's what it's like. You do, you treat it as another class, as an underclass. Yes, that's exactly how it feels.

The women's sense of their own marginalisation was rarely discussed or presented so directly. More often, the women would choose their words carefully, adding caveats and clarifying their accounts, caught in a tension between some kind of acknowledgement and then a deflection of their position (Skeggs, 1997; Shildrick and MacDonald, 2013). An account of this kind was offered during the first wave of fieldwork, by another 'old girl' who was studying at the local college at the time:

> I think when you are a student ... you are at the bottom. When I get through, I will be in the middle. I could be up the top. ... But I think it is stupid when they say classes ... really. ... It doesn't bother me. Some people get intimidated though. Like, I am not being thing, but you are from Cardiff and people think Cardiff is snobby. You are a student, so I could say you are down the bottom, like me, see, which I wouldn't say that because I look at you as like a doctor standing over by there, that doctor is right by there. But you don't look at people like that, but some people do. I think it is stupid. (Lifeline girl, 2009)

This excerpt is illustrative of the ways in which the women's narratives wove together a set of ideas or proxies for their class location relating to geographical, educational, employment or occupational status and associated ideas of hierarchy, mobility and equality. Each of these exchanges and commentaries spoke in different ways to the women's repeated exposure to forms of symbolic violence, the degradations and diminishments that punctuated everyday life, which they attempted to disavow (Sennett and Cobb, 1972).

Perhaps most notable were those narratives that arose in relation to the state's surveillance of the intimacies of family life, accomplished through the presence of various 'professional trouble workers', including social workers, health visitors, educational psychologists and the new category of parenting experts that had emerged (Walter, 1977: 153; Steedman et al, 2016; Jensen, 2018). Most of the women relied on the state to put food on their table and a roof over their heads, but there were numerous, stigmatising interactions with the state beyond welfare eligibility interviews. Their marginalisation was evident in the extent and intensity of their exposure to these kinds of encounter, which were at times framed as deeply intrusive and diminishing, prompting frantic preparations, especially if the professional was coming into the home. Years later, one woman remembered feeling panic at the prospect of preparing for a health visitor and thinking:

> It was just, well, oh my God, my house is not clean enough. Oh my God, this is not done. Oh my God, I've not got time to do ... I was really bad. Oh my God, she's going to come here and he's coughing, she's going to think I'm a bad mother. My anxiety would go through the roof. (Lifeline girl, 2021)

When the boundary between the domestic space of family life and the state becomes porous in this way, it is very clear that 'personal problems are political problems' (Hanisch, 2006).

The women's accounts also spoke to the ways in which stigma and hardship were experienced concurrently. We know women, and lone mothers in particular, are vulnerable to both recurrent and persistent poverty (Dermott and Pantazis, 2017; Reis, 2018). And like others in this situation, the girls refrained from describing themselves as 'poor' or using the word 'poverty' (Chase and Walker, 2013; Shildrick and MacDonald, 2013). It was only in later interviews, perhaps because their circumstances had changed, that some were open to discussing in more granular detail a life of 'just existing' with little money. Still, just one woman used this terminology, and on only one occasion, saying: 'There was a lot of strain back then, a lot … and it just got to the point where … you just feel poor.' In earlier conversations, the women were more likely to suggest that 'it's not too bad', before going on to describe 'just about coping', 'eking things out' and 'getting by'. Academic analyses of these kinds of commentaries tend to emphasise the sense of personal agency such phrases connote and the hidden activity involved in navigating the world in these circumstances (Skeggs, 1997; Charlesworth, 2000; Shildrick and MacDonald, 2012; Daly and Kelly, 2015; McKenzie, 2015; Dagdeviren et al, 2016; McDowell, 2017; Pemberton et al, 2017a; Dagdeviren and Donoghue, 2019). It is possible to romanticise these practices as thrifty or frugal to the neglect of the 'strain' implicated in the demoralising and frequently overwhelming effort to 'get by' (Orr et al, 2006; Gillies, 2007; Harrison, 2013; Hall and Holmes, 2017; Pemberton et al, 2017a; 2017b; O'Hara, 2020). Poverty 'is a condition of limit', a 'way of being' that involves restrictions to agency and autonomy rather than an infinitely replenishable and virtuous capacity for resourcefulness (Shildrick, 2018: 6; Donoghue and Edmiston, 2020). For these women, 'getting by' consisted of taken-for-granted, rather than noteworthy or remarkable, practices (Canvin et al, 2009; Batty and Flint, 2010). It involved careful calculation and extremely tight money management every single day because money ran low and could run out (Daly and Kelly, 2015; Hill et al, 2016). Descriptions of outgoings were confined to the essentials, with little scope for the experimental or the ethical, and 'no extras' in the way of leisure or luxury. One woman summarised her food shop succinctly: 'I buy Asda's green and white [then the store's budget range] and that's it – nothing else – you buy what you can afford.' It was a case of 'making sure' there was enough money for gas, electric, water and the telly licence, as well nappies, wet wipes, milk and food in the cupboards, but also money for school trips and school uniforms – 'things like that, and there is always something'. This was 'mundane ground', punctuated by 'everyday emergencies' (Mitchell, 2020: 238; Hall, 2020). The impossibility of saving meant daily life was textured by 'a pervasive sense of insecurity' (Pemberton et al, 2017a: 1164), of 'walking tightropes that could start wobbling at any time' (CRESR Research Team, 2011: 44). Some habits or incidents seemed to stick in the memory years later as acute expressions of the extent of the precarity and anxiety; 'having enough' was a persistent concern. One woman remembered going to the shop with a calculator knowing that she would have to pay for gas and she would have very little left. Another remembered borrowing money to pay for her child's shoes, a situation that filled her with dread as she knew it would make her short the following week. Another recalled 'trying to make it fun' for her children but 'thinking have we got enough for food?'.

For most, motherhood necessarily meant a withdrawal from some social engagements, but these were also avoided simply to save money from going 'down the drain'. A particular Christmas lingered in the memory of one woman:

> I loved Christmas, and I still love Christmas, but I've got to be honest, that Christmas was horrible. It was her first Christmas and she was in her walker, and everybody obviously had gone out ... it was still at that point. And then I was, like, sat there thinking: 'Oh my God, I'm totally on my own here, like at Christmas. I'm totally on my own.' (Lifeline girl, 2021)

For some, a night out with friends was framed at that time in their life as obviously a complete impossibility. One remembered this clearly: 'Because how am I gonna manage the rest of the bloody week? So you just can't do it, you can't.' This could mean cutting off important sources of comfort, support and fun (Pemberton et al, 2017a).

That mothers prioritise their children is well documented; self-sacrifice is not uncommon among parents living on low incomes – they tend to cut back on their own needs to try and protect their children (Daly and Kelly, 2015; McKenzie, 2015; Hill et al, 2016; Main and Bradshaw, 2016; Millar and Ridge, 2017; Daly, 2018). In our earlier conversations in particular, the women took time to explain that they would often 'make do' and 'go without' for the sake of their children, shielding them from hardship and any associated sense of shame: 'You don't want to see them without, so there is a lot that you go without as well to give them [what they need].' There was a general sense that if their children were okay, then they were okay, even though they 'scrimped and saved' and 'had basically nothing'. Treats were reserved for the children, and providing them with small pleasures was regarded as an important demonstration of love, even though it put additional strain on financial resources (Tirado, 2014; Daly and Kelly, 2015). Special occasions, often restricted to children's birthdays and Christmas, could mean having to ask for loans from family and friends, the credit union or the Prov[1] (for one woman, turning to the latter one Christmas added up to a crippling debt 'hanging over' her for years). Reflecting on these circumstances years later, one woman argued that the income from benefits 'is not enough', explaining the 'eating or heating' dilemma she faced:

> It is not enough to live on. … It's not. When you've got to feed your kids, you've got to make that choice. Do I not put the heating on today and feed them, or do I not feed them and put the heating on? How do you make that choice? (Lifeline girl, 2021)

Balancing the life-limiting constraints of a low income with being a good mother was *the* most acute pressure point for most of the women, a recurring feature of their narratives in both waves of research. They 'had to make sure' there was enough for their children, and as one explained, 'if it was just me … I wouldn't care'.

All this suggests that the management of precarity – of 'getting by', 'just about coping' and 'eking out' – involves a set of deeply gendered, moralised responsibilities, commitments and practices (Jensen, 2018; McDowell, 2017; Hall, 2020). The women's accounts of their relationships with their children's fathers, which varied greatly across instances and over time, also provide insights here. A small number had remained in a steady relationship with the fathers, and a smaller number still had consistently lived with them. But most had some experience of being a single mother, either maintaining, moving into or passing through lone parenthood. Several described the fathers of their children as men who had walked away and 'just stopped all contact'. The stories told by one of the women during our first interview detailed her own experience of abandonment but also a belief that her situation was not uncommon on the estate. She began by describing the enjoyment she derived when she had a job (a time she associated with having an income of her own and the freedom to enjoy nights out, new outfits, holidays, etc.) before she 'caught' pregnant. She went on to explain that she had decided not to return to paid work, but to stay at home with the baby, not least because the father of her child reassured her that this was for the best:

> When we were still together … he said to me: 'Well, you will have to finish, but don't worry about it because I am going to be working.' So, I didn't worry. I just assumed that everything was hunky dory. … You know, things happen. I was just left and I was just thinking, ah shit, what am I going to do? (Lifeline girl, 2009)

Angry and resentful, she went on to explain:

> *He* had a child too, you know, not just me. … I am struggling to make sure that she has got absolutely everything. … He works but he doesn't

> give me nothing. ... He was going to Las Vegas for the boxing and I was really pissed off 'cos I thought gambling all that money now, when you have got a kid in the house that needs it more .... When it comes to money, he will not part ... I will ring him up and say 'Look, I am really on my arse, like, can you please get her a jacket or something?' ... I do everything, everything. ... He is not even worrying. (Lifeline girl, 2009)

And she suggested this was an experience shared by others:

> All his mates, each and every one of them, have done exactly the same to their partners as what he done, and they are all in it together – one huge big group of people going to Las Vegas when their kids are in the house. One girl was taking her boyfriend, her ex-boyfriend, to court, and he put cockroaches through her door. ... Oh, you wouldn't believe they are really like that, you wouldn't believe it. Honest to God, I am not lying to you – that is the God's honest truth. And his own child, his little boy, was there in that house. (Lifeline girl, 2009)

Mindful of the broader stereotypes of working-class fatherhood limited to absenteeism or fecklessness (Neale and Davies, 2016; Jensen, 2018), these kinds of stories revealed more general social processes and laid bare structures that are normally hidden (Sayer, 1992). The women related these kinds of experiences to a double standard of sexual morality and observed that they were partly the product of the misogynistic air they all breathed, a reconfigured culture of machismo that signalled, 'it's a man's community ... and a man can walk away from his family at any time and nothing gets said'.[2] This representation of a distinct group of 'missing men' circulated widely on the estate, with fathers framed as either unwilling or unable to provide for their children. Protracted resentments and disputes over non-existent or inadequate and irregular child maintenance payments were not uncommon (Ridge and Millar, 2011; Millar and Ridge, 2017). For these women, the lack of material support from their children's fathers was deeply distressing; they couldn't understand how fathers could be content seeing a child 'living like this'. One asked: 'Why wouldn't you want to support them, even if he didn't support me?' The power and advantages men held over women were a common point of discussion, and some could only reconcile themselves to this circumstance with a resolute assertion that 'we are better off without him' or a dismissive 'what was I thinking?'

More troubling still were the personal accounts of domestic violence that circulated, which were a notable feature of the later interviews in particular. Some women framed the fathers of their children as an unpredictable and malignant presence, responsible for sexual violence, physical and verbal abuse, harassment, intimidation and forms of coercive control. As one explained of her persistently abusive ex-partner: 'He left me on my own with the baby, but did not leave *me* alone.' These were relationships that 'just went from bad to worse'. For some, it had taken time to 'find the strength' to cut ties because they 'didn't know any different', though in hindsight they knew they 'should have run a mile'. Again, in these instances, the women's foremost concern was their children, and among those with experience of domestic abuse and violence, it wasn't unusual to hear the sentiment: 'I don't care what he does to me as long as he doesn't touch the children.'

Others described having tried, or still trying, to make it work through the ebb and flow of sometimes 'turbulent' relationships. In these circumstances, fathers were likely to be positioned as an occasional and unreliable source of financial security and emotional support, including those who could 'just disappear for a few months' or who 'wouldn't have a clue' how to look after their children. In a small number of cases, bad debt racked up by an ex-partner in a woman's name added further injury. In contrast, several presented more sympathetic accounts, acknowledging that the fathers of their children 'didn't have the best life either' and that they themselves had 'a lot of issues, life issues, you know'. In these circumstances, and despite the difficulties they caused, these men were among those seen as 'good' fathers who provided a measure of financial support and were involved in their children's lives when and how they could be. This was also generally the case for those who had maintained long-standing relationships with the fathers of their children, even if they had not lived with them for extended periods of time (this could be due to a caring commitment taking a partner away from the family home, a prison spell or because precarious and unpredictable paid work and the associated frequency of signing on and off benefits meant it was just easier if they didn't live together). In these cases, men were framed predominantly as a nurturing presence, even if the family were not consistently living together.

The mothers each expressed a strong moral and emotional attachment to their commitment to caring for children (Haylett, 2003; Hennessy, 2009), and at the point in time when they were participating in the Lifeline project, the importance of 'being there' for their children was such that paid work tended to be framed primarily as a constraint on this activity (Duncan and Edwards, 1999; Lewis, 2005; Lynch and Lyons, 2009; McCarthy and Edwards, 2022; Andersen, 2023). On rare occasions, working mothers were framed as 'selfish' (see Hennessy, 2009), and mothering was framed as an important contribution and 'hard work' or a 'job in itself' (see Lynch and Walsh, 2016; Andersen, 2023). But mostly, it was simply that 'feelings got in the way' of paid work:

> I was like this single parent with an ill baby. ... Well, she was my child, and she was sick anyway, so I wanted to be with her. ... I was expecting

to go back to work. ... I was expecting to go back to work, but then after having her, I think everything totally changed because I didn't want to go back straight away. I wanted to be with her. ... You want that little bit of freedom of going to work because you know that would be brilliant, but it doesn't happen that way. I mean, your feelings get in the way. You think, oh well, I don't really want somebody else raising my child. (Lifeline girl, 2009)

The assertion that they wanted paid work that 'fitted in with their caring responsibilities' was commonplace (Millar, 2019: 91). The precarious and unpredictable employment available – often involving working early mornings, late evenings and weekends – together with the prohibitive cost, or just lack of, childcare made it unworkable (Haux, 2013; Graham and McQuaid, 2014; Patrick, 2014; Javornik and Ingold, 2015; Cain, 2016; Andersen, 2023). Earlier accounts tended to include descriptions of wrestling with the question of whether to take paid work that meant 'working odd hours all week' and needing to find childcare when there was very little, if any, extra money, and trapped in a low-pay, no-pay cycle that was difficult to escape from (Thompson, 2015; Forster et al, 2018). Many shared this sentiment, believing that 'if it were up to the Jobcentre', they 'would probably ... be somewhere stuck in a dead-end job'. They were convinced of their relegation to a secondary, gender-segregated labour market that meant the jobs on offer were 'absolutely crap ... the crap on the bottom'. Drawing on a combination of pragmatic and moral reasoning, most concluded that the paid work on offer could not compensate for 'not being there' for their children – 'letting them down' 'just for a job' they would 'hate'. It was 'difficult to shed domestic identities' (Wright, 2023: 46).

The small number who did try to balance paid work and unpaid care were only able to do so because of the support of close family. But many were not in a position to rely on informal help with childcare, and in fact their own caring roles extended also to close family members, friends and neighbours. Many were caring, some intensively, for parents and grandparents as well as informally 'adopted' children of former and new partners and family members. Some also actively participated in their wider community, taking part and volunteering in toddler groups, after-school clubs, youth groups, adult education classes, cooking clubs and 'other little things'; at times their participation was relied on to keep the activities going (Hall, 2020). As one woman explained, 'to me, that isn't doing nothing'. These roles mattered to them, and comments like 'I have always looked after people' and 'I naturally help someone if they are in trouble' peppered their narratives. Caring was the core medium through which they were able to value themselves and develop a sense of dignity and belonging (Graham, 1983; Skeggs, 1997). The following assessment one woman offered of her own character was typical: 'I am a very caring person … if someone is upset, I like to comfort them. … I like to take on people's problems, but I am, deep down, I am a very, very caring person. If I can help someone, then I will.'

Close personal relationships could play an important role in the management of everyday life, bolstering the women both materially and emotionally. But this kind of support relied on connections with close family, friends and neighbours, and the strength and nature of these sorts of relationships varied (Ghate and Hazel, 2002; Harrison, 2013; Daly and Kelly, 2015; McKenzie, 2015; Dagdeviren et al, 2016; Gill and Orgad, 2018). Some spoke of sustained, warm, 'marvellous' relationships with family members and not knowing where they 'would be without them' to offer a shoulder to cry on or give a helping hand (for example, by picking up children from school, cooking meals, getting in shopping or providing small loans or gifts in an emergency). These were descriptions of close-knit bonds of comfort and guidance that involved sharing confidences, responsibilities and resources. But, at times, even these kinds of relationships of care and concern were freighted with anxiety. Years after participating in Lifeline, one woman remembered someone from her extended family offering to help out by giving her some nappies. She knew 'the Social … would take the money for the pack of nappies off' what she was 'claiming', and she 'couldn't lie', so she refused the gift.

For others, there were limits to family support as benign relatives were overburdened themselves, perhaps because they were juggling paid work and their own caring commitments or maybe because they were older or in poor health and not in a position to help to any great degree either financially or emotionally (Daly and Kelly, 2015; Millar and Ridge, 2020). But more commonly women described the difficulties of 'a tough upbringing', and there were numerous accounts of ongoing familial estrangement, of 'strained' or 'broken' relationships with one or more family members. For these women, narrating their life history was akin to 'opening up a can of worms'. Stories of exposure to bereavement, abandonment, neglect, domestic abuse, sexual violence and exploitation in childhood were shared, and with greater frequency and detail in our later conversations as the slight inconsistencies or contradictions that were stumbling features of earlier accounts were fleshed out. This included descriptions of mothers and fathers who, for a range of reasons, had not been in a position to protect and care for their children: parents who 'could never support me', who 'weren't there much' or who 'weren't bothered really'. There were numerous accounts of either witnessing or being on the receiving end of 'pastings' and 'batterings'. A small number gave personal testimony of sexual abuse during childhood at the hands of predatory men who were either family members or had close links to their families. In these contexts of neglect, violence and abuse, several had moved out of the family home as children to live with or move between relatives – grandparents, aunts or uncles who were able to offer some support and comfort. One woman remembered 'jumping from school to school' as she moved between refuges with her mother. Another recalled a period of homelessness as a teenager, living in hostels or sleeping at friends' houses, 'going here, going there'. These experiences could be associated with privation; one woman described living with 'nobody to support me – I had nothing'; another explained that she 'literally had nobody'. Stories of truncated childhoods – 'the sense of growing up overnight'– were not uncommon in the face of extremely difficult circumstances in the family home. Some were young carers for younger siblings or adult family members experiencing chronic illness or substance misuse issues. One woman observed that as a child, she 'would be the one then' to step in or up. Another made reference to 'going without', 'trying to take care' and having 'to repair for people ... and do for others'. Some narrated their commitment to their own children through these experiences. It meant they wanted to 'protect them even more'. These kinds of personal circumstances also meant that for a significant number, it fell to them alone, with no savings and only limited and sporadic financial and emotional support, to make ends meet and 'keep going'.

For some these kinds of life histories, which meant growing up 'believing I'm no good', were associated with sustained periods of poor mental health across the life course. As one woman explained, 'just going through all that', you 'don't ever forget'; you 'just put it to the back of your mind as much as you can'. A small number recounted memories of traumatic events that could be triggered by the most routine happenings in later life, like a song, a type of food, a bath – 'little stuff' that 'no one would ever really think about'. Unsurprisingly, some of these women faced very difficult circumstances as adults, including experiences of homelessness, substance misuse, the criminal justice system, chronic debt and poor physical and mental health. References were made to chronic low self-esteem, distress, depression and compulsive behaviours, including self-harm and eating disorders, each of which were related to experiences in childhood and family circumstances, and compounded by the persistent anxiety of living on a low income. For many, prior to their engagement with Lifeline, a great deal of time was spent at home on their own with young children and there was an attached sense of isolation, restriction, and confinement. In our later conversations, talk often turned to an associated set of concerns, including experiences of depression, obsessive thoughts, compulsive behaviours and reclusiveness. A small number despaired at their cleaning routines, recalling how they ironed bed sheets every day, arranged and rearranged cupboards or painted their home in an ongoing cycle, moving 'from room to room'. Some detailed a sense of overwhelming desperation, a time of 'just constantly feeling bad', when they 'couldn't function', 'couldn't deal with life' and 'honestly thought' they were 'worth nothing, nothing at all'. These examples and others spoke to a sense of 'ontological insecurity' – a persistent and damaging disorientation produced through deep anxiety and a loss of connection with other people (Shildrick and MacDonald, 2012; O'Hara, 2014; Patrick, 2017; Pemberton et al, 2017a). Lisa McKenzie (2015: 170) captures this well in her description of a life lived in 'a pressure cooker, filled with fear, anger, desperation and fragility'. At the time, these circumstances had seemed fixed and unshakeable; as one of the women explained: 'You can't understand that this isn't the way life is supposed to be, you know?'

In this 'pressure cooker' environment, benefit reforms jarred sharply, ratcheting up anxiety and fear. While the women often spoke of a strong family history of 'going out to work' and relatives who had 'good jobs', they also mentioned those whose working lives were punctuated by recurrent periods of unemployment and underemployment – experiences at the margins of the labour market that they themselves had often shared. Many, and some from a young age, had worked, and worked hard, prior to having children, typically taking cleaning, retail or hospitality jobs and work in the informal economy. For most, paid work was confined to 'just jumping' from job to job or 'juggling' a 'couple of no-good jobs going … nowhere' for 'the minimum of money'. It was commonly felt that relatively poor academic records and sometimes interrupted schooling had restricted their progression. Only a small number had 'enjoyed education, enjoyed learning' and left school with good qualifications. More had left school with very few qualifications or none at all. The reasons offered were varied. Some enjoyed 'having a laugh' at school and didn't consider themselves particularly academic. Others felt undervalued at school and simply met the low expectations they felt their teachers had of them; as one woman said, 'they'd make you think that you were thick and [you would] sit at the back'. Yet others 'tried their best' with little success or could not 'be bothered with it' after 'not getting on'. One of the Lifeline project workers explained that 'perhaps some left school early … perhaps some didn't go at all', because a lot of them had 'tough upbringings'.

Reflection

Relaying the life stories of this small group of women necessarily involves a series of emphases and suppressions, and an attempt to take care to avoid distortions and embellishments that form, in the words of Nicky Wire, a well-known musician from the Valleys, 'the caricatures of working-class life' (Connolly, 1998). And while the girls could only 'make themselves' through the beliefs of others, within 'these constraints they deploy[ed] many constructive and creative strategies to generate a sense of themselves with value' (Skeggs, 1997: 162; Sayer, 2005). In various ways, each woman's life story told of the central value they placed on their caring commitments even while 'getting by' could involve not so much one thing after another as everything all at once. There was certainly no sense that claiming benefits was a strategic grift, that they had 'chosen the circumstances in which they live' (Wright, 2016: 243). One woman took time to explain just how far removed signing on for benefits as a single mother was from any premeditated preference or calculated self-interest:

> The Jobcentre was a nightmare because I'd never, because I'd always worked so I'd never had to deal with that side of things, and so I never knew what I could claim. I never knew what I had to do. I never knew anything on that side because I had my first job when I was 13. I always had to do, because of the life I had, I always had to do things on my own. I went out and got a job at 16, so I never experienced the fact of claiming anything, and so I didn't have a clue. I think I'd had my son for about five months before I knew I could claim anything for him. (Lifeline girl, 2021)

As another succinctly put it years later: 'I didn't have a clue what I could claim, what I couldn't – straight up, I didn't have a frigging clue.'

These women were neither saints nor sinners (Thane and Evans, 2012), and they weren't 'passive victims' either (Domosh, 1997: 82; Wacquant, 2002; Hanley, 2012). But their life stories do give good indication as to why it is unfeelingly irrational to conceive of ourselves as capable of drifting free of the complexities of personal circumstance – our social, cultural and historical moorings (MacDonald et al, 2005). This sense of constraint and limit was starker in later accounts, when the women placed greater stress on their lack of freedom and the lack of resources available to them to fashion their futures as they wished (Daly and Kelly, 2015; Wright, 2016; Reay, 2017). Lydia Morris (2019; 2020) reminds us that while debates over the relative value of our choices take place through the rhetorics and abstractions of the public sphere, they are also negotiated in concrete institutional settings (see also May, 2010). Lifeline was one such setting and these women looked to it for a 'a second chance' at a time when they were 'just trying to make better things' for themselves. But, interactions with the Social or the Jobcentre were also growing in significance, and this is the focus of the next chapter.

6

The interview

> I don't want to be another statistic. I don't want to be categorised.
> Lifeline girl, 2009

> All they wanted you to do was get a job. They didn't see the thing behind that was going on. You can't get a job if … you're not in a steady way. … They pushed for me to get these jobs. I had no qualifications; I had no skills. … I was timid, I was scared. I didn't like to ask the bus man for a bus ticket. … I wouldn't really look at people. I didn't have the confidence to go to someone and be like I am now. … I would feel anxious all the time.
> Lifeline girl, 2021

Appreciating how welfare restructuring unfolds in everyday life involves understanding its concrete institutional settings (Wright, 2012; Morris, 2019; 2020). Each of these settings can be understood as an active, social accomplishment, involving the enactment of policy by public officials through the state apparatus of street-level governance and the management of these interactions by those entitled to benefits. New classifications and practices – reflective of changing conditions of eligibility – are produced through this day-to-day activity. Of interest here are the 'work-focused interviews', first rolled out under New Labour in 2002 for new lone parent claimants with older children (Millar, 2006; Knijn et al, 2007). By 2008, during the first wave of this study, a six-monthly interview was mandatory for all lone parents other than those claiming on incapacity grounds, regardless of the age of their youngest child; and although job seeking and training activities were not compulsory, the introduction of financial sanctions meant non-attendance at interviews risked partial loss of benefits (Whitworth and Griggs, 2013). Each lone parent claimant was allocated an adviser, who provided guidance relating to searching for paid work, working out the financial implications of paid work, access to childcare and meeting the costs of transitioning to work, as well as some limited opportunities for education and training. At this time, those whose youngest child was 12 or older were being recategorised as 'jobseekers' and were required to demonstrate that they were available for and actively seeking paid work (Haux, 2013). Lone parents were no longer wholly released from the obligation to paid work by virtue of their parental status.

These developments meant that when we first met, for many of the Lifeline girls, the single most significant interaction with the state, and particularly so for those with older children, was their welfare eligibility interview at the local Jobcentre. The interview was a critical marker of a wider political culture of restructuring. An interaction where 'the state meets the street' (Zacka, 2017), it set out the contractual grounds for benefits eligibility and was developed as a mechanism engineered to change claimants' behaviours and beliefs. A further step change occurred during the years that followed as 'creeping conditionality' (Dwyer, 2004) gave way to 'ubiquitous conditionality' (Dwyer and Wright, 2014). The Jobcentre emerged at the frontline of a 'violent bureaucracy' when the requirements made of claimants intensified and punitive financial sanctioning for non-compliance expanded (Redman and Fletcher, 2021). We explore these developments through the accounts shared by women living in the Valleys. This includes the reflections of two of the Lifeline girls from the second wave of the study (2021–22): the first, from Sarah, consists of recollections of a work-focused interview that took place during the era of 'creeping conditionality', and the second, from Nicole, during the era of 'ubiquitous conditionality'. We then hear from two labour movement activists, both born and raised in the Valleys: Cheryl from Unite Community and Nadine from the Public and Commercial Services Union. They each share very different narratives of resistance to the intensification of welfare conditionality in the region.

During the first wave of the study (2007–10), the significance of welfare restructuring and the work-focused interview itself emerged in ethnographic work over time, as the women anticipated and reflected on their interactions with the Jobcentre. They 'hated going in there, absolutely hated it', 'hated it with a passion', attending reluctantly and at times in fearful apprehension. The interview was framed as an exacting exercise in coercion even then, and in the aftermath the women tended to dwell on how well they acquitted themselves, mostly concluding with a note of relief that it was at least 'done' for now. The interviews were cast as intrusive and generative of a sense of inferiority and deviancy; a belief that 'you're not good enough' and that 'even with nothing to hide, you still feel like you have something to hide'. The interviews involved attracting unpleasant, unwanted and unhelpful scrutiny; these were interactions freighted with mistrust and scepticism. At that time, one particular lone parent advisor – described by the girls as 'nasty', 'viscious' and 'horrible' – had gained a degree of local infamy. In meetings with this person, the women felt they had been weighed and measured, and found wanting.

Several women chose to speak at length about these interactions in each wave of research interviews. Telling stories – chronicling what happened, who was involved, what was said and felt – was a way of making sense of these events and their lives more broadly. Stories set scenes, establish characters, detail plots and raise personal troubles (Plummer, 2019). When we tell stories, we also craft explanations and justifications to account for our actions. When our adherence to social norms is in doubt, storytelling is a form of reparative work that allows us to present a morally sound self; through our narratives or 'vocabularies of motive', we attempt to present and preserve our moral character by accounting for our choices and actions, and finding a way through any suggestion of moral digression or transgression (Mills, 1940: 907). By attending to the ways the women chose to talk about these events, we can begin to better grasp their personal and societal significance. Here, we can follow a vein of sociological inquiry that explores the linkages between storytelling, the moral presentation of self and wider societal structures (Mills, 1940; Scott and Lyman, 1968; Riessman, 1990; Frank, 2002). In particular, scholars have attended to the ways people manage a 'spoiled identity', including that of 'claimant', by drawing on various available cultural scripts. Accounts of this kind might be textured by tacit or explicit acceptance, but also resistance and dissent, and authors use terms like subversion, minimisation, resignation, deflection, disidentification, disassociation, disengagement and more to describe these responses (see, for example, Piven and Cloward, 1971; McCormack, 2004; Wacquant, 2008; Luna, 2009; Pulkingham et al, 2010; Tyler, 2013; Daly and Kelly, 2015; McKenzie, 2015; Patrick, 2016; 2017; Edmiston and Humpage, 2018; Dwyer, 2019; Peterie et al, 2019; Donoghue and Edmiston, 2020; Mitchell, 2020). Typically, the stories told by the women who took part in this study enrolled many such strategies, illustrating how fluid and complex accounts of this kind can be.

Just two stories, emblematic of what the women chose to share about these experiences, are presented in some depth here. The first, part of a longer biographical account, was shared by Sarah in 2021. When we first met, in 2008, Sarah had been claiming benefits as a lone parent for five years. By the time we met again in 2021, she was settled in a 'good job' in the NHS. She was working long days and often picked up extra shifts, but the additional hours meant the pay was 'really good'. During this later conversation, she opened up a great deal, offering lengthy narratives of various aspects of her life history. This included reflections on her first work-focused interview, which had taken place not long before we first met:

> To be honest, I didn't want to claim. I didn't even want to claim when I knew I had to claim. It was my mother that said you're going to have to, you haven't got a choice here now. ... I went through my savings. ... God, I think I had like £60 left in my bank and then I thought, okay, I will now. ... I remember the first time I went down there, and it was nerve-wracking ... I'll never forget it. It was one of the girls that used to work with me actually ... so I was, like, freaking heck!

I mean, don't get me wrong, it wasn't her fault, it wasn't her fault, but I really, really didn't want to go. ... It was really embarrassing. ... I'd never claimed ... I'd never had to. ... I felt awful. And I was like oh my God, you know, what am I going to do? ... Obviously, you can't give up that money – that's your only money. I was thinking how am I going to cope? If I went back to work, who is going to have [my child]? Do I want to go back to work? But then, in my head, it was always oh God, I'm on benefits, like, I'm scrounging. It was awful ... and this pittance, what you're claiming, and then you're thinking oh my God ... how am I going to survive on this? How? And I'd be like oh my God, this is horrendous – I honestly can't cope. I didn't want to leave [my child] ... but I wanted to work. I needed, not wanted, to. But I needed to go back to work at that point. But ... I had no confidence, none whatsoever. It had all gone from me by then. I had none. It felt as if I was lying to them. ... It's not wrong – sometimes you can't help it, you don't want to be out of work. ... If I was the person I am now, I would probably shut them down, but like I didn't have that back then. So, I'd sit there like a sheep. I was like, mmm, yeah, whatever you say, three bags full, I'll do this, I'll do that. ... I think ... they need to realise that people are people, that some people do want to go back to work and not everybody's the same and just want benefits. I didn't want to be on benefits – no way did I. ... Obviously, you constantly feel guilty ... you're taking money really for nothing. But then it's not enough money is it? ... It's not really enough to live on. ... I always felt embarrassed about being on benefits – always. ... You didn't want to go down there anyway, and I don't care what anyone says, nobody really wants to go in that place and be made to feel like a fool – nobody does. ... You try and explain things, but they don't really hear you, do they? They don't really care, do they? They just want you back in work. ... So, really, you don't care what's happening when you're sat there. ... You just want to get out – I want to go now, thank you very much, I want to go. ... I'm not stupid, thank you very much. But you always were made to feel like you were stupid. ... If they were doing their jobs properly, then there should be some background information about this person – why are they not going back to work? (Sarah, Lifeline girl, 2021)

It is clear from this account that over a decade later the interaction still sits hard and heavy in Sarah's mind. Its detail is striking in its foreshadowing of the commentary that emerged in relation to the intensification of welfare conditionality that followed: a system in development, with a 'singular emphasis' on paid work that devalued unpaid care and used bare material need and crushing stigma for leverage (Andersen, 2023: 56; Wright, 2023;

Tyler, 2020). That claiming benefits was the only recourse in the face of destitution was a common assertion. Many of the women were frightened, wrung out with despair; they had never expected to claim, they did not want to claim, and they hoped that they would never have to claim again. Sarah was both dismayed and outraged at the distorted representation of herself as a 'scrounger'. Still, it was felt even then, that an isolated expression of resistance risked serious consequences. Even if the income from benefits was anxiety-inducingly low, it was impossible to manage without it.

While those taking part in the work-focused interview may have hoped to author their responses freely, it was a highly regulated interaction, produced through a set of standardised requirements and conditions that discouraged disruption (Lipsky, 2010). Explicitly understood as a pretext for their movement into a labour market (Haylett, 2003), the interaction was underscored by the assumption that people should, but won't, accept any job, however suitable or sustainable. As one of the girls explained, 'they just want you back in work' (Lindsay, 2007; Lindsay et al, 2007; Beck, 2018; Andersen, 2023; Wright, 2023). For their part, the women often valorised the work ethic while also challenging the legitimacy of a system intent on disregarding their personal circumstances, capabilities, commitments and preferences (Hennessy, 2009; Davies, 2012; 2015; Whitworth and Griggs, 2013; Rafferty and Wiggan, 2017; Wright, 2023). Their stories consistently illustrated the disconnections between the institutional framings and the complexities of personal life, showing that officials were enrolling an extremely limited understanding of what and who had value (Skeggs, 1997; 2004; Sayer, 2005; 2011; Morris, 2019; 2020). There was scant evidence of interest in the women's plans and hopes for the future; most reported being directed towards gendered, low-status, low-paid, insecure jobs in areas such as care work, fast food and retail (Smith et al, 2008; Grant, 2009; Ingold and Etherington, 2012). This kind of homogenising, mass processing silenced the knotty troubles and concerns of personal life, leaving women feeling as though they had not been heard: 'You try and explain things, but they don't really hear you, do they?'; 'They don't really care, do they?' Detailed explanations were prohibited or met with disinterest; there was no room for the kind of 'background information' that fills everyday life (Griffiths and Smith, 2014).

Perhaps most plain was the enduring sense of degradation that was a pronounced feature of these kinds of narrative. Sarah had a deep desire to be treated with respect – in Martha Nussbaum's words, 'as a dignified being whose worth is equal to that of others' (2000: 79), or as Richard Sennett expresses it, as a valuable citizen 'whose presence matters' (2003: 3; McKenzie, 2015). In telling her story, she was attempting to regain or retain some dignity, reshape the classification imposed on her and reconstitute herself as a subject of value (Tyler, 2013; Tarkiaien, 2017; Arnade, 2019).

Other accounts too were replete with the 'colloquialisms of shame' (Chase and Walker, 2013: 743); Sarah and others used terms like 'fool' and 'stupid' to describe and explain how they felt. It was also not unusual for them to recall managing these events by attempting to disassociate to some degree with their immediate environment, shamed into silence and sinking into a state of passive endurance: 'You don't care what's happening when you're sat there ... you just want to get out.' It was an event productive of what Andrew Sayer described as a sense of 'intense, sometimes burning shame' (2005: 153). These 'horrendous' interactions left deep impressions and provoked strong feelings years later as recollections spoke directly to their 'psychic price' (Halpern-Meekin et al, 2015: 7; Roberts et al, 2022). For Sarah, the interview proved to be a scarring interaction she would 'never' forget, one with profound consequence for her sense of self: she still remembered feeling 'guilty' for getting something 'for nothing' (see Wright, 2016; McGarvey, 2017). Each story described what Imogen Tyler (2020) later termed 'stigmacraft' – a coercive technology of governance produced through a process of classification and a set of disciplinary practices.

As the years passed, with the benefit of some distance, the women articulated their resistance to the work-focused interviews more freely and with greater surety. To return to Sarah's statement: 'If I was the person I am now, I would probably shut them down.' She offered a clear-sighted appraisal – rejecting the premise of the intervention and explaining that 'nobody really wants to' claim benefits, because the experience is fraught with shame and in reality 'it's not really enough to live on'. Policy makers needed to realise that 'people are people' and not assume everyone is morally suspect; intentions are often sound and cases are genuine. Officials should compassionately gather information by asking people why they are not going back to work and truly listening to the answers.

The 'policy environment became much more hostile' in 2010 when Labour lost power to the Conservative-led Coalition government (Wright, 2023: 50). Sanctioning rose as the decade wore on, peaking in the middle of the decade, at which point the state apparatus was indisputably punitive (National Audit Office, 2016; Webster, 2016; Fletcher and Wright, 2018; Wright et al, 2020; Redman and Fletcher, 2021). Conditionality measures were intensified and extended through an approach that required people to spend full-time hours either in paid work or job seeking as a matter of default; the system made use of an online vacancy portal to facilitate surveillance and act as a 'sanctions evidence-maker' (Fletcher and Wright, 2018: 338; Dwyer, 2019; Wright and Patrick, 2019; Wright et al, 2020). Sanctioning – the withdrawal or partial withdrawal of benefits – became the frontline workers' lever of 'first resort' (Wright, 2023: 122). Some of the Lifeline women reflected on these developments during the second wave of interviews, often because either they, or someone they knew, had claimed and experienced sanctioning for non-compliance. It was in this context that Nicole recalled the impacts of her interactions at the Jobcentre. She took the time to reflect on this period in her life when, having left her childhood home after experiencing years of abuse and neglect, she tried to make a fresh start. She introduced the interaction through her memory of a menacing atmosphere, featuring 'big, butch' security men:

> I was back and fore to the Jobcentre … because I had a work coach … but no interest – didn't, no eye contact, just: 'Oh, what would you look into?' I was like cleaning, that kind of thing. They were like that, do these many hours of search. The first one I went on … I was capable to look for work. … That's what took me over the edge. That's what was enough then for me. I couldn't do it – I was sanctioned. I was sanctioned and I was sanctioned for nine weeks. And the girl I was staying with, I had to have her to buy me food or cook me food. And I was trying to borrow money off certain people … to get me over. And then when I had my payment, I was paying out my debts. Do you know what I mean? And it really did mess me up for the first three months. I was broken. Do you know what I mean? I was like that, I don't know what I'm going to do. Do you know what I mean? … Somebody genuine as me who needs that help at the time. No. I just felt I had just more and more pressure, and how it didn't take me over the edge good and proper I don't know because money is a big stress to people. Do you know what I mean? It was one of mine. I had no stable home. I was staying with somebody who was feeding me and I couldn't contribute, do you know? And I think then she's going to get sick of this, she's going to kick me out. Do you know what I mean? I had all that going through my head at the same time. Do you know what I mean? … That killed me mentally, and physically I lost all my weight. (Nicole, Lifeline girl, 2021)

Nicole's account chimed with others of this era, illustrative of a sense of being funnelled down through a system, a set of perfunctory, dehumanising organisational practices involving 'no eye contact', a scripted, tick-boxed, computer-assisted, and flow-charted process (Clarke and Newman, 1997; Matarese and Caswell, 2017; Wright, 2023). She described, in a couple of sentences, a process of classification embedded in a wider political culture of welfare restructuring that involved aggregating groups of people into a codified totality, a category to be activated. This was accomplished through a series of shallow assessments and the selection of minimal amounts of information to determine eligibility and categories for action: making someone 'fit for work', applying 'intensive work conditionality', triggering a 'did not attend' sanction (Wright, 2023). Nicole's case, a first sift resulting in the ill-made judgement that she was in fact 'capable of work', only adds to the wealth of research suggesting that the welfare conditionality requirements were assessed under conditions of duress and distress (Goodin, 2001; Dwyer and Ellison, 2016; Dwyer, 2018; Andersen, 2023; Wright, 2023). The role of the official was predominantly to ascertain whether claimants were fulfilling the mandatory requirements, as opposed to providing guidance (Haux, 2013; Whitworth, 2013; Patrick, 2017; Dwyer, 2018; Andersen, 2023): formal behavioural criteria while extensive and intrusive, detailed little useful support. The interview inhibited meaningful forms of advocacy because the drivers of welfare policy 'collide' with the complexities of people's lives (Morris, 2020: 277).

The evidence that conditionality measures of this kind are futile, counterproductive and only add 'more and more pressure' is also considerable (Dwyer, 2019; Wright and Patrick, 2019; Andersen, 2023; Wright, 2023). For Nicole, they 'took' her 'over the edge' because, like many others, she found she simply could not comply. Managing work-related requirements (full-time, onerous and often unproductive job search activities and/or poor-quality paid work) with the complexities of personal life was challenging, especially under threat of sanction (Patrick, 2017; Johnsen and Blenkinsopp, 2018; Wright et al, 2020; Andersen, 2023). Sanctions were applied rigidly and could be triggered by a single, fleeting, trivial lapse in compliance, 'an honest mistake' or a 'genuine' reason (Wright, 2023: 104). Repeated sanctioning was 'almost always irrational, unjust and unrelated to work efforts', the result of neither 'deliberate and sustained rule breaking' nor 'work avoidance', but rather 'hostile changes to the social security system' (Wright, 2023: 99).

Already 'broken', sanctioning almost pushed Nicole over 'the edge' 'good and proper'. The financial implications mounted up rapidly because the 'very low rates' of 'benefits mean[t] that seemingly small reductions can have major impacts' (Wright, 2023: 107). For Nicole, the situation escalated quickly, rippling outwards, because the 'removal of essential income meant having to rely on others for cash, food, utilities or shelter' (Wright, 2023: 115). Immense harm was inflicted by both threat of and actual sanctioning and Sharon Wright (2023) compellingly conceives of the intensification of welfare conditionality as a form of state-perpetrated abuse given its impacts on women, including those with experience of domestic abuse (Johnsen and Blenkinsopp, 2018; Andersen, 2023). Nicole found herself in a vulnerable, subordinate position, faced with a state concerned with coercion and control; essential income was withdrawn 'without warning and with little recourse' (Wright, 2023: 24).

In places like the Valleys, these developments led to a wave of sanctioning and an erosion of social security benefits that far exceeded the scale of any perceived transgressions (Wright and Patrick, 2019; Redman and Fletcher, 2021; Pattaro et al, 2022). The magnitude of the issue was such that at the point when we met and spoke in 2017, Cheryl, an activist with the Unite Community, had been organising protests and advocating for welfare claimants in the Valleys for over three years.[1] She explained her views of the system by sharing a story about a recent demonstration outside a local Jobcentre:

> You get to speak to people. I'll give you an example. I spoke to a young lad and he couldn't read or write. ... He had been working for, you know, the companies that repair the railways .... Now he didn't have to read or write to be able to do the job. He'd got the job, word of mouth, you know: 'Oh, they're looking for people with us.' And when he got there, the foreman would say: 'Right, I need you to take that bit of railway track up and lay this bit of railway track.' And he just did the job that he was doing. He didn't need to read or write. Well, anyway, he was laid off so he went to the Jobcentre and said: 'I've been laid off.' So the Jobcentre said: 'Right oh, you need to fill in these forms.' 'I can't fill in the forms.' So they helped him fill in the forms and then they said: 'Right, now you've got to go online and do a CV.' Well, he can't read or write, so he couldn't do it. So they sanctioned him then for four months, so he had no money at all for four months. Now this wasn't a bad man, right. This man was married with two children. He was putting food on the table until he lost his job. He's not a bad man. But he was sanctioned because he couldn't read and write is the end result. We spoke to him and we said: 'Well, did you appeal?' And he said: 'I didn't know you could.' Well, you've got to be able to read and write to win. ... You've got to be able to read and write to access the system, and they can't. So we said: 'Right, well you really do need to appeal.' So what we did was we set him up with someone that could help him to do it, erm, one of the ladies from Unite Community, erm, could help him to do it ... and she done all the appeal for him. Erm, but it's those sorts of situations, you know, that people do need help for. And we had quite a few from that day that needed help, erm, for whatever reason, people that didn't even know that you could appeal – they didn't know how to appeal. When we said you've got to do it online, they didn't have access to computers to be able to do it. So, alright, they may have only, we may have only helped, I don't know, six or eight people on that day, but it's six or eight people who needed help. (Cheryl, activist, 2017)

This story is illustrative of the dispossessed and disadvantaged – and not 'bad' – 'people who do need help' but were unable to comply with welfare conditionality requirements. At this time, decisions about benefits eligibility were both unpredictable and difficult to challenge (Cain, 2016; National Audit Office, 2016; Caswell et al, 2017; Nothdurfter, 2017; Dwyer, 2018; Wright, 2023). The regime was 'unyielding' (Wright, 2023: 24), and even for those who lacked the basic literacy skills on which the entire system depended, there was a paucity of easily accessible guidance and support. The requirement to search for employment full-time was particularly challenging in the Valleys due to the lack of suitable jobs in the region (Beatty et al, 2019; Wright and Patrick, 2019; Beatty and Fothergill, 2020; Wright et al, 2020). Some people simply weren't aware that they could request any easement in the conditions of their claim or appeal a decision; others didn't feel comfortable or confident enough to do so (Stinson, 2019).

Cheryl went on to describe confrontations with Jobcentre officials who were angry and upset that their offices were being targeted by protesters. Within the scaffolding of broader policy structures, the day-to-day decisions and practices of these street-level bureaucrats 'effectively become the public policies they carry out' (Lipsky, 2010: xii). They sit at the intersection between our personal and public lives, and to the extent that they have autonomy, they can bestow and deny the rights of citizens. Analyses often focus on the attributes of these frontline officials – the degree to which they are able to exercise discretion and work attentively, respectfully and sympathetically. Earlier studies of welfare reform did point to instances of warmth, empathy and practical support that could be a feature of claimants' relationships with frontline workers, but as time passed, such findings tended to be limited to rare exceptions (Finch et al, 1999; Ridge and Millar, 2011; Chase and Walker, 2013; Millar, 2019; Wright, 2023). In theory, as welfare conditionality intensified, frontline workers did retain some discretion in setting mandatory requirements (including tailoring the hours of job search and the type and location of the work to caring responsibilities), but there was little evidence to suggest this happened to any great extent in practice (Andersen, 2023; Wright, 2023). Claimants' assessments of officials became less favourable, with reports of the latter demonstrating apathy, thinly veiled contempt or intentional stigmatisation (Wright; 2016). In later interviews, the Lifeline women would comment on this shift: in 'the early days it didn't bother me – it was once, twice a year – but towards the end they were quite, they'd speak down to you'. Descriptions of a series of predictable 'knock backs' and 'put downs' were evidence of a menacing cycle of degradation and shame (Daly and Kelly, 2015).

Perhaps the strength of received wisdom is such that some street-level workers do not appreciate the nuance of the causes, consequences and risks of living in poverty and so apply an individualised, behaviouralist logic and assumptions about personal culpability with little empathy (Wright, 2003; 2016; Morris, 2020; Treanor, 2020). But officials also have grievances in these kinds of pressurised work environments, and their capacity to attend to need with compassion is often constrained. In 2015, one Valleys resident, Nadine, a trade union representative who worked for the Department for Work and Pensions, took the time to discuss the concerns that developed among her members as ways of working changed and the public service ethos and attendant relationships with claimants deteriorated over the course of decades:

> Things changed and the way of working changed as well, so people find that really difficult. … I got to know my customers, and … you would have a really good relationship with them, obviously not with everyone … but … you don't get to know your customers at all … you haven't got that rapport with people any longer. (Nadine, activist, 2015)

As caseloads became overburdened and interactions shortened, attending to need and providing support and advice gave way to enforcing conditionality (Fletcher, 2011; Patrick, 2017; Work and Pensions Committee, 2018; Andersen, 2023). For Nadine, this involved an associated set of deeply troubling practices:

> I do sometimes feel that maybe they are targeting the most vulnerable, and certainly the sanctions – they say there are no targets but I am sure, somewhere there are. Because in offices where there are [trade union] reps, I don't see any problem, but in some offices where there are not reps, we have been told … that management are exerting pressure to have a certain percentage of people put on sanctions, so otherwise they will be on sort of a warning as a member of staff. But again, we have got no evidence because people are not prepared to come forward to talk about it. … It's clear in guidance, there are no percentages – it's only if it's appropriate. So, what people have said they do is that they look at the most vulnerable, which could be people with learning difficulties, someone who they think is not going to appeal against the sanction. So, it is really perverse behaviour they are encouraging. (Nadine, activist, 2015)

Nadine's 'feeling' was well founded: officials were working against 'benefit off-flow targets' directed at 'the most vulnerable' (Redman and Fletcher, 2021; Webster, 2016; Dwyer, 2018; Dwyer et al, 2020). 'Behind the scenes, hidden from view and accountability' (Wright, 2023: 33), the benefits system was subject to a 'disentitlement strategy' resulting in 'mass impoverishment' (Fletcher and Wright, 2018: 337; Redman and Fletcher, 2021). New targets meant radical changes to the behaviour of frontline workers; a new 'street-level calculus of choice' determined 'how, on whom and to what extent' sanctions were applied (Kaufman, 2020: 205). Beyond, the concerns raised by Nadine around the vulnerability of some in this system, commentators pointed to the social relations of gender, race and class through which these interactions are mediated, which meant frontline workers were 'sometimes harsher, sometimes more lenient than policies lead us to expect' (van Berkel, 2020: 194; Watkins-Hayes, 2009; Brodkin and Marston, 2013; National Audit Office, 2016; van Berkel et al, 2017; Wright, 2023). Nadine, adding another layer of analysis, argued that some of these variations might be explained by the presence or absence of visible and active trade union representation within the Jobcentre itself. Critically, she explicitly linked this 'perverse behaviour' to the internal appraisal and disciplinary processes in place for frontline workers:

> We have our appraisals, what box mark can you get at the end of the year. ... We have got 'must improve', which is obviously lowest, then you have 'achieved' and then you have got them 'exceeded'. They change them every year. ... So, if you are in the 'must improve', you are probably on a warning ... and it could be disciplinary, which in the end, if you don't improve, could lead to dismissal. So no one wants to be in that category. And then there is a difference in your pay, because you don't get paid properly. So there is these bonuses attached to what box you are in and now if you are on a 'must improve', you ... don't get any bonus at all. So it is a real worry for people. ... I think managers have pressures on them to put a certain amount of people into those categories. (Nadine, activist, 2015)

Street-level workers themselves were working with the threat of sanction, fearful of losing pay and even their job. They faced the prospect of an accusation of 'doing something you shouldn't', orchestrated through various performance management policies that might be breached and result in 'a penalty or a warning'. These included disciplinary processes for not meeting 'standards of behaviour' relating to data protection, electronic media, social media or a simple dress code. And in practice, the need to meet certain targets led to a focus on the 'most vulnerable' claimants (Soss et al, 2011: 207). Subsequent academic study identified the intensity of this drive to misapply sanctions to meet targets, the intense pressure that employees were under and the existence of 'perverse' incentives to meet targets (Redman and Fletcher, 2021). Frontline workers were negotiating a 'moral eco-system' (Zacka, 2017) that involved navigating multiple layers of policy documentation across multiple layers of organisational governance, relating to their own behaviour and that of claimants (van Berkel et al, 2017; van Berkel, 2020; Wright, 2023). A number made public statements taking issue with the complex and onerous administrative work, the relentless and pressurised use of targets and the aggressive forms of sanctioning designed to move people off benefits

(Viney, 2014). One, Angela Neville, wrote a play (*Can this Be England?*) about the 'everyday absurdity' of a welfare system that removed the capacity of workers to take care. She described how diminishing resources meant less capacity 'to genuinely support' people, to the extent that the job became 'morally compromising' because 'the work almost became the persecution of some of the most vulnerable people in society' (O'Hara, 2015).

Reflection

These women – claimants and activists – understood welfare reform well, and while sharing their stories is straightforward enough, it is harder to adequately capture the depth of feeling these interactions prompted. Each understood that the intensification of welfare conditionality made the Jobcentre an 'intensely anxiety-inducing and intimidating location' (Friedli and Stearn, 2015: 45; Gilliom, 2001; Darab and Hartman, 2011; Chase and Walker, 2013; Daly and Kelly, 2015; Patrick, 2017; Patrick and Simpson, 2020). Sarah's story was illustrative of the ways in which the material and cultural dimensions of claiming welfare are deeply entwined, experienced concurrently; she described being near destitution and the benefits as being a 'pittance' to 'survive on' and a process of claiming entangled with feelings of shame and humiliation. The work-focused interviews were events that produced 'enforced narratives', discussed for how the interaction and its fallout made people feel more than for what was said, by whom, and why (Steedman, 2000: 25). Nicole's story reminds us how serious the fallout could be. Street-level work was highly scripted within a set of rules and structures, with little allowance for attending to the particularities and complexities of individual cases. Officials developed routines of practice to process their clientele en masse, working with systems of automation produced formally through bureaucracy. They were likely to experience alienation because moments of creativity and genuine responsiveness were rare and they were unable to control the pace of their work and its outcomes. Of course, their own performances were also assessed, compared and either rewarded or penalised.

Sanctions were easily triggered, sometimes due to poor administration; sometimes the product of very normal, day-to-day ebbs and flows of caring for young children or someone with a chronic health condition (Andersen, 2023; Wright, 2023). Given 'the strength of enduring expectations that women will provide informal care', sanctions that hit them for fulfilling caring responsibilities were among the most egregious (Wright, 2023: 99; Pulkingham et al, 2010; Wright, 2012; Patrick, 2014; Andersen, 2023). Studies investigating the impacts of the intensification of conditionality on specific groups, including single mothers, have consistently concluded that while sanctions do increase exits from benefits, only a minority move into employment, and any progress or rise in income is typically short-lived (see, for example, Goodwin, 2008; Griggs and Evans, 2010; Loopstra et al, 2015; National Audit Office, 2016; Reeves and Loopstra, 2017; Dwyer, 2018). Sanctions-backed conditionality also tends to result in lower earnings over time because claimants accept less secure employment at a low occupational level, regardless of their level of education: for most, and notably so for single mothers, employment trajectories are confined to low-paid, insecure work. (Arni et al, 2013; van den Berg and Vikström, 2014; Andersen, 2023). The inefficacy of the system is made worse by the adverse impacts of sanctioning and even the prospect of sanctioning (Dwyer, 2018; Wright et al, 2018; Wright and Patrick, 2019; Wright et al, 2020; Wright, 2023). Welfare conditionality both compounded women's disadvantaged position in the labour market (Grover, 2007; MacLeavy, 2007; Letablier et al, 2011; MacLeavy, 2011; Ingold and Etherington, 2013; Boyer et al, 2017; Neitzert, 2020) and led to greater hardship for claimants (Wright et al, 2018; Cheetham et al, 2019; Patrick and Simpson, 2020; Robertson et al, 2020; Wickham et al, 2020). But a countercurrent, 'a way out', was pulling the Lifeline girls in a different direction. Reflecting on her interactions with the Jobcentre one of them explained, the project 'showed us it's not like that, it don't have to be like that'. In time, the Lifeline project workers became 'sick of writing' to the Jobcentre to provide evidence of the women's ongoing education, creating their own pro forma document with an instruction for officials to 'contact the project with any issues'.

7

The working activists

Beyond the call of duty.
Lifeline girl, 2008

We know what's needed, and then the person [the worker] has to fit that. And that's why local people doing a bit of activism on the ground [is the way]. Because they don't have to be taught. … Absolutely, those people are then accountable to their community, and it is just built in – doesn't have to be, it's just there naturally.
Lifeline worker, 2021

One feature of the contemporary dispersal of the welfare state is the emergence of alternative spaces of governance within civil society, connected to but distinct from hegemonic street-level bureaucracy and involving forms of paid work neither directly controlled by the state nor commercially driven by profit. Analyses of these settings make the range of possible or available welfare initiatives and interventions more visible and cast light on the choices governments make (Beck, 2018; Pollard and Tjoa, 2020; Phillips, 2022). Research in this field tends to reach beyond the practices of the Jobcentre's 'activation' workers to suggest that (well-funded) civil society organisations can be more responsive to local and individual needs and circumstances (Damm, 2012; Egdell et al, 2016; Irvine et al, 2024a; 2024b). The activity of Lifeline's 'support workers' was also illustrative of these developments. Here, we attempt to make sense of their performance and the practices that sustained Lifeline as a 'space of contestation' that enjoyed a degree of conditional autonomy ((Newman, 2001: 138; Clarke, 2004). Of primary interest are the 'vocabularies of motive' (Mills, 1940: 907) articulated by this set of workers – claims productive of a logic of action and a sense of collectivity that frame who they are and how and why they act. These are the vocabularies that form the 'code of ethics' that underpin their accomplishments and legitimise a set of shared values and beliefs (Wacquant, 1998: 47; Mills, 1940).

More intensive in focus and more expansive in scope than the work of the Jobcentre's frontline workforce, these women might best be understood as worker-activists positioned 'within and against the state' to mitigate the worst excesses of welfare conditionality (Craig and Mayo, 1995: 105; Newman,

2012a; 2012b). In creating this grass-roots initiative, these women were engaging in a form of paid work at the 'interface of activist commitments and governmental programs and projects' (Newman, 2012b: 476). Bold but fundamentally law-abiding, they were social reformers rather than agitators, balancing their day to day practices with the master frames and associated institutional demands of government policy. The Lifeline workers were intent on generating new behaviours and beliefs among the women, but with a view to supporting them to 'get on' and resist their coercion into poor-quality work. The Jobcentre, as one worker explained, 'wouldn't understand this'.

All occupations are guided by a code:

> A set of rules and stipulations that define proper character, conduct, and intercourse to and amongst its members. In some occupations, this code is formalised, recited, even sworn to. In others, it is a loosely strung assemblage of norms and guidelines, learned and deployed in the very process of going about one's business. (Wacquant, 1998: 47)

Within Lifeline, a 'loosely strung assemblage of norms and guidelines' (Wacquant, 1998: 47) cohered around the proximity of the workers to the women's lives, and an extraordinary degree of intimacy, familiarity and enduring relationships of respect, concern and compassion developed. In the words of the founder, Diana, 'staying close to the girls', 'speaking to them all the time' was 'crucial' – 'that's *the* way'. Fostering new capabilities and capacities involved creating social relations of care, cultivating trust and attending to personal concerns and troubles.

In the absence of lengthy periods of formal, occupational training or socialisation, the project borrowed and reshaped the folk symbols and practices of more-established, allied professions and para-professions (for example, those of social work, action research and community development) to construct an ideology. This was not a tightly defined and bounded regime subject to strict standardisation and limited to a scripted set of interventions (Lipsky, 2010); routinising this kind of work was not possible (Bélanger and Edwards, 2013). In the absence of explicit rules and directives steeped in bureaucracy, workers were expected to exercise their judgement to recognise and respond to need. Their success was understood as depending on this lack of prescription. As one worker explained years later: 'You don't see jobs written like that. I don't think you could have a rule book … if you put too many rules in, I don't think it'd be the same.' For the women, this was unfamiliar territory. Impressed and touched by the workers' dedication, they often took the time to pay tribute to them. Their narratives, both during their participation in the project and later, cited many examples of these women not 'just sticking by their job title' or 'job detail', but routinely working 'beyond the call of duty' when surely 'they didn't have to'. Except they were doing exactly the kinds of things that they were expected to do. Close and frequent connections were not to be guarded against, but actively sought out. Their accounts and interactions are foregrounded in this chapter to offer insights into the commitment of these women who, as activists, brought their personal experiences, attributes and values to bear in their day-to-day working lives.

The women who participated in the project were mostly recruited through community playgroups and parenting initiatives or via word of mouth; they were invited to attend a coffee morning to introduce them to the project and get to know the workers. Recognising how daunting 'walking through the door' could be, the workers described this aspect of their work as a process of 'catching and then keeping', 'making people feel as comfortable as possible' and dispelling any unease that might prevent them 'settling in' and 'getting on'. The approach was careful, so much so that the fieldwork for this study was postponed until after this induction period. As Diana explained, they 'would like to get them settled in first – it's a very difficult time when they first come up'. For the women's part, many recalled the workers' skill at putting them at ease. One remembered: 'I was a wreck, Hel … I was a nervous wreck … but then I think it come so naturally because they were so calm and just so welcoming.' The project was framed by workers as 'those first steps' or a 'soft entry' into education, involving a 'totally different way of learning'. It was a place where you could 'come along, have a cup of tea and a chat, get out of the house, come and meet people in [a] friendly atmosphere'. Days unfolded through timetabled lessons with fluid boundaries that allowed for unexpected phone calls, late arrivals or early departures, even while expectations were high: 'We explained what we were about. We explained that we would expect commitment. Yes, it is very sociable. Yes, it is very relaxed. … But we do expect them to achieve things and we want them to achieve things so that they can move on'. The 'relaxed' and 'sociable' rhythms were in place to allow the women to 'find their feet at their own pace'. Critically, the workers were there with them 'all the time', attending lessons, taking breaks, drinking tea together. They were on hand to help with studies, learning 'to read a room', 'see who is uncomfortable or not coping' and acting as a reassuring presence (perhaps explaining the material in a different way, checking spelling or assessment criteria, making additional notes or phoning with reminders when assignments were due). In turn, the women positioned the presence of a 'support worker' as critical to their engagement:

> If I had to go by myself … I would've just rang them and said, 'I'm sorry, I can't make today. I'm ill or the baby's not been well.' It would've

just been excuse after excuse after excuse after excuse. That's what life was like. It was always easier to find an excuse. Just knowing that she was coming with me just to sit with me, just to be there with me … just got me through it. (Lifeline girl, 2021)

The workers didn't censure or sanction the women, because 'they'd been there before'; but they were persistent, as one woman described:

She gone beyond the call of her job … 'cos it's like if someone don't turn up, she think they got problems, she will knock their door, 'Come on, put the kettle on.' You know, someone normally … like if it is an employer, they wouldn't do that, would they? … Not chasing you up all the time. Even now with [one of the girls], she's finished college, you know, a good few months, and she still haven't given up on her. 'Oh I will give her a ring see what she is up to, and if I can't help her that way, I will help her another way', she said. … She don't have to … like, she left. (Lifeline girl, 2009)

Visits to the homes of women who hadn't attended for a day or two were 'part of the job'. Several recalled 'days when she would be at my door', asking 'why haven't you been today?'; they concluded that without that knock on the door, perhaps they wouldn't have gone back to the project.

Workers focused on 'coaching' or 'coaxing' the women through the everyday knocks and crises they faced, which, as one woman explained later, meant the project was 'never just in that one room, always outside as well'. Recognising and attending to need was framed as a process of 'personal development', building 'confidence', 'self-esteem' and 'resilience'. One pointed out that this involved:

a process of coaching them through situations themselves … so when they come against that again, they don't get that knockback. It might be a temporary … they might think about it, but it doesn't ruin their whole week. … They have been at such a low ebb they can't, you know what I mean? … It's really, really hard to try and turn that around. (Lifeline worker, 2009)

Another said:

Through the course of the year we are trying build up their resilience I think is what I am getting at. It is their resilience to life's knocks so that they can brush themselves off and carry on, and that's the most important things we do for people. … We … don't have to manufacture occasions … because we know these things will happen as they come through the process of change with us. They come [up] against lots of things … we know they are going to happen.' (Lifeline worker, 2009)

This reading of 'resilience' involved 'respecting' the women's ability to 'make choices for themselves', while making 'life easier' for them, making sure that 'if they do fall, they can get back up' and 'find their own way' to stay on 'the straight and narrow'.

A practice of regular one-to-one reviews, including some home visits, was in place to gather the women's opinions of the tutors and the course content, but also to collect more detailed information relating to their personal circumstances. The women remembered the more formal sessions as an opportunity to 'have a chat, have a cup of tea, bring your favourite cake in' and get something 'off your chest', a 'weight off your shoulders'. For workers, these reviews and other more spontaneous interactions were intended to build rapport and create an environment in which the women could 'talk things through' 'without hiding anything': the process provided insights into what was helping or what else might help. For their part, the women described the workers as people in their lives to whom they 'can divulge anything' because 'nothing fazed' them.

The workers got to know the group and their personal troubles and issues well. They were immersed in the women's lives, as one explained during the first wave of interviews:

> The beauty of it is because we spend so much time together, I know their children's names, I know if they have been up half the night, I know if they have been boozing the night before, you know? I have had a tutor say to me: 'I really don't feel that so and so is engaging, are you sure that they can cope at this level?' And I will reply: 'Actually, I know they can cope at this level – they do this level for every other subject. That isn't the problem. Just take my word for it – it's self-preservation. I know that person needs to protect themselves from that subject.' I know so much about them. Obviously, as the year goes on, I know more and more about them and they can appreciate that I am here to help them and I will help them in any way that I can. (Lifeline worker, 2009)

By simply spending a lot of time with the women, the Lifeline workers were able to 'appreciate the concerns of the girls' because they were 'that much closer to their lives' and were able to 'understand their needs'. And the girls realised quite quickly that they could be trusted confidantes. As one worker explained at the time, 'when the shit hits the fan, they want to come more and more'; and another said years later, they 'knew they could depend on you … they knew you could help them'. The quality of support was a notable feature of many of the women's commentaries when they were participating in Lifeline, but also, and even more so, in later years. Statements like 'things going on in your life, you always had someone to talk to' and they were 'just there for me really if I need[ed] anyone or to talk at all' were commonplace. One woman neatly remarked that the workers were 'just there … an A and E, part of your life'.

With the benefit of some distance, the women articulated the importance of these interactions:

> There was never any crisis. They'd be like: 'Let's have a cup of tea and we'll talk about it. Don't panic now – we'll talk about it.' … There was no shouting or screaming or drama. … It was always calm. … You'd be thinking oh my God, I can't do this and I can't do that. … I've done this, done that and then you'd go in there and you'd talk about it and you're thinking what am I stressing for? I've got somebody to talk to. I've got somebody to help me. (Lifeline girl, 2021)

> I remember just sitting there, and I cried and I cried and I cried, and she was just like: 'It's fine – we can deal with it.' I cried and I cried. At this time, I was having a really, really, rough time. (Lifeline girl, 2021)

The workers similarly understood themselves to be 'on call' if any of the women needed help. They described attempts to move through the anxieties, frustrations and crises of daily life with the women in ways that meant the boundaries of work were not formally delineated but renegotiated depending on the immediate circumstances. Work self-consciously consisted of tasks that other street-level workers 'just wouldn't do' and amounted to providing 'whatever they require in their lives … in any shape or form that we can'; the attitude was, 'let's just do it'. Recognising and responding to need, the workers ensured that what mattered got done (Morrison, 2006). In turn, the the women described workers who 'helped with everything … just every day-to-day thing', and they 'always felt … that' and that meant they could 'cope' and make 'right' or 'good' choices.

Workers offered practical help, which included all sorts of things. When a house was being cleared a few doors down from the community centre, a worker called over to ask 'what you doing with that stuff?' and before long everybody was carrying bits of furniture and household items – a settee, a rug, a bed – for one of the women who had 'next to nothing'. On another occasion, when one of the women was sitting an exam, a worker looked after her baby, wheeling the pram along the road, because it 'needed doing'. Other examples included: getting hold of food vouchers from a local foodbank in an emergency; offering the use of the centre phone to let the women take advantage of a local call rate; making appointments with specialised advice services when bailiffs showed up at the door, and helping to prepare for that appointment; and checking benefit entitlements, including discretionary crisis payments. One woman explained that she got help with moving home:

> They helped me with moving ... sorting all the forms out with [the] council. They have wrote me letters to get from there, because it was really rough up there and I wanted to be close to my mother. They wrote me a letter so I could swap. ... She wrote me a fantastic reference to say that I was having a lot of trouble, I wasn't sleeping and things like that. Absolutely fab. They do give you so much support. (Lifeline girl, 2009)

In other situations, more support was needed. These were the times when workers realised someone was 'so vulnerable' that they would go along with them to get the help they needed. In one example involving domestic violence, the Lifeline worker helped a woman first with accessing support for new locks and police checks, then with getting emergency rehousing and returning the perpetrator's belongings 'so he didn't have any excuse to come back'. In another case, a worker spent a period of time helping a woman by 'knocking them out of bed' in the morning, making sure her children were having breakfast and calling the school if the children were going to be late. The worker explained, she was 'very capable, but didn't have the support there'. In another case, a woman recalled having been made 'homeless, effectively' and that the worker came 'to the appointment with me, sat there with me' to get a bed at a local hostel until more permanent accommodation was available.

A consistent feature of this kind of story was the women's need of, and appreciation for, an advocate. The workers knew that it could be difficult for the women to bridge the divide between themselves and 'often disrespectful' public officials:

> It's about ... being respectful of them because a lot of them are not used to be treated in that way, especially when they come [up] against authority. If they have got to go to the council or whatever to deal with people, that's often not the case, and some will be job advisers even. If they are single parents getting called in for interviews, they can't deal with that sort of thing well, to stand up for themselves. (Lifeline worker, 2008)

As one of the women explained, the workers were responsive and dependable, and sometimes simply having someone to be there with them was enough: 'I'd only have to text ... and one of them would say "What time is your appointment? We'll be there."' This extended to interactions with the Jobcentre, and there were instances of workers sitting in on welfare eligibility interviews, either over the phone or in person. They could also be an influential presence, part of a process of debriefing in the aftermath of these encounters. One woman recounted that the words of a worker shored up her decision not to take 'any old shit job' when she had felt ready to cave under pressure from the Jobcentre:

> She said: 'You are not going to be back and fore signing on … your job will probably be long term. … If you listen to them, you would … last 10 minutes … [and be] back in.' … In the long run … I am going to be better off … I am not gonna have to sign back on the Social. … I am gonna have a job for a long time. I haven't got to rely on the government funding. (Lifeline girl, 2009)

As the years passed, many of the women were struck more forcefully by the workers' presence in their lives. For one, the memory of being *asked* if she 'would *like* to tell them about' something troubling her stuck with her. The repeated requests for the girls' reflections on the project were also suggestive of the respect the workers demonstrated:

> I can remember the one time they were asking what they wanted next … did you want this, did you want that, you know. Would you be interested in this? What would be a nice idea for the kids? And just any and all opinions, and even on the bad things. If it was like something that wasn't as enjoyable, they'd want to know. … I can remember her pulling me aside to ask about a tutor. … She was like, 'Well, what's he like?' and he was right there. I'm like, 'Well he's not fucking deaf!' (Lifeline girl, 2021)

The project's tools of pedagogy were democratic. The women's opinions, attitudes and beliefs were stitched into the approach, and many expressed the often novel experience of being 'respected and listened to', referring to interactions that made them feel 'just that you were normal'.

With remarkable consistency over time and across instances, the women described the workers as 'just stepping in' and providing 'the backup' or 'that stepping stone' at 'a real shit time'. Workers themselves described being there 'because you can see how difficult things are' and because in some cases they 'have no one'. The following story offered by a worker expresses the depth of intimacy:

> She had a phone call to say to go to the hospital. … She gathered it wouldn't be good news. She didn't feel that her mother was a massive support. … I went with her. She finds out she is pregnant, we go

for a scan and the baby is dead. ... Obviously then it is my role to support her any way that I can. ... If it makes life easier for her, then that's fine. ... That day was probably one of the most horrendous days I have ever lived through because her emotions were so erratic it was unbelievable. ... You go through a process of shock. I can't say anything else. She was completely and utterly shocked. Then we went through the process ... while they were explaining the technicalities to her. At this stage, she is not even ... 'yeah, yeah, yeah' but hasn't actually grasped the situation. ... She has gone. She has knocked off now, she knocked off two hours ago. She knocked off when she was lying on that bed and they are saying to her 'Are you aware that you pregnant and there is no heartbeat?' At that point, she's gone. It's then my role to say: 'Right, well, come on. That's awful, but where do we go from here?' Because obviously my main objective is to get her back on the straight and narrow as soon as I can so that she's obviously going in the right direction. (Lifeline worker, 2008)

This – the 'job' of keeping someone 'going in the right direction' even when she has 'gone' – is an example of a difficult and sorrowful kind of emotion work that is ill-defined and undervalued because of its associations with women's domestic care (James, 1989). Being what the women described as the 'constant who was going to be there through it all' involved working with raw, unfiltered emotions. Distressing disclosures and experiences were not uncommon; each of the workers recalled occasions when they had 'shed a tear' or felt their 'blood run cold'. Doing 'whatever it takes' meant making sure there was 'light at the end of the tunnel', and this took a toll at times. The workers routinely came together to share concerns and work out the best course of action in any given situation; having each other to call on made it easier.

The women grappled with how to articulate these relationships and their accounts were peppered with the suggestion that it was 'really hard to explain' the 'unique bond' they shared. To the extent that these relationships were firmly categorised, many concluded that 'the only way to describe it' was that the workers were 'like family'; it was 'as if' they were mothers, aunties or sisters. This, the idea of 'fictive kin' or 'what might be thought of as non-kin kin' (Ball, 1972: 300), provided a way of understanding these relationships and the feelings they evoked that conformed with established cultural codes (Zadoroznyi, 2009). In this sense, the Lifeline workers took on obligations, 'instrumental and affectional ties similar to those of conventional kin' (Sussman, 1976: 225). Contextualising the resonance, one woman said: 'She is like my mother ... I think because of the life I had ... she just overtook the role of being my mother. She stepped up and just helped me with everything.' More broadly, the accounts offered were implicitly suggestive of the social relations – the affectionate and pragmatic bonds – that make up family life and personal community, those people who feel important to us whether they are kin or not (Spencer and Pahl, 2007; Wellman and Wortley, 1990):

> I got ... the answers to everything I need now. ... I don't think I am going to go that low again 'cos every time something goes wrong for me ... I know I got the people to turn to, I know I got the answers I am looking for. I got somebody to talk to, I got places to go, do you know what I mean? Whereas before [when] something goes wrong for me, I think, right, I have got nobody to talk to, who can I turn to? I would have just hit rock bottom. But now if anything goes wrong, I just pick up the phone ... and she is there, do you know what I mean? She seems to have all the answers, all the pieces are there like. (Lifeline girl, 2009)

> You could see they always wanted what was best for you ... every single one of them was exactly the same in wanting what was best for you, in supporting you to be able to achieve that. (Lifeline girl, 2021)

These kinds of description, indicative of the practical, emotional and instrumental support that folk understandings of family life tend to emphasise, signified the warmth and closeness of the personal attachments that were formed. In some cases, workers explicitly understood their contribution as a form of compensation or substitution, made in the absence of 'those people who you would expect to be really supportive', an absence which meant some of the women 'couldn't imagine why on earth anyone would do anything for them'. There was also a sense that the role was familiar to workers, with caring practices well rehearsed in the domestic sphere playing out in the workplace (James, 1989; Kessler et al, 2015). The activity chimed with analyses of 'the labour involved in dealing with other people's feelings' (James, 1989: 15), which often consider how tacit skills honed in the home are reproduced in the workplace. As with forms of paid care work, their contribution was positioned ambiguously between the personal and public spheres (Ungerson, 1999; Ungerson and Yeandle, 2007), and the distinctive sets of cultural meanings and practices associated with the family, civil society and the state were collapsed (Massey, 1994; Zadoroznyi, 2009; Newman, 2012a; 2012b).

For Diana, when appointing staff, 'making sure they were the right people and had the right attributes to be the right person' was critical. Again, as in forms of paid care work, personal characteristics were seen as important; expertise resided within the workers themselves (Kessler et al, 2015). Possessing a set of personal attributes suggestive of the 'right' values, attitudes and beliefs was a key criterion. Self-consciously borrowing from community development ideology, Diana explained:

> Some of the key principles ... for engaging people are more around the principles of community development, and I think that's about openness, honesty, integrity, doing the job for the right reasons, ... being able to build up trusting relationships. And unless you have got those sort of qualities going on, people won't engage with you, full stop. (Diana, 2008)

The workers' narratives frequently alluded to these characteristics of openness, honesty and integrity. In various ways, each of them invested heavily in the importance of their personal biography: understanding *who* they were was framed as central to understanding how and why they worked. Most often, this was accomplished through 'common ground' narratives – of people 'who understand the culture' or 'who have similar experiences' – that conferred a sense of belonging to the estate and with the women. This 'common ground' allowed workers to finely calibrate their interventions, to gain 'trust', exert 'influence' and support 'change'. Each of the workers was recruited through a local connection. As Diana explained, 'We didn't bring in people from outside when we didn't need to.' Diana took the time to detail the significance of her deep roots in the community:

> I was born and brought up on the ... estate, grew up in the local schools in the sixties and seventies ... and I have daughters who still go to the same local schools here ... and I have still got family who live on the estate. ... Obviously, working in, with community regeneration, ... it's a big plus to be from where you work, from the community's point of view, because obviously I understand innately why they think the way they do, what the culture is. (Diana, 2009)

Among most of the workers, this kind of expertise, born out of prolonged and intensive immersion in the locality, was combined with the kind of 'innate' knowledge that could only be gleaned from personal experience of adversity. You needed 'to have been through shit yourself'. This included accounts of living on a low income:

> I knew that if you didn't have money, it changed, you know. I am not saying that having money made your life perfect, but if you didn't have it, it was a damn sight harder, and I think from day one I appreciated that. ... From where I was growing up, I knew very early on that money was important and, without it, life was very, very hard. (Lifeline worker, 2009)

Other shared experiences included young motherhood, domestic abuse, mental health concerns and returning to education as an adult:

> An awful lot of these girls are on the journey where I started. ... An awful lot of their situations are things where I have been. ... I was 22 with three babies under the age of three. I had a mortgage through the roof, which I couldn't afford to pay, and my house was repossessed. ... I have lived within a very abusive relationship. I have been on Prozac for quite a while. I had horrendous postnatal depression. I have had a baby later on in life, when I least expected or wanted [that to happen], to be honest. ... I know how it feels to leave school with very few qualifications. I know how it feels to try to re-enter education. I know how hard it is to sit there listening to people speak to you and they could be speaking Spanish 'cos you can't understand a word they are saying. I hope that through my life experiences I can make theirs better. ... I am not saying that someone maybe who has had a perfect life can't come in and do just as good a job, but that's what I feel really, you know. (Lifeline worker, 2008)

And experiences of ill health:

> I was on the sick for years because I couldn't work. And I think it's a case of not judging people – I think that's one of the biggest things, is not to be judgemental. Because right, okay, it's easy to point the finger at somebody, but we never know at any point. ... More often than not, it's about peeling layers back, and then when you do that, it's like you've got this vulnerable person and you think, well, I probably would be exactly the same, behaving exactly the same if I had been through that. So I think it's got a lot to do with things that I have been through, and like I said, I can identify with people. (Lifeline worker, 2021)

Another worker simply said: 'I know how it feels to really ... like you have let everybody down.' In these cases and others, accounts of personal life experience, which were connected to a sense of privileged insight and cultural sensitivity, demonstrated suitability for this sort of work. It was felt that without this kind of understanding of what local women were going through, it was 'hard to get people', hard to 'catch' and 'keep' people involved in the project. Working well in charged conditions and with intense emotions was dependent on being able to build trusting relationships, and at times workers shared their own biographies as part of the give and take needed to build these connections (Strauss et al, 1982). During one conversation, one worker was described by the women as someone 'on the same level' and in 'the same league', who then became 'one of us'. In turn, the worker noted that 'that is exactly how I want them to feel because, to me, I am one of them'.

Reflection

The position of the Lifeline worker was ambiguous, 'neither here nor there; ... betwixt and between' the roles we tend to recognise that are 'assigned and arrayed by law, custom and convention' (Turner, 1969: 95). That the intervention extended well beyond the classroom in the community centre was well understood; the intention was to provide 'everything the girls needed, really', and the degree of autonomy afforded to project workers allowed for work invested with empathy and kindness (Bolton, 2005; Wharton, 2009; Bolton and Wibberley, 2014). They were able to act responsively and creatively to the women's needs and expressed satisfaction in their work; one described the work as 'so bloody rewarding it's unbelievable'. Each demonstrated a strong attachment to the work itself (Gill and Pratt, 2008). The significance of the workers' commitment was well understood and appreciated by the women. Years later, they spoke of the impacts on them, but also on the workers themselves:

> It made a difference then when you could see that, and you do feel good when you can see how they were, you know, changing *their* lives really ... and they said themselves ... how much it had changed their lives. They enjoyed helping people. They wanted to give it their best. It mattered deeply to them. (Lifeline girl, 2021)

These worker-activists were attending to need and intent on shoring up a personal and collective capacity for resilience, not least in response to increasingly coercive and punitive governing agenda. They were on hand when someone needed a 'breather' or help to work through a difficult day. Resilience 'is a highly contested concept', condemned 'because of its associations with neoliberal logics ... and the shedding of responsibility from states to citizens and third sector organisations' (Nicholls et al, 2025: 1). A policy rationale enrolling resilience 'promises' that people will be equipped with 'the wherewithal to empower themselves', while also 'promising a smaller, more economically efficient state' (Donoghue and Edmiston, 2020: 24). In actuality, those in receipt of social security benefits endure precarity and hardship and are subject to a disciplinary welfare regime produced through sanction and stigma, despite the development of resilience requiring 'some degree of material and ontological security through which to manage and overcome adversity' (Donoghue and Edmiston, 2020: 24; Brown et al, 2017). But the roots of Lifeline can be found in a different cultural and political history of grassroots organising, resistance and resilience (Nicholls et al, 2025). Among this group of women, there was a sense of being seen, listened to and understood, and of a space where they could untangle concerns and troubles, secure their place in the world and reassess their beliefs around what might be possible in the future:

> There is somebody out there that knows that we want to learn and that we need the support. Yeah. 'Cos I don't think, I got to be honest, I don't think any of us girls would have stuck it out if we didn't have that support behind us. Definitely not. (Lifeline girl, 2021)

The framing of this sort of care work as a 'natural' extension of a domestic role can belie its complexity and its contribution (James, 1989; Zadoroznyi, 2009). One woman, trying to articulate the enormous significance of the Lifeline workers' presence in her life, explained: 'They believed in me, you know? They believed that I could go on and do. That's what made it for me. ... That's what they do. They believe in you, and that is huge.' Another summed up the sentiment by saying that the workers were 'validating I am a person. That is just huge, you know ... when you're in that mindset where you feel like you're crap, you're not worth anything'. Yet another explained that the workers were women who would 'bend over backwards to make sure that you get whatever it is, and not just what you need but what you deserve'. They drank in what was described as the 'constant praise' of workers, who were a bolstering and inspiring presence – women who 'lit the torch' and 'never let us feel like we were worthless'. The workers' efforts were magnetising, drawing all these women together as a collective: creating 'a little world for us'.

8

Solidarities

It wasn't just me anymore.

Lifeline girl, 2021

Everyone was the one.

Lifeline girl, 2021

The concept of solidarity is often used to explain forms of social cohesion that emerge in contexts of social, political and economic instability. Founded through shared beliefs and practices, solidarity can be understood as an ongoing social accomplishment concerned with the allegiances we share with others and a sense of a collective future (Evans Jr and Evans, 1977). Our intrinsic interdependencies and interconnections are emphasised alongside the potential we each have to enhance the lives of others, particularly in a context of struggle. In both academic and folk accounts, the term often refers to class-based alliances of mutuality and trust established through a common interest in and commitment to contesting the intensification of capitalism (Gill, 2009). Here, relationships of solidarity are produced through intentional and explicitly disruptive forms of activism, with a related tendency to concentrate on the practices of protest and resistance that most obviously draw our attention: those 'dramatic, iconic, glamorous and heroic' acts with a 'readily-representable legacy' (Horton and Kraftl, 2009: 16).

One thread of literature attempts to extend these framings by suggesting that we also attend to smaller, quieter acts of solidarity (Martin et al, 2007). These approaches resist the tendency to understand activism as unambiguously disconnected from mundane routines and rhythms of everyday life and direct our attention to more banal or modest practices (Bayat, 2000; Dyck, 2005; Laurier and Philo, 2006; Pickerill and Chatterton, 2006; Kraftl and Horton, 2007; Jupp, 2008; 2017; Horton and Kraftl, 2009; Chatterton and Pickerill, 2010; Staeheli et al, 2012; Askins, 2014; 2015; Hankins, 2017; Pottinger, 2017; Hall, 2020). Here, authors consider the political character of unobtrusive and unassuming acts of 'implicit activism' (Horton and Kraftl, 2009). This includes those values and practices of reciprocity that are created through the ebb and flow of our day-to-day social engagements – non-commodified, personal, intimate relationships of care that are embedded within wider social formations and 'part of a broader continuum of movements for change' (Askins, 2015: 475; White, 2009; Hall and Ince, 2017; Pottinger, 2017).

Sarah Marie Hall's (2020: 247) ethnographic study of austerity in everyday life in the north-west of England draws on these ideas to cast light on the ways in which people are 'getting by' and 'speaking back' through embodied expressions of collectivity as subtle as 'a smile, a nod, a mutter of encouragement, [or] a brief conversation'. Similarly, Askins' (2015: 476) work on befriending encounters between refugees and residents in the north-east of England considers the political dynamics and import of sustained encounters – 'in homes, neighbourhoods, cafes, going for walks in the local park, and to local shops' – in contesting discourses of exclusion and marginalisation. Horton and Kraftl's (2009: 14) exploration of the interactions between carers and parents at a children's centre at risk of closure in the Midlands of England also attends to everyday practices of resistance found in local spaces – again, those 'small acts' and 'kind words' often neglected in conventional accounts of political activism (Horton and Kraftl, 2009: 14; Martin et al, 2007). We follow these contributions here in understanding the quietly political as being embedded in beliefs and practices of care and commoning. The Lifeline project can be positioned as another 'less obvious' space of quiet activism, a collective response to local women's marginalisation – of managing stigma, precarity and hardship – that was created through and enmeshed in a set of personal interconnections and interdependencies etched into the wider social fabric (Horton, 2016: 352; Held, 1993). The work of everyday life – of collectivity and community – was sustained through practices of conviviality, reciprocity and mutuality (Pahl, 1984; Massey, 1991; Domosh, 1997). Adopting this framework involves identifying patternings of sociality and relationality – those acts of communing generative of a sense of belonging and togetherness (Wills, 2012; 2016; Studdert and Walkerdine, 2016; Blokland, 2017; Neal et al, 2019).

The women's stories, textured by anecdotes, jokes and tributes, were replete with expressions of the affection and respect they held for each other. They spoke to the depth of fellowship that endured among them, which was often described through recollections of the numerous 'small acts' and 'kind words' (Horton and Kraftl, 2009: 14; Martin et al, 2007) that textured their interactions and were a feature of ordinary rhythms and routines. Later memories were striking for the references to the enjoyment they felt in the communal atmosphere of Lifeline; it was the social round of smoking together on the stoop, 'forever' drinking cups of tea, 'chipping in between us' and 'taking it in turns to cook for everybody' that lingered in minds. As one woman explained, the atmosphere was convivial: 'And it was just relaxed, wasn't it? The kettle was always on. ... Somebody was always making a brew. Somebody was always baking cakes and bringing them in. So it was like it's like morning tea with everyone.' Reminiscent of a kind of happy domesticity, these kinds of communal routines set the tone and the terms of the space, providing the basis for interactions (Pottinger, 2017; Hall, 2020). Woven through this simple social activity was a great deal of humour. When looking back, the women commented with notable consistency on the rounds of bantering, teasing and gossiping 'along the way', which meant there was 'never a dull moment' and 'there wasn't one day that we weren't laughing'. The gathering could be raucous at times. It was fun and as one of the women explained, this was compelling:

> The first week I was just into it. I was like, oh this is great ... and I used to go home and I'd be like, I can't wait to go back in tomorrow, you know. Get the kids off to school. Let's get up there, because we'd have such a laugh. Even though we were working, we were working hard, it was just such a good laugh. (Lifeline girl, 2021)

Attendance tended to mark the end of an extended period of isolation, of rarely being 'out of the house' and 'permanently looking after the kids'. Conversation was lively and stimulating, and the company was welcome. Gathering together meant spending pleasurable hours in the presence of other like-minded women, which in itself went some way toward offsetting the difficulties and disappointments of the world outside.

The project offered a place to meet where there were few hard and fast rules and little formality. Tutors brought order to the proceedings when leading a lesson and working through the material, but they left time for interpretation and lengthy discussion. During their time in the classroom, the women supported each other, drawing on their strengths to buttress each other's weaknesses; while some could be depended on for help with English, others were there to help with maths. When it came to the submission of coursework, one woman was there to call on, because her file was 'always perfect'. The women became aware of their different capabilities and worked together to overcome them – offering words of praise and nods of encouragement, going through their books and asking 'how are you with question one?', someone replying 'I don't know about that' and then supporting each other to get the work done. One woman described how she benefited from the other women providing advice and guidance in this way:

> I'm no good academically. I'm no good in the classroom, I'm not. I don't have the attention span for it. So when I started struggling, I'd have girls there. When people use big words that I don't understand ... the girls would notice my ... they'd be like, 'it means this'. They could ... see me drifting off. I'm not getting it, so they'd take time out of doing their work to help. (Lifeline girl, 2021)

Another, who had often helped those around her, described the amusement and camaraderie that sometimes flowed from these kinds of interactions:

> So, it would be Sam next to me and then Gemma, and we were doing maths, and I could see Sam like this, looking over to mine and that. And Gemma was like this to Sam: 'What is it? What has she put down? What is it? What is it?' And it went all quiet. Sam went: 'Shut up, she hasn't finished yet.' She was copying off me, and then Gemma was copying off her. (Lifeline girl, 2021)

This light-hearted anecdote pinpointed the way in which sharing knowledge and skills – a sense of 'give and take' – textured day-to-day classroom life.

A large part of the curriculum involved extended discussion of subjects within the social sciences and humanities – for example, there was a seminar on women's history and the role of the local workhouse, and another on changing cultural understandings of family life. The approach, as with adult education programmes in local communities more generally, attempted to 'build the curriculum from the interests, aspirations, and problems that people experience in their everyday lives' (Forster et al, 2018: 1). This was a conscious experiment, a process of selecting, adapting and modifying content that was calculated to transform how the women saw their place in the world. These topics and others drew the women in, provoking questions, debate and even heated argument on a set of (quietly feminist) issues. They were pushing themselves to foreground their views:

> I was sat in History and I was thinking, still a man's world, what really has changed? Still a woman who has to do everything, definitely may have more opportunities, still then men benefiting. Look in people's houses, go and find that house – the women are in the houses, one hundred percent a man's world. ... Women haven't really got a choice. If you are a single girl, this is a man's community – old values round here, men get away with a lot more. A man can walk away at any time and nothing gets said. We are the ones holding the babies. (Lifeline girl, 2009)

Many of the women recalled talking without restraint and sharing their stories and opinions during their time at Lifeline. The convivial atmosphere instilled an openness to different points of view and a ready exchange of ideas; it was a place to doubt and to disagree without being labelled strident or stupid. It was also a place to share difficult experiences of marginalisation and exploitation. For some, this kind of free expression came unbidden; as one woman explained of the chilling impact disclosures of her past made: 'I've never seen a room full of women just go quiet and go, oh my God.

They're like, you can just speak to us all day long. And I had to sit there and just talk shit … that's what I needed from them.' Others recalled being impressed by the others, even becoming overawed and a little 'timid' at first, content to just listen to the talk that swirled around a table where women could be, and could learn to be, outspoken. For the more cautious, opening up took time: 'People would talk and say, you didn't have to talk or whatever, but some people would say they felt this or this or that and whatever. And eventually then I started saying my bit.'

Either way, as time passed, the women shared more of their lives with each other. The topics often prompted personal reflections and contributions, and many chose to reveal something of themselves – about their families, their partners, their friends and their community. At times, this meant locating concerns and troubles in close relationships that had been undermined or ruined, and this was complicated by the question of whether and how they might sustain those ties. One example involved a series of conversations concerning one woman's relationship with her alcoholic father; in this case, talk turned to how she might reconsider his actions and perhaps move toward forgiveness and attempt reconciliation. Another focused on a woman's struggle to secure child maintenance payments from the father of her child, whom she knew was working and living locally; here, talk turned to her position as a single mother in a community where 'old-fashioned' gender stereotypes prevailed. On one occasion, the women were studying awareness of domestic abuse and its impact, including how to identify abuse, the allocation of support and the process of referral within domestic abuse strategies (important for those with plans to work in healthcare, social care, childcare, education and housing sectors). The learning materials included definitions of domestic abuse and the tools used by practitioners in cases when current or historic abuse is suspected. Years later, one woman recalled the personal significance for her of working through the definition and the discussions that unfolded:

> Being able to talk to other people as well, it made me realise, hang on, what he's doing isn't right, as well, in that sense. I knew it wasn't right, but it confirmed it then, and it wasn't just me … because you talk about things. So they pointed out, no that's not right, he shouldn't be following you all the time like that. It just cements it in, so you're not losing the plot and it's not just you thinking things. So, in that sense, to stand up for myself then. (Lifeline girl, 2021)

She wasn't the only woman to work and talk through these course materials and think 'that's me'.

These kinds of conversations – being able to speak openly with feeling – perhaps more than any other activity sedimented the importance of the collective for the women. The sustained interactions deepened the connections between them. As one explained, sharing stories and offering honest advice was one of the ways the circle helped each other:

> But being out there then, it was different. We were all good friends who helped each other and said it as it was. If we needed advice on anything, everybody would give their own advice, whether it was something we wanted to hear or not, do you know what I mean? (Lifeline girl, 2021)

Having 'somebody to talk to' on fair and frank terms was often framed as 'different' or novel. Lifeline was a place where the women could 'have a rant some days and … let off some steam'. Talking with friends eased the pressures of day-to-day life. And, of course, as one woman noted at the time, 'You haven't got to say anything. You could just go for a cuppa, just a chat.'

These practices were produced through and productive of a recognition among the women of their common ground. Ties of solidarity were forged through shared experiences of stigma, hardship and precarity (Squire, 2018), and a related sense of inclusivity and equality that was still keenly remembered years later. They were 'all equal' because they 'were going through the same … not every situation was exactly the same, but it was mostly the same'. These were framed as authentic, reciprocal relationships. The women spoke of being 'able to just be yourself with others that are in the same position as you'. It worked 'because they all shared stories'. As one woman explained:

> You could just, you could be open and you could talk about anything really. And everyone was understanding, and they all had their own stories of why they were there and they've had experiences in life and things, And yes, it was just amazing, and we all bounced off each other, as well, so the conversations just flew. (Lifeline girl, 2021)

Lifeline was a place for free thinking and open discussion, honest exchanges about difficult subjects, but also a place where contributions were met with respect, kindness and empathy. The significance of the latter was a recurrent theme within and across the women's accounts, at the time but particularly so in later years:

> People who had similar things, who felt the same. I can't explain to my friend who's got this perfect life, … because it's embarrassing. It's not just that. They don't understand, I don't think. Until you go through something yourself, they don't understand. And they've always had everything, they don't really realise. … I wasn't judged when I went there. I just felt everyone was the one. (Lifeline girl, 2021)

> No one judged, no one pretended to care. People were there for you, they would show up for you and be there for you, they would listen, we would talk. (Lifeline girl, 2021)

> The bad days where we were having a shit time and we would just turn up and sit there and cry, and nobody judged you. (Lifeline girl, 2021)

Sometimes developing this respect for one another involved dispelling or abandoning the kinds of prejudices that tend to circulate with only distant or passing acquaintance, as one of the women recalled when thinking of someone who in time became a friend: 'It's like, oh my God, she's rough, we're not bothering with her, she's a bit dodgy. And then … you think she's really tidy, she is. And then it gives you a different outlook onto different people as well.' Critically, Lifeline was framed as a place free of censure, where the women could find a measure of dignity. It was engaging, and it was safe. It 'was nice, really, really nice'; 'it felt tidy'.

The women described building relationships of care or 'gaining relationships' of 'trust', exactly the kinds of interdependencies and interconnections that might have been unfamiliar. Several, while reflecting later on what the project had meant to them, spoke to the dawning significance of these new connections, their own heightening awareness of the bonds they were developing:

> That's really the full-on acceptance and realisation that you weren't on your own, that you weren't on your own, feeling, thinking or going through. It could even be just an off-the-cuff comment like sharing our experiences and thinking, oh. (Lifeline girl, 2021)

> Trust, gaining relationships with people. Being able to talk openly without being judged. Actually knowing that you're not going to be let down by these people. But forming relationships, having them sort of things. (Lifeline girl, 2021)

The women gathered on terms of such intimacy that it could be disconcerting for a newcomer: 'You kind of feel like the outcast first of all because they're all like family. They all know each other and they're all familiar, but you soon … they include you straight away so you quickly feel like you're part of that family.'

Sharing their stories had brought the women together and they quickly learnt they could rely on each other for a gentle nod of encouragement or a cwtch (a hug) but also other, more concrete forms of mutual aid. As one of the women remembered, Lifeline was a place where practices of mutuality were commonplace: 'Everybody just like helped each other.

I remember one of the girls was moving and we were all over there one day, just like helping her in her new house and stuff and ... because she moved across the road. But it was lovely, I've got to be honest.' The pleasure that undertaking acts of this kind provided was widely articulated, and the women regularly came together to provide assistance to those who were experiencing especially tough times. The solidarity among them was perhaps most clearly visible during the 'everyday emergencies' that punctuated the women's lives (Millar, 2014: 34; Michell, 2020). At times and in response to pressing need, they worked together to help collect and redistribute basic goods, including food, clothing and furniture. Other examples included providing small loans or gifts or offering a spare bed or couch for a short time. Given the paucity of social security, these small-scale, everyday acts – practices of collective organisation, of commoning and care – that met need in times of crisis (Hall and Jayne, 2016; Jupp, 2017), were critical avenues for managing the gendered fallout of hardship and precarity (Jupp, 2017). In time, many of the women banded together into smaller groups, developing friendships in twos or threes. The members of one trio each independently chose to discuss the strength of the bond between them during their later interviews. This friendship, like others, was sustained beyond the classroom. Each remembered talking, laughing, studying and watching television together, sometimes late into the night. They would become very close, 'an extended family' whose 'kids grew up together ... [and] forged their own type of friendship'. It was 'nice', but it was also needed. The significance of these smaller groupings was prominent in accounts of (often protracted) crisis, involving experiences of deep trauma and privation. One of the three, a survivor of abuse and neglect, offered this tribute to their friendship:

> Because I'm on my own, I'm protecting myself. I haven't got, I'm not eyeing anybody who's in my life. It's because of these girls taking me under their wing. ... Some of them know a little bit because I'm open and honest about it. I've got nothing to be ashamed of ... I'm a survivor from it and I certainly have not let it define me. ... But them girls didn't call me a liar. ... They said, 'We'll get you back up.' And, fair play, they did – they stuck by their word. They'd never let me go without. They were getting me ... blankets and stuff, to get me started off. ... It was obviously needed ... the support was there. The girls were rallying round ... when I was going through them really bad breakdowns. It was them that were 'We're on our way.' They'd be at my door, do you know what I mean? When the police were getting called, they were at my door. When I was up the hospital seeing the crisis team, they were at my door. 'We've got you. We'll get you through this.' Do you know what I mean? (Lifeline girl, 2021)

These were women who 'stuck by their word' and helped her 'back up', first by believing her when she confided in them, then by providing basic necessities when she was waiting for her benefits claim to be processed, and later by being there 'at her door' when the 'shit hit the fan'. This friendship was one of many that spoke to the active role the women willingly took in helping each other manage insecurity and stigma, a quiet activism that bonded them together and penetrated their private, interior worlds. For this relationship, as with others, reciprocation did not 'need to be immediate', nor 'of the same form', nor 'involve a precisely calibrated scale of obligation' (Bowlby, 2011: 612; Bunnell et al, 2012). Often 'showing up' was seen as enough. At the time, one woman explained that the collective meant they weren't on their 'own anymore'. The tight-knit interdependencies and interconnections of the circle meant 'there was always somebody watching your back', and 'all the girls just being there' through the conditions of everyday life, including times of emergency and acute crisis, was productive of what Hall terms a 'politics of togetherness' (2020: 247; Akins, 2014).

During both waves of the research the women spent time reaching for precise descriptions of these relationships, which meant 'everyone was involved with each other'; attempting to articulate what their togetherness – 'having that community' and what Studdert and Walkerdine (2016: 76) refer to as those 'meanings-in-common' – meant to them. At the time, those on the most precarious footings framed these relationships as filling a void in their lives, because 'not everybody is privileged enough to have the backing of family and friends and the support network'; this collective was like 'a big family'. Others, typically those on surer foundations, suggested that these relationships were shoring up their lives, adding something valuable. In each case, narratives were deeply scored with a motif of belonging: these attachments were concerned with 'feeling part of a larger whole, through social, familial, emotional bonds *with others and to place*' (Askins, 2015: 474; original emphasis). As one women observed later, meeting people who were 'all in the same boat … people … who were going through the same things … made you feel you were a community. It was being a part of something. … You feel, you do feel like you're part of something'. These 'collective imaginaries' (Peacock et al, 2014: 388) conferred a sense of belonging: of feeling 'at home' and 'secure', but equally of being 'recognised and understood' (Wood and Waite, 2011: 201; Ignatieff, 1994). Accomplished through everyday practices of being with and there for each other (Mee and Wright, 2009), a sense belonging is suggestive of the close social bonds that we yearn for, the kinds of connections we would like to have and sustain (Stratford, 2009; Probyn, 2015). Belonging to this collective evoked a sense of 'pride, esteem and efficacy' (Peacock et al, 2014: 396).

These ties were created quick and strong under the pressures of hardship and stigma, but they were also lasting. When the project was running, many of the 'old girls' would go 'back and forth', introducing themselves to a new cohort and helping out when needed. As one explained: 'you're supposed to have a year there and they take on new people every year … but we were going back and forth there, every single year for one thing or another. … We would go back and help the girls as much as they needed.' These relationships continued to unfold after the project itself ended in 2014. Even though many no longer remained in daily contact, each reunion, formally organised or otherwise, had an easy warmth, as shown by the prevalence of comments such as 'we still slip into exactly the same conversations that we used to', they are 'still all connected' and 'you see somebody … it's like, oh God, a big cwtch … you know, it's lovely'. The descriptions of these relationships also showed that the care and concern for others remained as one woman said: 'there are plenty of girls … that I will still drop everything for if they need help'.

Reflection

The sense of belonging together created by the girls was produced through shared experience, the close intimacies of personal life and a set of associated practices of care and commoning (Antonsich, 2010; Askins, 2014; Pottinger, 2017; Hall, 2020). This quietly political circle of women was worked in response to conditions of precarity, in recognition and mitigation of the hardship and stigma that textured everyday life (Squire, 2018). Engaged in a common project of creating social ties that offered a measure of security and comfort, they cultivated a space for moral action – attentive, purposive acts of mutuality, reciprocity and conviviality that involved caring for each other (Horton, 2016; Jupp, 2017; Hall, 2020). These often spontaneous, improvised and inventive acts made a real difference to the women's lives, producing outcomes, both felt and seen, that were commonly understood and appreciated. The women were attending to material and emotional needs through relationships infused with respect and dignity, engaging in a common project of repairing and strengthening social ties and bonds that offered a measure of security and comfort.

Friendship is often considered less significant than our familial and romantic connections, and subordinate to the role of educators and mentors in shaping the trajectories of our personal lives. Yet, these relationships are important, profoundly influential on the way we live every day. For those with the closest bonds, these attachments formed the basis of long-standing, intimate relationships. These solidarities, enacted through intimate interpersonal relationships, were anchored in broader structures of political and cultural economy; they were created through social-historical processes of welfare restructuring, hardship, precarity and in stigma. Responding to need, sharing personal stories of marginalisation and suppression, and 'speaking out', sometimes for the first time, can be seen as political acts as opposed to purely therapeutic endeavours (Hall, 2020). Neither ideologically driven nor explicitly linked to any established social movement, the women's quiet activism amounted to a set of everyday practices that made implicit claims to substantive rights; acts of citizenship that were a protective and productive form of resistance (Isin, 2013). Through this lens, values and practices of mutuality, reciprocity and conviviality 'enter politics' (Staeheli et al, 2012: 640), and 'seemingly mundane acts or micropolitics' can be understood as a form of 'ordinary citizenship' (Staeheli et al, 2012: 630; Staeheli, 2011). Here, our understanding of citizenship extends to the activity of alternative or divergent spaces and those forms of often overlooked or unnoticed uncommodified, mutual aid and care provisioning that feature in accounts of civic engagement (Alexander, 2008; White, 2009; Fraser, 2016).

Of course, grumbles and spats reared up from time to time, but mostly it *was* 'just nice'; Lifeline offered the comfort and support of being in the company of women who shared what they had experienced in the past, what they were all experiencing together and what they hoped for the future. These practices of solidarity were productive of a sense of hope that was stirring, and the women would draw on the collective to reshape their perspectives on the future: it was through collective engagement that their hopes, and the power they had to bring those hopes to fruition, crystallised. The women came to see their engagement with the project as a pivotal moment in their life stories; it was framed, at the time and years later, as opening up new capabilities and possibilities, new ways of being and living. Their orientations towards education, paid work and unpaid care consciously altered as the sentiment that 'we are in this together', 'we are doing this together', 'together we are stronger' strengthened. Being part of the circle helped fuel enthusiasm for the future, bolstering and boosting their capacity to 'get by' but also 'get on'.

9

Trajectories

I do look at things a lot differently. I like my life differently now. I look at my life differently now.

                                                                          Lifeline girl, 2009

They've all given me that hope.

                                                                          Lifeline girl, 2021

The aspirations of individuals, in relation to employment at least, are of central importance to politicians, and we are told keeping our aspirations 'high' is good (Roberts and Evans, 2013). Nonetheless, our aspirations tend to be calibrated to the likelihood of success, and a rich vein of scholarship evidences the ways in which our plans and hopes for the future develop through a prism of the personal capacities, commitments and environments that make up everyday life. Hardship, stigma and insecurity make for truncated futures, cut off by the need to 'get by' and attend to the familiar and pressing concerns of the present moment rather than more distant horizons (Shipler, 2005; Boon and Farnsworth, 2011; Shildrick et al, 2012; Tirado, 2014; Bryant and Ellard, 2015; Daly and Kelly, 2015; Carabelli and Lyon, 2016; Desmond, 2016; Hanley, 2016; Millar and Ridge, 2017; Major and Machin, 2018; Pemberton and Humphris, 2018; Arnade, 2019; Exley, 2019; Laurison and Friedman, 2020; Donaghue and Edmiston, 2020; Ravn, 2021). An associated sense of low self-esteem and poor morale make 'getting on' and even planning or hoping to 'get on' that much more difficult (Gallie et al, 2003; Hacker, 2019). The precarity of day-to-day life among the dispossessed and disenfranchised can foster ambivalence and resignation because the future does look bleak against a backdrop of chances and choices that fail to materialise or disintegrate (McCollum, 2011; Shildrick et al, 2012; Desmond, 2016; Exley, 2019; Treanor, 2020). Still, the futures people imagine – the plans they make and the hopes they have – do shift in response to circumstance and experience. The trajectories of lives can be redirected through shifting orientations to paid work, unpaid care, education, civic engagement and so on.

Certainly, a degree of reinvention born out of some combination of necessity and desire was a recurring feature of the life stories the Lifeline women shared. It was clear when we first met that they each felt their life was at a turning point, and most believed there was a real chance of escape from a set of highly restrictive personal circumstances. Over a decade later, their stories continued to frame this time in their lives as profoundly consequential, productive of real and enduring change. In these later conversations, the women were well placed to take stock and make connections between the various critical moments or episodes that had accumulated over time to redirect the paths their lives would take (Elder, 1985; Riessman, 2008a; Kupferberg, 2012). There were many of these kinds of stories, crafted to interpret experiences in an attempt to make 'significant wholes out of scattered events' (Ricoeur, 1980: 178). Taking some time to reflect on her life in this way, one woman remembered 'sitting on this bus one day … looking out the window … looking at all these people, all the druggies. And I was thinking my son's going to be like this … I've got to do something.' She remembered joining Lifeline, which she described as 'the start of my life really'. She remembered going on a day trip with the girls (something she hadn't done for years because she could never afford it). The trip was 'nothing special'. Except it was really. She could remember being bought food and thinking 'I haven't even probably eaten out in a food place for so long' and it 'was just nice to have that normalised feeling'. Then she remembered celebrating at her graduation from Lifeline and 'just crying' with an old friend 'because we were proud of ourselves and what we'd become' and 'thinking we were super cool' – 'look at us two!'. 'It was nice'. Then, winning 'pupil of the year or something' at college, being invited to a ball and getting a voucher to buy something to wear – 'and I can remember buying myself a dress to go … and I was like, look at me!'. 'I hadn't really dressed up and done stuff like that.' Then years later, after college, university and getting a job, she remembered taking a trip with her friends to the Grand Canyon, where this 'super big thing come over me', 'like a sense of, I don't know, like the best one' – 'me, this girl, has come to the Grand Canyon … look what I've achieved'. She does still look around 'sometimes at some of the people'. The other day, she bumped into someone she had been quite close to at one time. She knew her children had been taken away and she asked if the woman was alright. 'I was thinking, oh my God, that would have been me, and it really would have been.' She felt she had met her counterfactual, someone 'going under' rather than 'getting on'. She went on to say that now 'if I see anyone like me, I try to always help them or give them something because I feel like if I didn't have that, I don't know where I would be.'

In this chapter, we delve into these kinds of accounts of reinvention and redirection, which were commonplace. This involves moving between time frames, between each wave of the study, to consider narratives that were anchored in the past and present, but often orientated toward the future (Emirbayer and Mische, 1998). Studies of those who return to education are replete with examples of people seeking to leave aspects of their lives behind – metaphorically and literally – to secure a better perspective on the future (Rees, 1997; Hughes, 2002). The women who returned to education through Lifeline narrated their lives in this way. One, a lone parent of three children and a community volunteer at the time when she was participating in the project, described her 'old life' in the following terms:

> I think I was probably just more like a robot then, just living, well shall I say existing? ... I think I am living now, that's the best way to describe it. ... I think I was just drifting along, existing. Now, I think I am actually living my life now. So, yeah, that's the best way I can describe it. (Lifeline girl, 2009)

In response to a request for a 'life history interview', another of the women offered a rueful: 'What life? I didn't have a life until now.' In these instances and many others, 'old' lives were framed through ideas of passivity, stasis and deficit. Over a decade later, many of the women described deeply grooved routines of domesticity and unpaid care, sharing accounts of 'doing the same thing, day in, day out, day in, day out', 'over and over and over', cycles of waking, feeding, washing, brushing, cleaning, cooking, playing, watching, soothing, tidying and then 'doing exactly the same thing the next day'. At times, these kinds of narrative were inflected with dismay at 'the rut' they had found themselves in and included corresponding expressions of personal inadequacy, incapacity and self-recrimination: 'I sort of was that type of person, I couldn't do anything, I was useless at everything'; 'I didn't think I would try to be anything – I didn't have any, I didn't think I would try to be anything'; 'I was absolutely clueless, and I was just, like, I'm going to be on benefits for the rest of my life.' These character assessments cast inert figures who didn't move through the world so much as stay put, 'stuck' fast in it.

In the beginning, if nothing else, the project was cast as a reason to 'get out and about'. It gave days 'a structure', 'a routine of something' different. Most decided to 'just go along and see what happens'. Many 'didn't think it'd last' and they all knew they could 'always drop out'. What followed from their involvement was 'surprising' to them. With remarkable consistency, the women went on to describe a revelatory experience that 'opened up eyes' and generated a new awareness of their own capabilities and capacities to act (Forster et al, 2018). These were 'lightbulb' moments, times when the women either individually or collectively were able to 'see the light' and take the first of many 'big steps' into 'the big bad world'. Other stories detailed a protracted, incremental process, a case of 'building', 'slowly, bit by bit', which involved small but deeply consequential gains. For one woman, 'speaking out' in class and 'saying my bit' for the first time was remembered as a critical step. On one occasion, having worked through a long division problem, another burst into tears. She was proud of herself for the first time in a long time. Many of the women immersed themselves deeply in their studies, which were seen as challenging and galvanising. Exposure to a curriculum rich in the humanities and social sciences provided plenty of material for open discussion and engagement with societal issues and reflection on their personal lives. Connecting their experiences and circumstances to social and political theories and ideas pushed against the boundaries of their worlds. Counselling, a central touchstone of the approach, proved to be enormously popular and gave the women a therapeutic vocabulary with which to reassess their beliefs about not only themselves but also those close to them and the world at large. At the time, drawing on the vocabulary of 'personal development', and years later, this was framed as a period of acute introspection and ontological awareness. For some, it was understood to be totalising. One woman recalled questioning herself: 'What the hell am I doing? Who am I even?' Another explained: 'You question everything, and I've never had that before.' Yet another suggested the experience 'made us realise what life is about.'

Emboldened, the women were reimagining their futures. For most, the urge to 'break' with the past was keenly felt, and even if doubts resurfaced periodically, they felt that alternative pathways and trajectories were opening up. They were at a juncture and there were choices to be made: 'It's like life's choice, innit? ... To me now, it's like I will choose ... the way I see it now, I choose the path that's gonna make my life better quality or I don't.' The women made these kinds of plain statements in the belief that their circumstances could change for the better. At times, at their keenest, they offered optimistic accounts of futures defined by unfettered choice and mobility. Indicative of the strength of popular belief in meritocracy (Mijs, 2018), vocabularies of liberation and fulfilment, detached from the moorings of class, gender and place, were put to work. Well-trodden idioms ('the world is your oyster and it is what you make of it'), featured alongside more grounded, hopeful assertions that they were 'now', 'trying' to do their 'best', 'trying to make something of' themselves. One woman explained: 'Now, I believe that if you study something, if you really concentrate on something that you really want in your mind, you can get it.' On rare occasion, these kinds of arguments mingled with narratives that unpicked the myth of meritocracy with an ease born out of experience, as when one woman remembered her childhood expectations of having 'a lush house, lush job, lush partner'. Speaking ruefully and perhaps with a touch of scorn, she remembered imagining this stuff of 'fairy tales', before growing up and realising that 'it don't work out like that unless your parents are minted, like, unless you are born with a silver spoon in your mouth'. Nevertheless, the formula is powerful and did find traction among the women, who were far more likely to embrace the idea of working hard work to master their own destiny than to express outrage at those more fortunate than themselves.

A sense of injustice was only rarely articulated. Besides, the child who had once believed in 'fairy tales' didn't want things handed to her 'on a plate', even if she 'wouldn't mind just some help now and again'.

The careful, concrete plans that were made by the women alluded to the new sense of personal control they felt over how the future might unfold. Keenly aware of their own position, their interests lay in securing practical advantages in relation to their immediate situation. They went from defending and protecting what they had as best they could to attempting to make their lives differently and improve their position in the world. As one explained: 'I could see my plans ahead of me. I could see if I went to college and finished that course and then I could go to uni if I wanted to or then I could go out and get a job that I would enjoy doing'. In later years, another recalled the point when she thought: 'Well, I can do it. ... There is nothing wrong with me that I can't do it, do you know what I mean?' Even though studying well into the night was hard work, most remained resolute; they sketched out the contours of their intentions to 'get qualifications' and most wanted to go to college and some, to university. They didn't want the 'crap at the bottom' of the labour market. Most wanted to 'have a job', earn 'proper money', to 'take the kids on holidays and just pay the bills'. They wanted to work towards a 'career' (Wright and Patrick, 2019). These reappraisals of the future involved securing a 'better' life that retained a strong attachment to the Valleys and the tangible opportunities presented by the local labour market (Jamieson, 2000; Cairns, 2013; Lamberg, 2020; Ravn, 2021). They were hoping for a more 'normal', 'ordinary' life, and envisaging this 'different' life spurred them on. A 'good education' and 'good job' meant escape from a highly circumscribed position. Both came to be associated with empowerment, emancipation and enjoyment. The opinions of, often unnamed, others were an important motivation:

> I want them to [think], you know, she worked hard even though she didn't do very good at school. She worked hard. She sorted her life out. She brought her kid or kids up well and, you know, she got a roof over her head. The kids have all got clothes on their backs, you know, and she worked for it, do you know what I mean? (Lifeline girl, 2009)

> I wanna make something of my life. ... People, like, look down at me, 'you can't do it' ... but deep down in my heart I know what I want to do and I am not going to give in. (Lifeline girl, 2009)

These descriptions melded together the economic and cultural dimensions of marginalisation, yoking ideas of self-support and self-improvement to those of respectability and redemption (Walker and Bantebya-Kyomuhendo, 2014; Millar, 2019). The women wanted to be stable and secure, but they also wanted to be 'normal and good' (Sayer, 2005: 58; Savage, 2015; Millar and Ridge, 2017; Shildrick, 2018).

The political message that paid work is the defining feature of a responsible and fulfilled adult life was saturating (Braun et al, 2008). The 'steady withdrawal of their 'right to care' was associated with reorientations of the women's beliefs and everyday practices (Haylett, 2003: 809). Returning to education and taking employment, involved reappraising family life and while caring for children remained important, that the working definition of 'good' motherhood among the women was fluid was clearly articulated (Finch, 1989; Duncan and Edwards, 1999; Duncan et al, 2003; Holloway and Pimlott Wilson, 2016; Andersen, 2023):

> I did start changing my views about things and I did start becoming, … I didn't become less of a parent, I just realised that I was important as well … and that I still got a life. Even though they are still here, I can do things without being a bad parent. So, I mean that is always in your head as well, that you can be a bad parent if you do this, you are going to be a bad parent if you do that, you know. So then I just realised that, no, you know, you are not a bad parent. As long as you are there when they need me, then I can still do things. Before it gets too late, you know? So everything do change, from wanting to be with them, wanting to do everything with them. (Lifeline girl, 2009)

Moving away from traditional ways of 'being there' for children, at home and at the school gates, was a self-conscious adjustment that could be painful and for some doubts and concerns lingered. Over a decade later, one woman described worrying that she had overlooked her son's poor mental health. She remembered thinking: 'My son is depressed and I don't even know it – I have been too busy.' Another was concerned that she wasn't her caring for her youngest child in the same way as her older children, which 'wasn't fair'. These kinds of anxieties – the product of contradictory impulses and ambiguities about the 'right' beliefs, values and practices (Hochschild, 2003) – could be hard to shake. Still, in time, as children grew older and mothers committed more fully to their education and paid work, the matter became more settled (Braun et al, 2008; Hennessy, 2009). Realising the kind of future they wanted for their children was of central importance: the women wanted to give their children 'the chance to do it as well' and 'give them the push to go that bit further' (Daly and Kelly, 2015; Ravn, 2021). They also wanted to meet the Lifeline workers' expectations of them. One recalled that she didn't want to 'let them all down, because they'd invested a lot of time in us'; it became important to 'prove them right'.

While these hopeful narratives were congruent with the women's experiences at the time, it was by no means certain how they would fare in unfamiliar further and higher education settings, a weak local labour market and a decade of austerity politics and policies. Aspirations for 'normal' and 'ordinary' lives that hinged on securing a 'proper job' in the Valleys were far from modest. Perhaps unsurprisingly, the life trajectories that unfolded appear to resonate with others in similar circumstances and Jane Millar and Teresa Ridge's (2020) longitudinal study of low-income, lone mother families is a rich seam of research that provides some useful anchors here. When we met and spoke over a decade later, all but a small number of the women were in paid work. One qualified as a nurse and worked in the local hospital, but was facing the prospect of medical retirement having developed a chronic disease. Two, who had gone on to study successfully at university before taking on periodic volunteering roles, were recuperating with significant mental health concerns, the origins of which preceded their time with Lifeline. For another, a long-term health condition had intensified over the years to the point of debilitating unpredictability, disrupting both her education and her employment. In short, for some, life events either ruled out the possibility of pursuing education and paid work or made sustaining these activities extremely challenging. Still, in general, as time progressed, most found stable jobs, often with a strong element of care work. A few made an uncomplicated move straight into sustained work; usually, they did so by sharing their own caring responsibilities with family and with the benefit of assistance from a good employer (Millar and Ridge, 2017; 2020). Some, having completed further qualifications at college or university, or having pursued opportunities when in work, progressed into skilled jobs with a degree of seniority and good wages for the area. Women with older children were more likely to share this experience, able to move into further and higher education to study nursing, social work or social sciences. But for those with younger children, it was often a case of moderating or tempering aspirations and pursuing the 'next best thing', as many of them realised quite quickly at the time:

> The next best thing after the nursing would be working with children ... because with them now I would probably have to wait a year or two now, and it would still probably be awkward because you have to go to uni to do nursing, you got to do a year in college and then three or four years in uni. And, like, I couldn't afford to do it with childcare, so I would have to wait. (Lifeline girl, 2009)

In these cases, employment choices were made pragmatically and often to make family life more manageable, with factors like the location of a workplace and working hours taking priority (Millar and Ridge, 2017; 2020). For those with little support from family and friends, education was difficult to sustain alongside caring commitments, especially with young children:

Some went to uni. Like, one girl went to uni. She had three children and she was a single parent. Did really, you know, could have done well, had the knowledge. … So I said it was too much, too much to do, with the kids and whatever. She was really good in the class, you know, you could see. She left school with no qualifications, but she had it. And then you've got like, you know, when they were younger, so you'd need somebody to pick the kids up from school and, you know, and if you haven't got family, it's really hard, isn't it? (Lifeline worker, 2021)

Women with younger children tended to choose shorter, less intensive college courses and often made quicker transitions into the labour market (Millar and Ridge, 2017; 2020), going into childcare, education or health and social care jobs. These routes were seen to demonstrate a good measure of responsibility and respectability. Embedding and sustaining work in day-to-day life sometimes took time, and perhaps involved volunteering at first or taking on a few hours of work while still in college, and possibly changing jobs several times (Millar and Ridge, 2017; 2020). But they 'learnt to make it work'. As children grew older and the responsibility of 'being there' eased, several women took the opportunity to move to 'better jobs' or work longer hours (Millar and Ridge, 2017; 2020). Again, those who secured some progression in the workplace usually did so by sharing caring responsibilities with family and through the support of a good employer (Millar and Ridge, 2017; 2020), and again these jobs often had a strong emphasis on care in the education, health and social care, and criminal justice fields. Some were working in what were thought of as 'good' jobs locally; they made modest advances that boosted incomes a little and provided a measure of security, allowing them to build up some savings and plan for the future. As one of the women said of her experiences of juggling frequently unpredictable jobs and family life before finding 'better' work in the NHS:

You're coming in and then you're going back out in the cold to go back out to do another job. So you're not really seeing the kids … you're literally saying there's your food, make sure your homework's done, change out of your uniform, I've got to go now. And I had to find childcare …. whereas … now I know they are older, don't get me wrong … I don't have to worry about it … whereas before … you couldn't plan anything. (Lifeline girl, 2021)

Several women discussed the complexities of taking paid work and the impact on their children. Accounts were both positive and negative, varying with the circumstances, including the age of the children and the terms and conditions of employment (Millar and Ridge, 2009; 2020; Andersen, 2023). However, a consistent thread over time and across instances was the women's belief that by studying and working they were being a 'good' role model for their children (Duncan and Edwards, 1999; Duncan et al, 2003; Holloway and Pimlott-Wilson, 2016; Andersen, 2023).

Critically, all but one of the women in work felt that the employment they secured marked a big 'step up', both from life on benefits and the kinds of informal paid work – the 'shitty little things' – they might have done in the past. For women, and mothers in particular, stability and security in employment are often more important than progression and mobility, even if the work available is of otherwise poor quality (Hennessy, 2009; Millar, 2019; 2020; Wright, 2023). Several were working at or just above the national minimum wage, often in the private sector providing care for people in their own homes or in residential settings. In these cases, incomes were low and likely to remain so, but care work was preferable to the very insecure and low-status work – like cleaning, dish washing and glass collecting – they might have had in the past. It was considered a 'better' job even if it didn't pay much more, and these women were aware of and tended to stick with the 'good employers' in the area. The work could be hard and heavy, particularly so during the COVID-19 pandemic, but (in part because it was difficult at times) it generated a great deal of satisfaction (Hebson et al, 2015). It was associated with a strong sense of, sometimes unexpected, accomplishment. Here, ideas of self-worth and self-support, respectability and responsibility were connected to taking care of others:

> Now I'm a carer. I'm going into elderly, vulnerable people and taking care of them, which I never thought I'd do. … I know what it's like to have nobody. … So look at me go. … Proud of myself. I've never accomplished nothing my life. I've had jobs that I've never stuck out. … I've never had nothing, so actually, oh my God, look at me. … I've got full control of my life again … not afraid of nobody else. … Because that was my biggest downfall, thinking of everybody else, oh, I can't … my life, my independence, my security, I've got everything back. (Lifeline girl, 2021)

The women felt this work put a floor on their economic and cultural circumstances (see Skeggs, 1997), even as they expressed dismay and sometimes anger at the low wages (see Andersen, 2023). These women expressed commitment to and passion for care work, which was a source of considerable pride. Most felt they were well suited to this kind of work because these jobs built on their extensive personal biographies of caring; they were bringing their private lives to bear in the world of work (Bolton, 2005). This position was sedimented by a desire for the greater degree of independence and sense of control that even relatively modest employment was understood to offer, something acutely felt by those with experience of abuse. As one of these women explained: 'I'm still doing everything on my own, but I've got the means to do everything on my own.' For these women, caring for other people in need was especially rewarding: 'my best thing now is I feel like I can support people who are going through these things and all, because I can relate to little things'; it was a way of giving 'somebody that second chance in life'. For others, caring was more self-consciously political, a way to 'fight' to help people, 'to stop them from being exploited' and to help them 'live to the best quality of life they can'.

More broadly, the presentation of a moral self in possession of a 'good work ethic' was deeply scored into many of the life stories that were shared over the course of the study (see Sidel, 2006; Shildrick et al, 2012; Katz, 2013; Shildrick and MacDonald, 2013; Daly and Kelly, 2015; Shildrick, 2018). And while most could point to workplace issues and concerns, all but one of the women who were working described their working lives positively (Andersen, 2023). They were 'definitely happier', to the extent that some suggested they 'could never, ever be without work now' or that they 'couldn't cope' without work – 'signing on' again would mean 'going backwards', it would mean 'losing their minds'. Staying in work involved 'pushing' through and 'fighting' on, and in some cases signing on and off benefits several times, in a struggle to gain that foothold. For example, one woman was dismissed because she 'caught' pregnant, and another was furloughed during the COVID-19 pandemic. In the Lifeline workers' assessments, women with these kinds of experiences were among the most eager to take paid work after their time with the project concluded, so they 'settled' early on for poor-quality jobs that proved tough to sustain. As welfare conditionality intensified, a small number of women also spoke of coming into conflict with the Jobcentre and officials who 'weren't happy' with their decision to pursue their studies in the hope of 'better' work. It was frustrating (Katz, 2013). One recalled realising that she was expected to look for paid work even though she was attending the local college. Another was told she needed to leave college because she had been offered paid work. Summarising her experience of trying to return to education after the birth of her third child interrupted her studies, one woman explained:

> I went back and started again and they told me at the Jobcentre, 'we're going to stop your money'. So it was oh great. ... I don't have any work, I don't earn enough money to feed my kids, I'm going to college and train and get a better job, you're not going to let me do it ... and that was the only choice in my head at the time I had. (Lifeline girl, 2021)

'Signing on' remained a difficult experience, as another detailed: 'I had to go down the other day to sign .... and I felt like a kid again. Back down to there. ... It's just like I know that feeling of going back to where I was.

And I felt, like, oh my God.' She had picked up three different agency jobs in the short time since then, which 'made her feel better again'. She was 'just getting by' but felt it was preferable to claiming benefits, such was the dignity found in working life (Lamont, 2009).

But focusing on concrete labour market outcomes offers only a partial insight into the kinds of life projects that the women narrated and there were several alternative expressions of value. Signe Ravn (2019) suggests that the term 'imagined futures' is useful in this respect because it is more encompassing than 'aspirations', which tend to be more narrowly confined to our employment goals. Over a decade earlier, most of the women offered accounts of their lives changing 'beyond all recognition', but the significance of the experience as a biographical turning point was only shored up over time. One woman remarked later: 'I still talk about it now … how they … helped me just move on in life. I think my life would've gone down a completely different track if I hadn't.' Here, and across many instances, the project was positioned as a 'starting point', an experience that was 'life-changing'. Some felt they had become 'a totally different person' living a 'completely different life'. Each took the time to narrate the arc of their biography through ideas of progression and advancement. Accounts resonated the stack of things – the actions, thoughts and utterances – they 'would never have done before', and the life-changing choices in relation to employment but also education, leisure, community life, personal well-being, friendships and romantic and familial relationships – changes that were attributed to the project and amounted to 'a tremendous impact'. They commented that it was 'much better now, much, much better' and that they lived in 'a different world … fabulous', marked by 'incredible' and 'surprising' 'changes'. Perhaps most notably, education wasn't calibrated solely in relation to the labour market. Many enjoyed their studies a great deal and they were understood to hold intrinsic value. Pursuing them often slayed old demons – they were 'bright' and they 'could do it'. Through education, they reinvigorated old friendships and built new ones, which gave them 'more life'. For some, participation in the project was critical to the decision to 'finally' sever the ties of deeply corrosive, intimate relationships. Years later, one woman remembered her time with the project as a tipping point: as she put it, she 'was, like, come and change my locks and everything!'. She explained:

> Lifeline, it made me, it did make me stronger. … I wouldn't have found the support then from my own friends again. I wouldn't have been strong enough to say that's it … my life has to change, and I'm not having it, I can't do this for the rest of my life, I can't. And that is when … it was slowly, nothing happens straight away, does it? You know, you have got to build everything up. I wish it happened straight away, but it didn't – it was me becoming me again, more confident,

laughing again, you know. I mean, I can't say I became more confident straight away, because that was something that I needed to work on. But it was like that was my starting point. I knew then that from there, I knew I could go forward. I did know I could go forward. ... And, like, now I cringe, oh, I do cringe thinking of the stuff that I put up with. ... To be honest, it is hard now to think back, and it is, it's horrible. Because if I was then who I am now, things would have been a lot different. (Lifeline girl, 2021)

For some, it meant being able to do things that most people take for granted, like talking to a stranger or making eye contact during a conversation:

It taught me so much, and it's like looking at you, when I'm talking to you, I'm looking at you and I'm looking at your eyes. I could never do that before. I'd be looking down like that or I'd look to the side. It's like, I'm just as good as you now. I am, I'm not inferior. I used to feel terribly inferior to people. ... I can look at you and talk to you, and even if I stumble, it doesn't matter. (Lifeline girl, 2021)

Often, the women's reflections came to rest more steadily on their capacity for resilience in the face of tremendous adversity. As one put it: 'I don't believe half of the shit I went through and look at me now ... how am I still standing?'; another said: 'I've come so far for what I've been through, the life I've had. I've turned it around and I keep telling myself every day I should be proud of myself.' Among the most marginalised, the project was positioned as 'a life saver' in accounts that traced biographical arcs of developing self-awareness, self-worth and self-belief. Poignantly condensing what many expressed, one woman explained: 'I am a good person, and I never thought that before.'

Reflection

Lauren Berlant argues that a political economy produced through meritocratic ideology is textured by a form of 'cruel optimism', an attachment to a brighter future, without an acknowledgement that its pursuit can be impeded by hardship, stigma and insecurity in everyday life and may deliver only negligible returns (Berlant, 2011). At play are the products of a political sleight of hand, those 'fantasies of upward mobility, job security, political and social equality and lively, durable intimacy' that promise a flourishing life (Berlant, 2011: 3). Optimism is the product of shallow engagement, limited to the capacity to envisage only inevitably positive outcomes, and while these imaginaries may be sustaining, they can also be diminishing and harmful (Berlant, 2012; Eagleton, 2015). In contrast, hope has an uplifting 'anticipatory logic' based on a sense of possibility and uncertainty; the capacity to imagine a different way of being, a desire for something that is valued but absent (Rigney, 2018: 370; Eagleton, 2015). When we first met, many of the women were hopeful and took the time to reflect extensively on their lives, reimagining their own attachments to a brighter future and taking measured steps towards it. Several referred to undertaking a personal 'journey' that was leading to 'a totally different outlook on life'. At the time, this term circulated widely. A phenomenon of a contemporary culture infused with a highly contested therapeutic ethos – the 'journey' referred to a revelatory process of self-discovery. Bearing little relation to an objective change in social position and limited to psychological or emotional wellbeing, the concept relates to a new state of mind rather than any material shift in circumstance. Through the 'journey', the individual is better placed to deal with adversity and to work on their emotions (of disappointment, anger, frustration and so on). For the women the term was part of a useful therapeutic vocabulary that could be put to work to help explain how 'getting out from that stuck place' was slowly becoming conceivable. The presence of hope, based on a sense of possibility and no small measure of uncertainty, was integral to these narratives, and its development can itself be understood as a biographical turning point (Sanders and Munford, 2008; Worth, 2009; Hardgrove et al, 2015; Neale, 2021).

The collective trajectory of the Lifeline girls that unfolded over time is familiar to us. Working-class women dominate much of the education, health and social care workforce and continue to endure inequalities in the labour market and in the patterns of family responsibility (Wheatley et al, 2018; Francis-Devine and Foley, 2024). As Willis (1978) argued of 'the lads' and later Skeggs (1997) of the 'care girls', our choices in relation to paid work and unpaid care are socially embedded, produced through formations of class, gender and race (Lewis and Giullari, 2005; Kintrea et al, 2015; Friedman and Laurison, 2020). We make both more and less genuine choices (Lewis and Giullari, 2005; Greve, 2009) through a calculation of what is likely to be possible (see Walby et al, 2012), and the 'quality of choice[s]' available to us varies a great deal (Beck, 2018: 7). For the women who took part in this study, workfare reforms meant once-dependable strategies of 'getting by' on social security benefits were becoming increasingly less tenable. The presence of the Lifeline project offered an alternative to days punctuated by well-worn domestic routines and perhaps the prospect of a 'dead-end job going nowhere', but also a space to cultivate relationships of care and concern and some peace of mind. Having cycled between self-blame, self-doubt and self-belief (Haylett, 2003), and despite living through a period of economic crisis, recession and welfare resettlement through austerity (Hall 2019b), most felt they had carved out a greater degree of stability and security than they might have. Those I met and spoke with felt they were better off than they were when they started and some markedly so. Their desire for fuller lives was better met, with so much of what they appreciated about their experiences relating to a greater sense of dignity and respect, and the value they were able to derive for themselves within and beyond paid work, as they moved through the world.

10

Conclusion

The reason I am where I am today is because somebody gave me that second chance.

Lifeline girl, 2021

There's nothing out there now is there? ... It's mad, you look back years and there was so much there, and now it's not, is it?

Lifeline girl, 2021

There are all these people now ... going through it, when they shouldn't have to go through it.

Lifeline girl, 2021

In *Landscape for a Good Woman*, Carolyn Steedman (1987) reminds us of our collective capacity to meet our basic needs. Growing up in the 1950s, she commented on the presence in her life of a post-war social democratic welfare state that framed social assistance as a universal right. For the architects of this settlement, the proper role of government involved a commitment to mitigating the worst excesses of capitalism and lessening inequality by providing social security benefits and freely available public goods, such as education and medical care. The settlement held the possibility of greater protections but also opportunity and mobility (Rees and Rees, 1980; Gray and Barford, 2018). Framed as social insurance for social progress, the creation of a contributory system of entitlements was an instance of cooperation between the state and the citizen, which, while flawed, did provide material and cultural gains for citizens (Titmuss, 1967/2000; Rees and Rees, 1980; Levitas, 2001; Pateman, 2004; Lewis, 2005; 2010). For her part, Steedman concludes: 'I think I would be a very different person now if orange juice and milk and dinners at school hadn't told me, in a covert way, that I had a right to exist, was worth something' (1987: 122). In the contemporary era, the retreat of the state – the disinvestments of de-industrialisation and welfare retrenchment – means citizens in the Valleys and elsewhere are less well shielded from hardship and stigma, and experience the deprivations and humiliations that arise when everyone must 'compete on the same terms, but without the same advantages' (Sayer, 2005: 161). While politicians came to frame people's reliance on social security benefits as a matter of preference based on shiftless self-interest, many of the women I spoke with described biographies consisting of a succession of knock-downs and setbacks. These were the corrosive, gendered impacts of living in protracted crisis in the Valleys.

Writing of de-industrialised communities, Kathryn Dudley (2020: 201) argues that people in these places have given up the possibility of hope; and certainly the early biographies of the Lifeline girls were suggestive of a sense of the 'loss of futurity' produced by ruinous economic and cultural violence. The ugliness of the societal decay across the UK was outlined by the United Nations Special Rapporteur on extreme poverty and human rights, Philip Alston (2018):

> I have talked with people who depend on food banks and charities for their next meal, who are sleeping on friends' couches because they are homeless and don't have a safe place for their children to sleep, who have sold sex for money or shelter, children who are growing up in poverty unsure of their future, young people who feel gangs are the only way out of destitution, and people with disabilities who are being told they need to go back to work or lose support, against their doctor's orders.

In the Valleys, the concentration of societal decay can be measured by the brute fact of stalling and falling life expectancy (Seaman et al, 2024).

The Lifeline project, an attempt to resist the orthodox, was one early response to these developments. Like Steedman's (1987: 122) 'juice and milk and dinners', this small experiment in concrete action left its mark. Its presence was felt directly and deeply. If nothing else, its legacy lies in making it clear to a small circle of women that they also mattered. Together, the women who participated in the project questioned their sense of themselves and their place in the world, confronting the fact of their own marginalisation. This included the gendered patternings of hardship, precarity and stigma in the place they lived, and for some, the punitive experiences of coercion and control in their homes that were mirrored in their relationship to the welfare state (Wright, 2023). They sought social acceptance and respect, and expressed their resistance to being positioned within the pool of workers for the 'crap at the bottom' of the labour market. A desire for something 'better' took root, and they acted on it. Most planned for their own absorption into the limited number of more privileged, better-educated working-class people. It was an attempt to break through established hierarchies and attain an extra measure of economic independence, security, and dignity. They were intent on moving 'higher', 'getting on' and finding a more comfortable pocket for themselves. Despite the paucity of the choices permitted to them, they began to challenge the authority of a more muscular Jobcentre to issue instructions on how to behave and the pressure to take a job, any job, regardless of its quality and sustainability. Often, after considerable personal struggle, they felt their plans and hopes were no longer so tightly contained. There was a general sense that their participation in the project gave them the chance to 'live' rather than 'exist'. They found new ways to negotiate the world and reformulated their orientations to education, paid work, unpaid care and civic engagement.

The women were remarkably emphatic in their admiration for the project's worker-activists – women who could gather others around them, who were openly critical of the Jobcentre's street-level bureaucrats and the job they had to do, and who were respected for their knowledge of the world and the care they took in it. They made a profound impact through a combination of material and less concrete but nonetheless important interventions. Of core concern was access to decent work. Their ethos was accommodative of the women's established preferences and commitments: the offer of a pathway to further and higher education was key, as was the provision of free childcare to ensure they could take it up. There was also practical information and advice for negotiating with the Jobcentre and various other arms of the state, including the housing, child maintenance and school systems. That the support reached deeply into personal life was critical. It was in these ways that worker-activists occupied a space that confounded 'neat divisions between public, private and personal', with a concern for 'new ways of living, working and doing politics' (Newman, 2012b: 472, 473). They demonstrated a strong commitment to a role that arose at the 'interface of activist commitments and governmental programs and projects' (Newman, 2012b: 473; Gill and Pratt, 2008). These worker-activists were radically minded and enjoyed some autonomy in a pragmatic approach that attempted to subvert the 'master frames' of welfare policy and practice (Emirbayer and Mische, 1998: 993). In turn, the women responded to the ethic of care and respect that textured these relationships and the scope for self-expression they provided.

The close, intimate bonds the Lifeline girls forged with one another also lingered in their memories, the product of a tight-knit housing estate and dense connections born of ready and intimate communication. Through a new set of ties, attentive to need and textured by mutual aid and solidarity, the collective developed a growing awareness of having more room to act in ways many felt fundamentally reset their personal trajectories. Their accounts spoke of learning to better trust their capabilities and overcome a sense of fatalism, and in time they found that life felt 'different' and 'better'. Here, we see the importance of relationships of care – of solidarity in friendship – in shaping who we are and what we become, and the obliquely political contributions others can make in burnishing hopes, steeling resolve and cushioning blows.

Over a period of several years, as the ambition and reputation of the worker-activists grew, the project expanded, and larger cohorts of local women came and went. But as the last decade progressed, the atmosphere for these kinds of experimental, grass-roots interventions darkened; with austerity measures, social provisioning came under sustained assault and the environment for activists working 'within and against' the state grew more hostile (Craig and Mayo, 1995: 105; Emejulu and Bassel, 2018; Williams, 2021). Embattled, Lifeline folded in 2014, the same year the project was hailed by the Welsh Government for exemplary community development practice. There was deep regret at the loss. Still, many of the women took the time to recall occasions, long after their own formal participation and even after the project had closed its doors, when they had returned to the collective. The reference to women who were 'always still there' and 'there with you' was one of the most consistent features of these later accounts. Some continued to spend a great deal of time with women they had met through the project, while others continued to 'pick up the phone' now and then to share news, good and bad. The workers also remained a reassuring presence: 'they're a message away or if you see them in the street'. On occasion, they could be relied on to provide a reference, suggest a good solicitor, source a good training course or offer help to fill in a form or make a difficult phone call. For their part, the workers spoke of still trying to doing their 'best' to help if and when they could and keeping loose tabs, but wishing there was more they could do in some cases. They also recalled serendipitous meetings, 'bumping into' women they had lost touch with over the years. One recalled a time in the pub when one of the women 'come straight up to me and give me a cwtch'; another recalled being in the queue at the supermarket and someone saying 'Oh my God, you saved my life!'. Later narratives were tempered with warm reminiscence; as one worker said: 'Everyone speaks of it fondly now, and it was really devastating when it finished.' Perhaps, testimony of this kind was infused with a little nostalgia: on occasion some of the women themselves wondered if they were sentimentalising these relationships and looking 'back on it now with rose-tinted glasses', before concluding 'no ... they were really good times'. Regardless, the collective memory was itself productive: the connection sustained the women in the years that followed even as bonds loosened or fell away.

Still, the impact of austerity cuts on women-centred activities and initiatives was felt on the estate, most obviously in the loss of community workers and communal space (Vacchelli et al, 2015; Studdert and Walkerdine, 2016; Jupp, 2017). A great deal of vibrant community development activity was stripped out or slowly disintegrated, and while there were attempts to manage the 'fallout' (Hall, 2020: 242), there was a strong sense of loss and uncertainty (Jupp, 2021): that 'there is nothing there anymore now, nowhere to go, nothing to help people' and 'there's hardly, you know, there's not a lot going on'. The Jobcentre's standing as a space freighted with anxiety was solidified as attention was directed towards encouraging self-recrimination among those claiming social security (Deacon and Patrick, 2011; Wright, 2012, Friedl and Stearn, 2015). Sharon Wright (2023: 2) is clear in her assertion that 'underlying threat formed a perpetual feature' of the system, that 'fear and foreboding is no accident': it was 'the intention of UK government to make women feel economically unstable'. The accounts of the intensification of welfare conditionality that circulated widely in the Valleys chimed with the broader evidence base, which is clear and damning: the measures entrenched existing inequalities, generating adverse impacts that rippled through families and across the locality (Arni et al, 2013; van den Berg and Vikström, 2014; Loopstra et al, 2015; National Audit Office, 2016; Reeves et al, 2017; Dwyer, 2018; Wright et al, 2018; Wright and Patrick, 2019; Wright et al, 2020; Andersen, 2023; Wright, 2023). In response to these developments, some commentators set out a range of modest policy recommendations – reforms that might well be accomplished with a fair wind, reasoned argument and a little care. Others put forward demands for root and branch change, requiring a significant redistribution of power to carry a radically alternative system into being. Each set of arguments offers important insights. They also share common ground in drawing the conclusion that any future welfare resettlement should better attend to the actualities of everyday life – the complexities of personal circumstances and capabilities, and their embeddedness in the social fabric of localities and wider formations and class, gender and race (Morris, 2020).

In contributing to these debates, scholars have developed forensic analyses of the social security system, often suggesting measures with a feminist impetus because the gains made from paid work and our orientations to unpaid caring are so deeply embedded in gender relations (see, for example, Andersen, 2023; Wright, 2023). Here, there are calls for a system that shores up women's independence, by tying benefits and wages to the costs of living, and improving the accessibility, affordability and quality of formal care. The quality of paid work should meet basic preconditions, and generous enough incomes and income protections should be provided in and between periods of paid work, with allowances and protections for caring responsibilities, disabilities and ill health. Here there are calls for street-level workers with specialist expertise to be given the time and resources to respond to the complexity of personal life (see, for example, Wright et al, 2018; Wright, 2023). All of this stands in opposition to a punitive and coercive system that instrumentalises the inadequacy of benefits, makes women vulnerable to coercion and control, disregards caring commitments that are not evenly distributed and fuels the 'bad jobs trap' (Warhurst, 2016: 823; Veitch and

Bennett, 2010; Bennett, 2012; Judge, 2013; Rubery and Rafferty, 2013; Field and Forsey, 2016; Brewer et al, 2017; Wheatley et al, 2018; Bourquin et al, 2019; Cominetti and Slaughter, 2019; McNeil et al, 2021; Andersen, 2023; Wright, 2023).

Proponents of radical reconfiguration argue forcefully in favour of moving well beyond economistic orientations that prioritise the search for paid work to the detriment of other pursuits. Nancy Fraser (1997: 62) asks us to 'imagine a social world in which citizens' lives integrate wage earning, caregiving, community activism, political participation and involvement in the associational life of civic society – while also leaving some time to have some fun'. A rich vein of scholarship argues that realising such an imaginary involves remodelling the welfare settlement through an alternative ethic of care, something which is understood to be of universal importance, a 'central concern' (Tronto, 1993: 180; Pateman, 1989; 2004; 2005; Fisher et al, 1990; Held, 1993; Cass, 1994; Tronto, 1995; 2015; Sevenhuijsen, 2000; Williams, 2001; Lynch and Lyons, 2009; Orloff, 2009; Fraser, 2016). Here, the interdependencies of personal life – the caring relations – that bind us together and on which productive, paid work relies are foregrounded (Bowlby et al, 2010; Cantillon and Lynch, 2017). The linkages between claims to citizenship and waged work, which have consistently marginalised women, are broken in an approach that better recognises and rewards the societal contribution of the range of activity that sustains us. This involves displacing both those economic 'mechanisms of distribution that systematically deny some ... the necessary means and opportunities by which to participate on a par with others in social life' and those 'patterns of cultural value that pervasively deny some ... the recognition they need in order to be full, participating partners in interaction' (Fraser, 1999: 39). Care becomes an alternative 'lens' through which we can make judgements about citizenship, the collective commitments we share and the responsibilities we each have to each other (Williams, 2001). This position resists the presentation of caring as a set of ordinary, tacitly understood practices or the taken for granted 'natural' performance of women; instead it reconsiders how informal and formal care activity, which is deeply gendered, classed and racialised, might be reorganised, redistributed and revalued in our homes, neighbourhoods and wider society. It involves investments in 'social infrastructures' sensitive to collective need, and moving beyond ideas of care as an individual responsibility directed towards those closest to us, a task that can be straightforwardly contracted out (Pearson and Elson, 2015: 26; Massey, 2004; Smith, 2005; Fraser, 2016; Hall, 2020). Centring care in this way also involves resisting the tendency to confine the investigation of inequalities to particular kinds of places through stigmatising framings that obscure the underpinning economic and political imperatives (Massey, 1984; Day,

2015). This involves understanding geographically even development to be dependent on the extent and type of available paid work, but also the qualities of the institutions and infrastructures of collective social provisioning (Rees and Rees, 1980).

While a reconfiguration of the welfare settlement might be imperative, it does not appear to be imminent, and it can be dispiriting to look back over the course of the past century. The story of the modern welfare state has been one of advancement and expansion followed by retreat and contraction, the disintegration of collective provisioning and its reconstruction in the interests of capital (Harvey, 2007). The countervailing proposals for radical resettlement tend to circulate as a matter of academic concern, gaining currency in spheres far removed from the day-to-day reckonings of street-level bureaucracy and those with direct experience of the benefits system. The challenge lies in building the collective will and consensus for a new political project – a fundamental reconfiguration of our public welfare imaginary and the development of a counter proposal to the dominant 'toxic poverty narrative' (O'Hara, 2020; see also Tyler, 2020). This involves developing arguments to refute the logics of psycho-social approaches that emphasise self-reliance, individualism and competition in the pursuit of wealth and status, and instead recognise that our capacity for resilience is not a matter of sheer will in the face of adversity but structurally embedded (Hall and Lamont, 2013; Lamont, 2023). Francesca Polletta (2020) argues that we need to reinvigorate the kinds of enduring bonds that provide the sustained solidarity required to make complex societies work more equally: moving beyond intimate acts of kindness with those close to us, requires connecting and cooperating with distant others, with whom we have 'imagined ties', to repair and expand our civic institutions and infrastructures (Polletta, 2020). These forms of collective mobilisation and organisation are galvanised and sustained by the interplay between a sense of injustice and the presence of hope in future progress (Castells, 2012). Yet, despite chronic, steeping inequality, there is little public outrage. The rising prevalence of persistent poverty 'is all too frequently ignored, increasingly demonised', and the contemporary welfare 'common sense' is deeply anchored (Shildrick, 2018: 1). The ideological climate since the turn of the century is one of growing intolerance for benefits claimants, even for groups like lone parents who were traditionally excluded from such thinking. Social attitudes have shifted and hardened (Hills, 2017). In the Valleys, there is evidence of political disengagement and disaffection: relatively low electoral turnouts and the growing presence of a vengeful and persecutory expression of the political Right, which clearly views the region as fertile ground (Davies, 2024b; Sturge, 2024; Thompson, 2024). The old pit towns and villages may remain a stronghold of trade unions in the UK, but that the forms and institutions of social cooperation and collectivism once found within them have fallen away is undeniable (Beynon et al, 2021).

Still, the neoliberal impetus is not all-encompassing; spaces of resistance and creativity can and do emerge through social relations of care and concern (Power and Hall, 2018). The collective biography offered here traces the response of a small circle of overburdened and under-resourced women, tracing their 'collective sensibilities' (Newman, 2012: 11) and providing a sense of the ways in which 'the personal is political' (Hanisch; 2006; Steedman, 2013). The worker-activists on the estate understood well the value of bringing women together to talk about their lives, to share their experiences and ideas. Theirs was an approach with a radical impulse, critical of the established order of street-level welfare bureaucracy and the formula for action it advocated. But active political and civic engagement can be incredibly difficult for women and especially working-class women, whose time and energy is more likely to be consumed by working in 'shitty' insecure and unpredictable jobs, doing the housework and caring for others (Rowbotham et al, 2013). Still, there is a long political tradition of discussion circles of this kind (Hanisch, 2006; Rowbotham, 2014), small pockets of grass-roots organisation attentive to personal troubles and concerns and the practical needs of women; a creative way of organising and doing politics. These are women who push against our conventional, popular frameworks of biographical inquiry, which can be narrow and confining (McCrindle and Rowbotham, 1979; Rowbotham, 2001; Newman, 2012a; 2012b). But writing of them isn't to speak for them (Gregson and Rose, 1992; Lister, 2004; Tyler, 2013; Shildrick, 2018; Williams, 2021) and claiming otherwise diminishes them (Rowbotham, 2014). Rather, Carol Hanisch (2006: 5) urges us to:

> listen to what so-called apolitical women have to say—not so we can do a better job of organising them but because together we are a mass movement. ... there are things in the consciousness of 'apolitical' women (I find them very political) that are as valid as any political consciousness we think we have.

Creating a space of quiet solidarity, this collective sustained a commitment to the idea that life could and should be 'different', and 'not just what you need but what you deserve with it'. Their life stories offer a biting critique of those who made welfare state law, and also contain accounts of personal success and expressions of value on many grounds. The significance of 'making eye contact', 'speaking out' and 'saying your bit' that marked turning points in the everyday lives of the girls is difficult to isolate and capture adequately here. While their biographies should not be overwritten with romantic tropes – some sense of forbearance and a quest of self-discovery followed by plenitude – most were sure their lives were 'better' for the time they spent together and some felt it 'saved' them. Providing a clear sense of the proper role of social security and protections, they built attentive relationships of care that offered a greater measure of dignity, security and possibility.

Notes

Chapter 1
1. The project name is a pseudonym, as are all the names used in the book.
2. In the intervening years, between the waves of research, I worked first as a community development worker under the auspices of the Communities First programme in Cardiff's Butetown, and with the Welsh Government's Knowledge and Analytical Services under the Communities and Tackling Poverty minister. I then continued to work on research in the South Wales Valleys, with WISERD (Wales Institute of Social and Economic Research and Data) at Cardiff University, mostly with a focus on the region's labour movement. Often by chance, this led to several lengthy conversations with activists on the impacts of the austerity project and welfare conditionality with people who lived in the South Wales Valleys. Two of these interactions are presented in some detail here – one with a Public and Commercial Services Union representative who worked in the region for the Department for Work and Pensions, and another with an activist in Unite Community.

Chapter 2
1. A number of scholars offer detailed analyses of the policies underpinning this resettlement, and this includes excellent contributions from Sharon Wright (2023) and Kate Andersen (2023) focusing on women and welfare conditionality. Their work guides much of the discussion here.
2. Measures to boost the incomes and protections for those working for low wages were particularly beneficial for women. The measures included the introduction of a minimum wage in 1999 and reforms to the system of tax credits for working people in 2003. Childcare provision was also expanded through the National Childcare Strategy in 1998.
3. For an excellent summary of the key welfare conditionality texts of this era, see Wright (2023).
4. Notably over this period, as conditionality for lone mothers was intensified further, measures were also introduced for the first time for the main carer of children within couples: as lead or responsible carers, these claimants were made subject to varying requirements depending on the age of the youngest child (see Wright, 2023, and Andersen, 2023).
5. Alongside the intensification of conditionality under Universal Credit, there has been an expansion of, and an increase in state assistance with, formal childcare provision, though the system remains woefully inadequate (see Wright, 2023).
6. Here, policy frameworks predicated on an employment imperative that assumed women enjoyed economic and cultural equality, and rendered caregiving invisible, were often entwined with narratives emphasising the organisation of family life through traditional gender roles as a 'source of moral order' (Newman, 2001: 3; Jensen, 2018).
7. EQUAL was funded until 2008, at which point its principles were incorporated into the European Structural and Investment Funds.
8. The Communities for Work and Communities for Work Plus programmes are active across the Valleys. Here, advisors attempt to build rapport and trust with participants by regularly meeting in person or over the phone. Working to boost claimants' confidence and motivation, they offer mentoring and specialist advice, access to training and work placements. The Welsh Government-funded evaluation of these schemes suggested they had a positive effect on employment outcomes overall, particularly among those with lower levels of qualifications and those who had been out of paid work for longer,

although the effects were estimated to be smaller for women and those with long-term health conditions (Davies, 2024a). While experiences and outcomes varied a great deal, participants were keen to emphasise how supportive advisors were in comparison with the Jobcentre's Universal Credit coaches (Holtom et al, 2023).

Chapter 3
1. The pub is named for Dic Penderyn, a martyr of the working class who was publicly hanged for his support of the 1831 Merthyr Rising (though the pub offers no further detail of the man or the event). The Rising was a period of political and social unrest, provoked by working conditions, wage cuts and layoffs in the mines and ironworks. A plaque on the wall of the old library opposite the pub memorialises Dic Penderyn, 'a working class hero, a folk hero, who has remained in the minds and the affections of all Welsh people' (Carradice, 2011). Merthyr Rising is the name of the local music, arts and ideas festival, which takes place on Merthyr's Penderyn Square each year.
2. Wetherspoon provides a potted local history for some of its pubs on a dedicated website (Wetherspoon, 2024), which includes images of the prints displayed in each of the pubs along with the accompanying text.

Chapter 5
1. Provident Financial, commonly known as 'the Prov', was a credit company that had been lending money and collecting repayments on doorsteps since the 1880s, before withdrawing from this business in 2021.
2. More broadly, the number of women claiming lone parent benefits rose substantially from the start of the 1980s, before peaking in the mid-1990s, with the job loss among men in older industrial regions and the erosion of the family wage emerging as a critical factor (Rowthorn and Webster, 2008; Beatty and Fothergill, 2017a).

Chapter 6
1. While the drive towards paid work has been retained, conditionality and particularly sanctioning has since eased, with rates falling back considerably in recent years (Redman and Fletcher, 2022).

References

Adamson, D. (2010) 'Community empowerment: identifying the barriers to "purposeful" citizen participation', *International Journal of Sociology and Social Policy*, 30(3/4): 114–26.

Alexander, C.L. (2008) 'Safety, fear and belonging: the everyday realities of civic identity formation in Fenham, Newcastle upon Tyne', *ACME: An International Journal for Critical Geographies*, 7(2): 173–98.

Alston, P. (2018) 'Statement on visit to the United Kingdom, by Professor Philip Alston, United Nations Special Rapporteur on extreme poverty and human rights', 16 November, www.ohchr.org/en/statements/2018/11/statement-visit-united-kingdom-professor-philip-alston-united-nations-special

Andersen, K. (2020) 'Universal Credit, gender and unpaid childcare: mothers' accounts of the new welfare conditionality regime', *Critical Social Policy*, 40(3): 430–49.

Andersen, K. (2023) *Welfare that Works for Women? Mothers' Experiences of the Conditionality within Universal Credit*, Bristol: Policy Press.

Antonsich, M. (2010) 'Searching for belonging—an analytical framework', *Geography Compass*, 4(6): 644–59.

Arnade, C. (2019) *Dignity: Seeking Respect in Back Row America*, Sentinel: Penguin.

Arni, P., Lalive, R. and Van Ours, J.C. (2013) 'How effective are unemployment benefit sanctions? Looking beyond unemployment exit', *Journal of Applied Econometrics*, 28(7): 1153–78.

Askins, K. (2014) 'A quiet politics of being together: Miriam and Rose', *Area*, 46(4): 353–4.

Askins, K. (2015) 'Being together: everyday geographies and the quiet politics of belonging', *ACME: An International Journal for Critical Geographies*, 14(2): 470–8.

Atkinson, R. and Kintrea, K. (2004) '"Opportunities and despair, it's all in there": practitioner experiences and explanations of area effects and life chances', *Sociology*, 38(3): 437–55.

Ball, D.W. (1972) 'The "family" as a sociological problem: conceptualization of the taken-for-granted as prologue to social problems analysis', *Social Problems*, 19(3): 295–307.

Barnes, M. and Prior, D. (eds) (2009) *Subversive Citizens: Power, Agency and Resistance in Public Services*, Bristol: Policy Press.

Barnes, M., Newman, J. and Sullivan, H. (2004) 'Power, participation, and political renewal: theoretical perspectives on public participation under New Labour in Britain', *Social Politics: International Studies in Gender, State and Society*, 11(2): 267–79.

Barnett, C. and Land, D. (2007) 'Geographies of generosity: beyond the "moral turn"', *Geoforum*, 38(6): 1065–75.

Batty, E. and Flint, J. (2010) *Self-Esteem, Comparative Poverty and Neighbourhoods*, York: Joseph Rowntree Foundation.

Bayat, A. (2000) 'From "dangerous classes" to "quiet rebels": politics of the urban subaltern in the Global South', *International Sociology*, 15(3): 533–57.

Beatty, C. (2014) 'Two become one: the integration of male and female labour markets in the English and Welsh coalfields', *Regional Studies*, 50(5): 823–34.

Beatty, C. and Fothergill, S. (2014a) 'The local and regional impact of the UK's welfare reforms', *Cambridge Journal of Regions, Economy and Society*, 7(1): 63–79.

Beatty, C. and Fothergill, S. (2014b) *The Impact of Welfare Reform in the Valleys*, Sheffield: Centre for Regional Economic and Social Research, Sheffield Hallam University.

Beatty, C. and Fothergill, S. (2017a) 'The impact on welfare and public finances of job loss in industrial Britain', *Regional Studies, Regional Science*, 4(1): 161–80.

Beatty, C. and Fothergill, S. (2017b) 'The long shadow of industrial Britain's demise', *Regions: Quarterly Magazine of the Regional Studies Association*, 308(4): 5–8.

Beatty, C. and Fothergill, S. (2018) 'Welfare reform in the United Kingdom 2010–16: expectations, outcomes, and local impacts', *Social Policy and Administration*, 52(5): 950–68.

Beatty, C. and Fothergill, S. (2020) 'The long shadow of job loss: Britain's older industrial towns in the 21st century', *Frontiers in Sociology*, 5(54): 1–12.

Beatty, C. and Fothergill, S. (2023) 'The persistence of hidden unemployment among incapacity claimants in large parts of Britain', *Local Economy*, 38(1): 42–60.

Beatty, C., Fothergill, S. and Gore, A. (2019) *The State of the Coalfields 2010: Economic and Social Conditions in the Former Coalfields of England, Scotland and Wales*, Sheffield: Sheffield Hallam University.

Beck, V. (2018) 'Capabilities and choices of vulnerable, long-term unemployed individuals', *Work, Employment and Society*, 32(1): 3–19.

Bélanger, J. and Edwards, P. (2013) 'The nature of front-line service work: distinctive features and continuity in the employment relationship', *Work, Employment and Society*, 27(3): 433–50.

Bennett, F. (2012) 'Universal Credit: overview and gender implications', in M. Kilkey, G. Ramia and K. Farnsworth (eds) *Social Policy Review 24*, Bristol: Policy Press, pp 15–34.

Bennett, F. (2019) 'UK: changing politics of crisis management', in S. Ólafsson, M. Daly, O. Kangas and J. Palme (eds) *Welfare and the Great Recession: A Comparative Study*, Oxford: Oxford University Press, pp 176–91.

Bennett, F. and Daly, M. (2014) *Poverty through a Gender Lens: Evidence and Policy Review on Gender and Poverty*, Oxford: Department of Social Policy and Intervention, University of Oxford.

Bennett, K., Beynon, H. and Hudson, R. (2000) *Coalfields Regeneration: Dealing with the Consequences of Industrial Decline*, York: Joseph Rowntree Foundation.

Berlant, L. (2011) *Cruel Optimism*, Durham, NC: Duke University Press.

Beynon, H. (ed) (1985) *Digging Deeper: Issues in the Miners' Strike*, London: Verso Books.

Beynon, H. (2019) 'After the long boom: living with capitalism in the twenty-first century', *Historical Studies in Industrial Relations*, 40: 187–221.

Beynon, H. and Hudson, R. (2021) *The Shadow of the Mine: Coal and the End of Industrial Britain*, London: Verso Books.

Beynon, H., Hudson, R. and Sadler, D. (1994) *A Place Called Teesside: A Locality in a Global Economy*, Edinburgh: Edinburgh University Press.

Beynon, H., Grimshaw, D., Rubery, J. and Ward, K. (2002) *Managing Employment Change: The New Realities of Work*, Oxford: Oxford University Press.

Beynon, H., Blakely, H., Bryson, A. and Davies, R. (2021) 'The persistence of union membership within the coalfields of Britain', *British Journal of Industrial Relations*, 59(4): 1131–52.

Birch, M. and Miller, T. (2002) 'Encouraging participation: ethics and responsibilities', in M. Mauthner, M. Birch, J. Jessop and T. Miller (eds) *Ethics in Qualitative Research*, London: Sage, pp 91–106.

Blokland, T. (2017) *Community as Urban Practice*, Cambridge: Polity Press.

Bloodworth, J. (2018) *Hired: Six Months Undercover in Low-Wage Britain*, London: Atlantic Books.

Boffey, D. (2012) 'David Cameron's back-to-work firms want benefits cut more often', *The Guardian*, 30 June.

Bolton, S. (2005) *Emotion Management in the Workplace*, Basingstoke: Palgrave Macmillan.

Bolton, S.C. and Wibberley, G. (2014) 'Domiciliary care: the formal and informal labour process', *Sociology*, 48(4): 682–97.

Boon, B. and Farnsworth, J. (2011) 'Social exclusion and poverty: translating social capital into accessible resources', *Social Policy and Administration*, 45(5): 507–24.

Bottrell, D. (2013) 'Responsibilised resilience? Reworking neoliberal social policy texts', *M/C Journal*, 16(5). doi: 10.5204/mcj.708

Bourquin, P., Cribb, J., Waters, T. and Xu, X. (2019) *Why Has In-Work Poverty Risen in Britain?* IFS Working Paper W19/12, *Institute for Fiscal Studies*.

Bowlby, S. (2011) 'Friendship, co-presence and care: neglected spaces', *Social and Cultural Geography*, 12(6): 605–22.

Bowlby, S., McKie, L., Gregory, S. and MacPherson, I. (2010) *Interdependency and Care over the Lifecourse*, Oxford: Routledge.

Boyer, K., Dermott, E., James, A. and MacLeavy, J. (2017) 'Men at work? Debating shifting gender divisions of care', *Dialogues in Human Geography*, 7(1): 92–8.

Bradley, H. (1986) 'Work, home and the restructuring of jobs', in A. Waton, S. Allen, K. Purcell and S. Wood (eds) *The Changing Experience of Employment: Restructuring and Recession*, Basingstoke, Palgrave Macmillan, pp 95–113.

Bramley, G. (2018) 'Poverty and local public services', in D. Gordon and C. Pantazis (eds) *Breadline Britain in the 1990s*, London: Routledge, pp 193–212.

Braun, A., Vincent, C. and Ball, S.J. (2008) '"I'm so much more myself now, coming back to work" – working class mothers, paid work and childcare', *Journal of Education Policy*, 23(5): 533–48.

Brewer, M., Finch, D. and Tomlinson, D. (2017) *Universal Remedy: Ensuring Universal Credit is Fit for Purpose*, Resolution Foundation.

Brodkin, E.Z. and Marston, G. (eds) (2013) *Work and the Welfare State: Street-Level Organizations and Workfare Politics*, Washington: Georgetown University Press.

Brown, K., Ecclestone, K. and Emmel, N., 2017. The many faces of vulnerability. *Social Policy and Society*, 16(3): 497–510.

Bryant, J. and Ellard, J. (2015) 'Hope as a form of agency in the future thinking of disenfranchised young people', *Journal of Youth Studies*, 18(4): 485–99.

Bukodi, E. and Goldthorpe, J.H. (2018) *Social Mobility and Education in Britain: Research, Politics and Policy*, Cambridge: Cambridge University Press.

Bukodi, E. and Goldthorpe, J.H. (2022) *Meritocracy and Populism – Is there a Connection?* SocArXiv Papers, https://osf.io/preprints/socarxiv/qgrkf_v1

Bukodi, E., Goldthorpe, J.H., Waller, L. and Kuha, J. (2015) 'The mobility problem in Britain: new findings from the analysis of birth cohort data', *The British Journal of Sociology*, 66(1): 93–117.

Bulmer, M. (1975) *Working-Class Images of Society*, London: Routledge.

Bunnell, T., Yea, S., Peake, L., Skelton, T. and Smith, M. (2012) 'Geographies of friendships', *Progress in Human Geography*, 36(4): 490–507.

Burawoy, M., Blum, J.A., George, S., Gille, Z. and Thayer, M. (2000) *Global Ethnography: Forces, Connections, and Imaginations in a Postmodern World*, Berkeley: University of California Press.

Burton, L.M., Purvin, D. and Garrett-Peters, R. (2015) 'Longitudinal ethnography: uncovering domestic abuse in low-income women's lives', in J. Hall (ed) *Female Students and Cultures of Violence in Cities*, New York: Routledge, pp 29–80.

Cain, R. (2016) 'Responsibilising recovery: lone and low-paid parents, Universal Credit and the gendered contradictions of UK welfare reform', *British Politics*, 11(4): 488–507.

Cairns, K. (2013) 'The subject of neoliberal affects: rural youth envision their futures', *The Canadian Geographer/Le Géographe Canadien*, 57(3): 337–44.

Cantillon, S. and Lynch, K. (2017) 'Affective equality: love matters', *Hypatia*, 32(1): 169–86.

Canvin, K., Marttila, A., Burstrom, B. and Whitehead, M. (2009) 'Tales of the unexpected? Hidden resilience in poor households in Britain', *Social Science and Medicine*, 69(2): 238–45.

Carabelli, G. and Lyon, D. (2016) 'Young people's orientations to the future: navigating the present and imagining the future', *Journal of Youth Studies*, 19(8): 1110–27.

Carradice, P. (2011) 'Dic Penderyn, the Welsh martyr', *BBC | Wales History*, 28 June, http://bbc.co.uk/blogs/waleshistory/2011/06/dic_penderyn_the_welsh_martyr.html

Cass, B. (1994) 'Citizenship, work, and welfare: the dilemma for Australian women', *Social Politics: International Studies in Gender, State and Society*, 1(1): 106–24.

Castells, M. (2012) *Networks of Outrage and Hope: Social Movements in the Internet Age*, Cambridge: Polity.

Caswell, D., Kupka, P., Larsen, F. and van Berkel, R. (2017) 'The frontline delivery of welfare-to-work in context', in R. van Berkel, D. Caswell, P. Kupka and F. Larsen (eds) *Frontline Delivery of Welfare-to-Work Policies in Europe*, New York: Routledge, pp 1–11.

Charlesworth, S.J. (2000) *A Phenomenology of Working-Class Experience*, Cambridge: Cambridge University Press.

Chase, E. and Walker, R. (2013) 'The co-construction of shame in the context of poverty: beyond a threat to the social bond', *Sociology*, 47(4): 739–54.

Chatterton, P. and Pickerill, J. (2010) 'Everyday activism and transitions towards post-capitalist worlds', *Transactions of the Institute of British Geographers*, 35(4): 475–90.

Cheetham, M., Moffatt, S., Addison, M. and Wiseman, A. (2019) 'Impact of Universal Credit in North East England: a qualitative study of claimants and support staff', *British Medical Journal Open*, 9(7): 1–9.

Clarke, J. (2004) *Changing Welfare, Changing States: New Directions in Social Policy*, London: Sage.

Clarke, J. and Newman, J. (1997) *The Managerial State: Power, Politics and Ideology in the Remaking of Social Welfare*, London: Sage.

Clarke, J. and Newman, J. (2009) *Publics, Politics and Power: Remaking the Public in Public Services*, London: Sage.

Cominetti, N. and Slaughter, H. (2020) *Low Pay Britain 2020*, Resolution Foundation.

Compton-Lilly, C. (2017) *Reading Students' Lives: Literacy Learning across Time*, New York: Routledge.

Conaghan, J. (2009) *Gendered Aspects of Activation Policies: The Limits of Welfare to Work*, Oxford: Foundation for Law, Justice and Society, University of Oxford.

Connolly, M. (dir) (1998) *Manic Street Preachers: From There to Here* [documentary], BBC.

Conradson, D. (2003a) 'Geographies of care: spaces, practices, experiences', *Social and Cultural Geography*, 4(4): 451–4.

Conradson, D. (2003b) 'Spaces of care in the city: the place of a community drop-in centre', *Social and Cultural Geography*, 4(4): 507–25.

Corden, A. and Millar, J. (2007) 'Qualitative longitudinal research for social policy – introduction to themed section', *Social Policy and Society*, 6(4): 529–32.

Corkey, D. and Craig, G. (1978) '"CDP": community work or class politics', in P. Curno (ed) *Political Issues and Community Work*, London: RKP, pp 36–66.

Cornwall, A. and Gaventa, J. (2000) 'From users and choosers to makers and shapers: repositioning participation in social policy', *IDS Bulletin*, 31(4): 50–62.

Cowie, J. and Heathcott, J. (2003) *Beyond the Ruins: The Meanings of Deindustrialization*, Ithaca, NY: Cornell University Press.

Craig, G. (2007) 'Community capacity-building: something old, something new …?', *Critical Social Policy*, 27(3): 335–59.

Craig, G. and Mayo, M. (1995) 'Rediscovering community development: some prerequisites for working "in and against the state"', *Community Development Journal*, 30(2): 105–9.

CRESR Research Team (2011) *Living through Challenges in Low Income Neighbourhoods*, York: Joseph Rowntree Foundation.

Crompton, R. (ed) (1999) *Restructuring Gender Relations and Employment: The Decline of the Male Breadwinner*, Oxford: Oxford University Press.

Crompton, R. (2002) 'Employment, flexible working and the family', *The British Journal of Sociology*, 53(4): 537–58.

Crompton, R. (2008) *Class and Stratification*, Cambridge: Polity Press.

Crossley, S. (2017) *In Their Place: The Imagined Geographies of Poverty*, London: Pluto Press.

Crow, G. and Lyon, D. (2011) 'Turning points in work and family lives in the imagined futures of young people on Sheppey in 1978', in M. Witterton, G. Crow and B. Morgan-Brett (eds) *Young Lives and Imagined Futures: Insights from Archived Data*, Timescapes Working Paper Series No 6, pp 12–26, https://timescapes-archive.leeds.ac.uk/wp-content/uploads/sites/47/2020/07/WP6-final10Oct.pdf

Curtis, B. (2013) *The South Wales Miners: 1964–1985*, Cardiff: University of Wales Press.

References

Dagdeviren, H. and Donoghue, M. (2019) 'Resilience, agency and coping with hardship: evidence from Europe during the Great Recession', *Journal of Social Policy*, 48(3): 547–67.

Dagdeviren, H., Donoghue, M. and Promberger, M. (2016) 'Resilience, hardship and social conditions', *Journal of Social Policy*, 45(1): 1–20.

Daly, M. (2011) 'What adult worker model? A critical look at recent social policy reform in Europe from a gender and family perspective', *Social Politics*, 18(1): 1–23.

Daly, M. (2018) 'Towards a theorization of the relationship between poverty and family', *Social Policy and Administration*, 52(3): 565–77.

Daly, M. and Kelly, G. (2015) *Families and Poverty: Everyday Life on a Low Income*, Bristol: Policy Press.

Daly, M. and Rake, K. (2003) *Gender and the Welfare State: Care, Work and Welfare in Europe and the USA*, Cambridge: Polity/Blackwell.

Damm, C. (2012) *The Third Sector Delivering Employment Services: An Evidence Review*, Third Sector Research Centre Working Paper 70, Birmingham: TSRC.

Darab, S. and Hartman, Y. (2011) 'Psychic wounds and the social structure: an empirical investigation', *Current Sociology*, 59(6): 787–804.

D'Arcy, C. and Finch, D. (2017) *The Great Escape? Low Pay and Progression in the UK's Labour Market*, London: Social Mobility Commission.

Davies, R. (2024a) *Evaluation of Communities for Work and Communities for Work Plus: Counterfactual Impact Evaluation*, GSR report number 04/2024, Cardiff: Welsh Government.

Davies, D. (2024b) 'Farage: Wales shows what a Labour government will do', *BBC*, 17 June.

Davies, L. (2012) 'Lone parents: unemployed or otherwise engaged?', *People, Place and Policy Online*, 6(1): 16–28.

Davies, L. (2015) 'Nudged into employment: lone parents and welfare reform', in M. Harrison and T. Sanders (eds) *Social Policies and Social Control*, Bristol: Policy Press, pp 151–66.

Day, G. (2006) *Community and Everyday Life*, London: Routledge.

Day, G. (2015) 'Sociology in and of Wales: an overview', *Irish Journal of Sociology*, 23(1): 62–82.

Deacon, A. (2004) 'Justifying conditionality: the case of anti-social tenants', *Housing Studies*, 19(6): 911–26.

Deacon, A. and Patrick, R. (2011) 'A new welfare settlement? The Coalition government and welfare-to-work', in H. Bochel (ed) *The Conservative Party and Social Policy*, Bristol: Policy Press, pp 161–80.

Dean, H. (2014) *Welfare Rights and Social Policy*, London: Routledge.

De Henau, J. (2018) *Social Security and Women: Briefing from the UK Women's Budget Group on the Impact of Cuts to Social Security Benefits since 2010 on Women*, Women's Budget Group.

Delanty, G. (2002) 'Communitarianism and citizenship', in E.F. Isin and B.S. Turner (eds) *Handbook of Citizenship Studies*, London: Sage, pp 159–74.

Delanty, G. (2009) *Community*, London: Routledge.

Dennis, N., Henriques, F. and Slater, C. (1969) *Coal Is Our Life: An Analysis of a Yorkshire Mining Community*, London: Tavistock Publications.

Department for Work and Pensions (2006a) *Making a Difference, Tackling Poverty, A Progress Report*, London: Department for Work and Pensions.

Department for Work and Pensions (2006b) *A New Deal for Welfare: Empowering People to Work*, CM6730, London: Department for Work and Pensions.

Department for Work and Pensions (2024) *Get Britain Working White Paper*, www.gov.uk/government/publications/get-britain-working-white-paper/get-britain-working-white-paper

Dermott, E. and Pantazis, C. (2017) 'Which men and women are poor? Gender, poverty and social exclusion', in E. Dermott and G. Main (eds) *Poverty and Social Exclusion in the UK Vol I: The Nature and Extent of the Problem*, Bristol: Policy Press, pp 95–114.

Desmond, M. (2016) *Evicted: Poverty and Profit in the American City*, New York: Crown.

Dicks, B. (2008) 'Performing the hidden injuries of class in coal-mining heritage', *Sociology*, 42(3): 436–52.

Domosh, M. (1997) 'Geography and gender: the personal and the political', *Progress in Human Geography*, 21(1): 81–7.

Donoghue, M. and Edmiston, D. (2020) 'Gritty citizens? Exploring the logic and limits of resilience in UK social policy during times of socio-material insecurity', *Critical Social Policy*, 40(1): 7–29.

Dorling, D. (2015) *Injustice: Why Social Inequality Still Persists*, Bristol: Policy Press.

Dudley, K.M. (2020) 'Precarity's affects: the trauma of deindustrialization', In M. Fazio, C. Launius and T. Strangleman (eds) *Routledge International Handbook of Working-Class Studies*, Abingdon: Routledge, pp 201–12.

Duncan, S. and Edwards, R. (1999) *Lone Mothers, Paid Work and Gendered Moral Rationalities*, Basingstoke: Macmillan.

Duncan, S. and Smith, D. (2002) 'Geographies of family formations: spatial differences and gender cultures in Britain', *Transactions of the Institute of British Geographers*, 27(4): 471–93.

Duncan, S., Edwards, R., Reynolds, T. and Alldred, P. (2003) 'Motherhood, paid work and partnering: values and theories', *Work, Employment and Society*, 17(2): 309–30.

Durbin, S., Page, M. and Walby, S. (2017) 'Gender equality and 'austerity': vulnerabilities, resistance and change', *Gender, Work and Organization*, 24(1): 1–6.

Dwyer, P. (2004) 'Creeping conditionality in the UK: from welfare rights to conditional entitlements?', *Canadian Journal of Sociology/Cahiers Canadiens de Sociologie*, 29(2): 265–87.

Dwyer, P. (2016) 'Citizenship, conduct and conditionality: sanction and support in the 21st-century UK welfare state', in M. Fenger, J. Hudson and C. Needham (eds) *Social Policy Review 28: Analysis and Debate in Social Policy*, Bristol: Policy Press, pp 41–62.

Dwyer, P. (2018) 'Punitive and ineffective: benefit sanctions within social security', *Journal of Social Security Law*, 5(3): 142–57.

Dwyer, P. (ed) (2019) *Dealing with Welfare Conditionality: Implementation and Effects*, Bristol: Policy Press.

Dwyer, P. and Ellison, N. (2009) '"We nicked stuff from all over the place": policy transfer or muddling through?', *Policy and Politics*, 37(3): 389–407.

Dwyer, P. and Ellison, N. (2016) 'Work and welfare: the rights and responsibilities of unemployment in the UK', in M. Giugni (ed) *The Politics of Unemployment in Europe*, London: Routledge, pp 53–66.

Dwyer, P. and Wright, S. (2014) 'Universal Credit, ubiquitous conditionality and its implications for social citizenship', *Journal of Poverty and Social Justice*, 22(1): 27–35.

Dwyer, P., Scullion, L., Jones, K., McNeill, J. and Stewart, A.B. (2020) 'Work, welfare, and wellbeing: the impacts of welfare conditionality on people with mental health impairments in the UK', *Social Policy and Administration*, 54(2): 311–26.

Dyck, I. (2005) 'Feminist geography, the "everyday", and local–global relations: hidden spaces of place-making', *Canadian Geographer/Le Géographe canadien*, 49(3): 233–43.

Eagleton, T. (2015) *Hope without Optimism*, New Haven, CT: Yale University Press.

Edmiston, D. and Humpage, L. (2018) 'Resistance or resignation to welfare reform? The activist politics for and against social citizenship', *Policy and Politics*, 46(3): 467–84.

Egdell, V., Dutton, M. and McQuaid, R. (2016) 'Third sector experiences of work programme delivery', *Journal of Social Policy*, 45(4): 729–46.

Elder, G.H. (ed) (1985) *Life Course Dynamics: Trajectories and Transitions, 1968–1980*, Ithaca, NY: Cornell University Press.

Emejulu, A. and Bassel, L. (2018) 'Austerity and the politics of becoming', *Journal of Common Market Studies*, 56(S1): 109–19.

Emirbayer, M. and Mische, A. (1998) 'What is agency?', *American Journal of Sociology*, 103(4): 962–1023.

England, K. (1994) 'Getting personal: reflexivity, positionality, and feminist research', *The Professional Geographer*, 46(1): 80–9.

England, K. (2010) 'Home, work and the shifting geographies of care', *Ethics, Place and Environment*, 13(2): 131–50.

Equality, Local Government and Communities Committee (2017) *Communities First: Lessons Learnt Full Report*, Cardiff: National Assembly for Wales.

Etherington, D. and Daguerre, A. (2015) *Welfare Reform, Work First Policies and Benefit Conditionality: Reinforcing Poverty and Social Exclusion*, London: Centre for Enterprise and Economic Development Research, Middlesex University.

European Commission, Employment and Social Affairs (2000) *EQUAL: New Ways of Tackling Discrimination and Inequality in the Field of Employment*, Luxembourg: Office for Official Publications of the European Communities.

Evans, A., Jr and Evans, A. (1977) 'An examination of the concept "social solidarity"', *Mid-American Review of Sociology*, 2(1): 29–46.

Evans, B. and Reid, J. (2014) *Resilient Life: The Art of Living Dangerously*, Cambridge: Polity Press.

Exley, D. (2019) *The End of Aspiration? Social Mobility and Our Children's Fading Prospects*, Bristol: Policy Press.

Fagge, N. (2010) 'Named and shamed: our sicknote capitals', *The Daily Express*, 29 June.

Farnsworth, K. and Irving, Z. (2018) 'Austerity: neoliberal dreams come true?', *Critical Social Policy*, 38(3): 461–81.

Ferge, Z. (1997) 'The changed welfare paradigm: the individualization of the social', *Social Policy and Administration*, 31(1): 20–44.

Field, F. and Forsey, A. (2016) *Fixing Broken Britain: An Audit of Working-Age Welfare*, London: Civitas.

Finch, H., O'Connor, W., Millar, J., Hales, J., Shaw, A. and Roth, W. (1999) *New Deal for Lone Parents: Learning from the Prototypes Areas*, Research Report 92, London: Department of Social Security.

Finch, J. (1989) *Family Obligations and Social Change*, Oxford: Polity Press.

Fisher, B. and Tronto, J. (1990) 'Toward a feminist theory of caring', in E. Abel and M. Nelson (eds) *Circles of Care: Work and Identity in Women's Lives*, Albany, NY: SUNY Press, pp 35–62.

Fletcher, D.R. (2011) 'Welfare reform, Jobcentre Plus and the street-level bureaucracy: towards inconsistent and discriminatory welfare for severely disadvantaged groups?', *Social Policy and Society*, 10(4): 445–58.

Fletcher, D.R. and Wright, S. (2018) 'A hand up or a slap down? Criminalising benefit claimants in Britain via strategies of surveillance, sanctions and deterrence', *Critical Social Policy*, 38(2): 323–44.

Flowerdew, J. and Neale, B. (2003) 'Trying to stay apace: children with multiple challenges in their post-divorce family lives', *Childhood*, 10(2): 147–61.

References

Forster, J., Petrie, M. and Crowther, J. (2018) 'Deindustrialisation, community, and adult education: the north east England experience', *Social Sciences*, 7(11): article 210. doi: 10.3390/socsci7110210

Francis, H. and Smith, D. (1980) *The Fed: A History of the South Wales Miners in the Twentieth Century*, London: Lawrence and Wishart.

Francis-Devine, B. and Hutton, G. (2024) *Women and the UK Economy*, House of Commons Library, Research Briefing, No 6838.

Frank, A.W. (2002) 'Why study people's stories? The dialogical ethics of narrative analysis', *International Journal of Qualitative Methods*, 1(1): 109–17.

Fraser, N. (1995) 'From redistribution to recognition? Dilemmas of justice in a "post socialist" age', *New Left Review*, 212: 68–94.

Fraser, N. (1997) *Justice Interruptus: Critical Reflections on the Post-Socialist Condition*, New York: Routledge.

Fraser, N. (1999) 'Social justice in the age of identity politics: redistribution, recognition and participation', in L.J. Ray and A. Sayer (eds) *Culture and Economy after the Cultural Turn*, London: Sage, pp 25–52.

Fraser, N. (2016) 'Contradictions of capital and care', *New Left Review*, 100: 99–117.

Freedland, M. and King, D. (2003) 'Contractual governance and illiberal contracts: some problems of contractualism as an instrument of behaviour management by agencies of government', *Cambridge Journal of Economics*, 27(3): 465–77.

Fremeaux, I. (2005) 'New Labour's appropriation of the concept of community: a critique', *Community Development Journal*, 40(3): 265–74.

Freud, D. (2007) *Reducing Dependency, Increasing Opportunity: Options for the Future of Welfare to Work. An Independent Report to the Department for Work and Pensions*, Leeds: Corporate Document Services.

Friedli, L. (2015) 'The politics of tackling inequalities: the rise of psychological fundamentalism in public health and welfare reform', in K.E. Smith; C. Bambra and S.E. Hill (eds) *Health Inequalities: Critical Perspectives*, Oxford: Oxford University Press, pp 206–21.

Friedli, L. and Stearn, R. (2015) 'Positive affect as coercive strategy: conditionality, activation and the role of psychology in UK government workfare programmes', *Medical Humanities*, 41(1): 40–7.

Friedman, S. and Laurison, D. (2020) *The Class Ceiling: Why It Pays to Be Privileged*, Bristol: Policy Press.

Furedi, F. (2004) 'Reflections on the medicalisation of social experience', *British Journal of Guidance and Counselling*, 32(3): 413–15.

Gallie, D., Paugam, S. and Jacobs, S. (2003) 'Unemployment, poverty and social isolation: is there a vicious circle of social exclusion?', *European Societies*, 5(1): 1–32.

Gane, N. and Back, L. (2012) 'C. Wright Mills 50 years on: the promise and craft of sociology revisited', *Theory, Culture and Society*, 29(7–8): 399–421.

Gater, R. (2022) "Dirty, Dirty Job. Not Good for Your Health": Working-class men and their experiences and relationships with employment', in *Education, Work and Social Change in Britain's Former Coalfield Communities: The Ghost of Coal*, Cham: Springer International Publishing, pp 107–26.

Geertz, C. (1973) *The Interpretation of Cultures*, New York: Basic Books.

Ghate, D. and Hazel, N. (2002) *Parenting in Poor Environments: Stress, Support and Coping*, London: Jessica Kingsley Publishers.

Gill, L. (2009) 'The limits of solidarity: labor and transnational organizing against Coca-Cola', *American Ethnologist*, 36(4): 667–80.

Gill, R. and Pratt, A. (2008) 'In the social factory? Immaterial labour, precariousness and cultural work', *Theory, Culture and Society*, 25(7–8): 1–30.

Gill, R. and Orgad, S. (2018) 'The amazing bounce-backable woman: resilience and the psychological turn in neoliberalism', *Sociological Research Online*, 23(2): 477–95.

Gillies, V. (2005) 'Raising the "meritocracy": parenting and the individualization of social class, *Sociology*, 39(5): 835–53.

Gillies, V. (2007) *Marginalised Mothers: Exploring Working-Class Experiences of Parenting*, London: Routledge.

Gilliom, J. (2001) *Overseers of the Poor: Surveillance, Resistance, and the Limits of Privacy*, Chicago: University of Chicago Press.

Glucksmann, M. (2000) *Cottons and Casuals: The Gendered Organisation of Labour in Time and Space*, Durham: Sociologypress.

Glyn Jones, T. (2021) Covid: South Wales Valleys' high death rates "caused by poverty"', *BBC*, 14 February, www.bbc.co.uk/news/uk-wales-56054655

Goodhart, D. (2020) *Head Hand Heart: the Struggle for Dignity and Status in the 21st Century*, London: Penguin.

Goodin, R.E. (2001) 'False principles of welfare reform', *Australian Journal of Social Issues*, 36(3): 189–205.

Goodwin, J. and O'Connor, H. (2015) 'A restudy of young workers from the 1960s: researching intersections of work and lifecourse in one locality over 50 years', in N. Worth and I. Hardill (eds) *Researching the Lifecourse: Critical Reflections from the Social Sciences*, Bristol: Policy Press, pp 63–80.

Goodwin, V. (2008) *The Effects of Benefit Sanctions on Lone Parents' Employment Decisions and Moves into Employment*, Department for Work and Pensions, No 511, HM Stationery Office.

Gordon, A.F. (2008) *Ghostly Matters: Haunting and the Sociological Imagination*, Minneapolis: University of Minnesota Press.

Gordon, E. (1987) 'Women, work and collective action: Dundee jute workers 1870–1906', *Journal of Social History*, 21(1): 27–47.

Graham, H. (1983) *Caring: A Labour of Love*, London: Routledge.

Graham, H. and McQuaid, R. (2014) *Exploring the Impacts of the UK Government's Welfare Reforms on Lone Parents Moving into Work – Literature Review*, Glasgow: Glasgow Centre for Population Health.

Grant, L. (2009) 'Women's disconnection from local labour markets: real lives and policy failure', *Critical Social Policy*, 29(3): 330–50.

Gray, M. and Barford, A. (2018) 'The depths of the cuts: the uneven geography of local government austerity', *Cambridge Journal of Regions, Economy and Society*, 11(3): 541–63.

Greer Murphy, A. (2017) 'Austerity in the United Kingdom: the intersections of spatial and gendered inequalities', *Area*, 49(1): 122–4.

Gregg, P. (2008) *Realising Potential: A Vision for Personalised Conditionality and Support*, an independent report to the Department for Work and Pensions, TSO.

Gregg, P. and Harkness, S. (2003) 'Welfare reform and the employment of lone parents', in R. Dickens, P. Gregg and J. Wadsworth (eds) *The Labour Market Under New Labour*, London: Palgrave Macmillan.

Gregson, N. and Rose, G. (1997) 'Contested and negotiated histories of feminist geography', in Women and Geography Study Group (ed) *Feminist Geographies*, London: Routledge, pp 13–48.

Greve, B. (2009) 'Can choice in welfare states be equitable?', *Social Policy and Administration*, 43(6): 543–56.

Griffith, A.I. and Smith, D.E. (eds) (2014) *Under New Public Management: Institutional Ethnographies of Changing Front-Line Work*, Toronto: University of Toronto Press.

Griggs, J. and Evans, M. (2010) *Sanctions within Conditional Benefit Systems: A Review of the Evidence*, York: Joseph Rowntree Foundation.

Griggs, J., Hammond, A. and Walker, R. (2014) 'Activation for all: welfare reform in the United Kingdom, 1995–2009', in I. Lødemel and A. Moreira (eds) *Activation or Workfare? Governance and the Neo-Liberal Convergence*, Oxford: Oxford University Press, pp 73–100.

Grimshaw, L. (2011) 'Community work as women's work? The gendering of English neighbourhood partnerships', *Community Development Journal*, 46(3): 327–40.

Grover, C. (2007) 'The Freud Report on the future of welfare to work: some critical reflections', *Critical Social Policy*, 27(4): 534–45.

Grover, C. (2019) 'Violent proletarianisation: social murder, the reserve army of labour and social security "austerity" in Britain', *Critical Social Policy*, 39(3): 335–55.

Guetzkow, J. (2020) 'Common cause? Policymaking discourse and the prison/welfare trade-off', *Politics and Society*, 48(3): 321–56.

Hacker, J.S. (2019) *The Great Risk Shift: The New Economic Insecurity and the Decline of the American Dream*, Oxford: Oxford University Press.

Halbwachs, M. (2020) *On Collective Memory*, Chicago: University of Chicago Press.

Hall, P.A. and Lamont, M. (eds) (2013) *Social Resilience in the Neoliberal Era*. Cambridge: Cambridge University Press.

Hall, S. (2021) *The Hard Road to Renewal: Thatcherism and the Crisis of the Left*, London: Verso Books.

Hall, S. and O'Shea, A. (2013) 'Common-sense neoliberalism', *Soundings*, 55(55): 9–25.

Hall, S.M. (2017) 'Personal, relational and intimate geographies of austerity: ethical and empirical considerations', *Area*, 49(3): 303–10.

Hall, S.M. (2019a) 'Relational biographies in times of austerity: family, home and care', in *The New Politics of Home*, Bristol: Policy Press, pp 63–86.

Hall, S.M. (2019b) 'A very personal crisis: family fragilities and everyday conjunctures within lived experiences of austerity', *Transactions of the Institute of British Geographers*, 44(3): 479–92.

Hall, S.M. (2020) 'The personal is political: feminist geographies of/in austerity', *Geoforum*, 110: 242–51.

Hall, S.M. and Jayne, M. (2016) 'Make, mend and befriend: geographies of austerity, crafting and friendship in contemporary cultures of dressmaking in the UK', *Gender, Place and Culture*, 23(2): 216–34.

Hall, S.M. and Holmes, H. (2017) 'Making do and getting by? Beyond a romantic politics of austerity and crisis', *Discover Society*, 44, 2 May, https://archive.discoversociety.org/2017/05/02/making-do-and-getting-by-beyond-a-romantic-politics-of-austerity-and-crisis/

Hall, S.M. and Ince, A. (eds) (2017) *Sharing Economies in Times of Crisis*, London: Routledge.

Halpern-Meekin, S., Edin, K., Tach, L. and Sykes, J. (2015) *It's Not Like I'm Poor: How Working Families Make Ends Meet in a Post-Welfare World*, Oakland: University of California Press.

Haney, L. (2000) 'Global discourses of need: mythologizing and pathologizing welfare in Hungary', in M. Burawoy, J.A. Blum, S. George, Z. Gille, T. Gowan, L. Haney et al (eds) *Global Ethnography: Forces, Connections, and Imaginations in a Postmodern World*, Berkeley: University of California Press, pp 48–74.

Hanisch, C. (2006) 'The Personal Is Political: the Women's Liberation Movement classic with a new explanatory introduction', www.carolhanisch.org/CHwritings/PIP.html

Hankins, K. (2017) 'Creative democracy and the quiet politics of the everyday', *Urban Geography*, 38(4): 502–6.

Hanley, L. (2012) *Estates: An Intimate History*, London: Granta Books.

Hanley, L. (2016) *Respectable: The Experience of Class*, London: Penguin.

Hardgrove, A., Rootham, E. and McDowell, L. (2015) 'Possible selves in a precarious labour market: youth, imagined futures, and transitions to work in the UK', *Geoforum*, 60: 163–71.

Harrison, E. (2013) 'Bouncing back? Recession, resilience and everyday lives', *Critical Social Policy*, 33(1): 97–113.

Harvey, D. (2007) *A Brief History of Neoliberalism*, Oxford: Oxford University Press.

Hatch, J.A. and Wisniewski, R. (eds) (1995) *Life History and Narrative*, London: Routledge.

Haux, T. (2013) 'Lone parents and activation – towards a typology of approaches', *Journal of International and Comparative Social Policy*, 29(2): 122–33.

Haylett, C. (2003) 'Class, care and welfare reform: reading meanings, talking feelings', *Environment and Planning: A Special Issue on Geographies of Care*, 35(5): 799–814.

Hebson, G., Rubery, J. and Grimshaw, D. (2015) 'Rethinking job satisfaction in care work: looking beyond the care debates', *Work, Employment and Society*, 29(2): 314–30.

Held, V. (1993) *Feminist Morality: Transforming Culture, Society, and Politics*, Chicago: University of Chicago Press.

Hemmerman, L. (2010) 'Researching the hard to reach and the hard to keep: notes from the field on longitudinal sample maintenance', in F. Shirani and S. Weller (eds) *Conducting Qualitative Longitudinal Research: Fieldwork Experiences*, Timescapes Working Paper Series No 2, pp 7–19, https://timescapes-archive.leeds.ac.uk/wp-content/uploads/sites/47/2020/07/WP2-final-Jan-2010.pdf

Hennessy, J. (2009) 'Morality and work—family conflict in the lives of poor and low-income women', *The Sociological Quarterly*, 50(4): 557–80.

Hick, R. (2016) 'Material poverty and multiple deprivation in Britain: the distinctiveness of multidimensional assessment', *Journal of Public Policy*, 36(2): 277–308.

Hick, R. and Lanau, A. (2018) 'Moving in and out of in-work poverty in the UK: an analysis of transitions, trajectories and trigger events', *Journal of Social Policy*, 47(4): 661–82.

Hill, K., Davis, A., Hirsch, D. and Marshall, L. (2016) *Falling Short: The Experiences of Families Living Below the Minimum Income Standard*, York: Joseph Rowntree Foundation.

Hills, J. (2017) *Good Times, Bad Times: The Welfare Myth of Them and Us*, Bristol: Policy Press.

Himmelweit, S. and Sigala, M. (2004) 'Choice and the relationship between identities and behaviour for mothers with pre-school children: some implications for policy from a UK study', *Journal of Social Policy*, 33(3): 455–78.

HM Treasury, Department for Work and Pensions, and Department for Children, Schools and Families (2008) *Ending Child Poverty: Everybody's Business*, HM Treasury.

Hochschild, A.R. (1983) *The Managed Heart: Commercialisation of Human Feeling*, Berkeley: University of California Press.

Hochschild, A.R. (2003) *The Commercialization of Intimate Life: Notes from Home and Work*, Berkeley: University of California Press.

Hodgson, L. (2004) 'Manufactured civil society: counting the cost', *Critical Social Policy*, 24(2): 139–64.

Holloway, S.L. and Pimlott-Wilson, H. (2016) 'New economy, neoliberal state and professionalised parenting: mothers' labour market engagement and state support for social reproduction in class-differentiated Britain', *Transactions of the Institute of British Geographers*, 41(4): 376–88.

Holtom, D., Burrowes, E. and Bryer, N. (2023) *Evaluation of Communities for Work and Communities for Work Plus: Stage 1 (Process Evaluation and Theory of Change)*, GSR report number 24/2023, Cardiff: Welsh Government.

Horton, J. (2016) 'Anticipating service withdrawal: young people in spaces of neoliberalisation, austerity and economic crisis', *Transactions of the Institute of British Geographers*, 41(4): 349–62.

Horton, J. and Kraftl, P. (2009) 'Small acts, kind words and "not too much fuss": implicit activisms', *Emotion, Space and Society*, 2(1): 14–23.

Hughes, C. (2002) 'Beyond the poststructuralist-modern impasse: the woman returner as "exile" or "nomad"', *Gender and Education*, 14(4): 411–24.

Ignatieff, M. (1994) *Blood and Belonging: Journeys into the New Nationalism*, London: Vintage.

Ingold, J. and Etherington, D. (2013) 'Work, welfare and gender inequalities: an analysis of activation strategies for partnered women in the UK, Australia and Denmark', *Work, Employment and Society*, 27(4): 621–38.

Irvine, A., McKenzie, J., Brass, C. and Kelley, A. (2024a) '"Working with the whole person": employability keyworker experiences of supporting people furthest from the labour market', *Social Policy and Society*, advance online publication. doi: 10.1017/S1474746424000022

Irvine, A., McKenzie, J., Sullivan, S. and Kelley, A. (2024b) '"Less money, less time, more complex clients": the impacts of short-term funding for third sector employability programmes and potential for moral distress', *Social Policy and Administration*, advance online publication. doi: 10.1111/spol.13089

Isin, E.F. (2013) *Democracy, Citizenship and the Global City*, London: Routledge.

James, N. (1989) 'Emotional labour: skill and work in the social regulation of feelings', *The Sociological Review*, 37(1): 15–42.

Jamieson, L. (2000) 'Migration, place and class: youth in a rural area', *The Sociological Review*, 48(2): 203–23.

Javornik, J. and Ingold, J. (2015) 'A childcare system fit for the future?', in L. Foster, A. Brunton, C, Deeming and T. Haux (eds) *In Defence of Welfare 2*, Bristol: Policy Press, pp 75–8.

Jenkins, J. (2017) 'Hands not wanted: closure, and the moral economy of protest, Treorchy, South Wales', *Historical Studies in Industrial Relations*, 38(1): 1–36.

Jensen, P.H. and Møberg, R.J. (2017) 'Does women's employment enhance women's citizenship?', *European Societies*, 19(2): 178–201.

Jensen, T. (2014) 'Welfare commonsense, poverty porn and doxosophy', *Sociological Research Online*, 19(3): article 3, www.socresonline.org.uk/19/3/3.html

Jensen, T. (2018) *Parenting the Crisis: The Cultural Politics of Parent-Blame*, Bristol: Policy Press.

Jensen, T. and Tyler, I. (2015) '"Benefits broods": The cultural and political crafting of anti-welfare commonsense', *Critical Social Policy*, 35(4): 470–91.

Jimenez, L. and Walkerdine, V. (2011) 'A psychosocial approach to shame, embarrassment and melancholia amongst unemployed young men and their fathers', *Gender and Education*, 23(2): 185–99.

Jimenez, L. and Walkerdine, V. (2012) '"Shameful work": a psychosocial approach to father–son relations, young male unemployment and femininity in an ex-steel community', *Psychoanalysis, Culture and Society*, 17: 278–95.

Johnsen, S. (2014) *Conditionality Briefing: Lone Parents*, Welfare Conditionality Briefing Papers, York: University of York.

Johnsen, S. and Blenkinsopp, J. (2018) *Final Findings: Lone Parents*, Welfare Conditionality Reports, York: University of York.

Jones, O. (2020) *Chavs: The Demonization of the Working Class*, London: Verso Books.

Judge, L. (2013) *Will Universal Credit Work?*, London: Trades Union Congress.

Judge, L. and Slaughter, H. (2020) *Working Hard(ship)*, London: Resolution Foundation.

Jupp, E. (2008) 'The feeling of participation: everyday spaces and urban change', *Geoforum*, 39(1): 331–43.

Jupp, E. (2017) 'Home space, gender and activism: the visible and the invisible in austere times', *Critical Social Policy*, 37(3): 348–66.

Jupp, E. (2021) 'The time-spaces of austerity urbanism: narratives of "localism" and UK neighbourhood policy', *Urban Studies*, 58(5): 977–92.

Jupp, E., Bowlby, S., Franklin, J. and Hall, S.M. (eds) (2019) *The New Politics of Home*, Bristol: Policy Press.

Katz, S. (2013) '"Give us a chance to get an education": single mothers' survival narratives and strategies for pursuing higher education on welfare', *Journal of Poverty*, 17(3): 273–304.

Kaufman, J. (2020) 'Intensity, moderation, and the pressures of expectation: calculation and coercion in the street-level practice of welfare conditionality', *Social Policy and Administration*, 54(2): 205–18.

Kearns, A. and Parkinson, M. (2001) 'The significance of neighbourhood', *Urban Studies*, 38(12): 2103–10.

Kessler, I., Heron, P. and Dopson, S. (2015) 'Managing patient emotions as skilled work and being "one of us"', *Work, Employment and Society*, 29(5): 775–91.

Kiernan, K., Land, H. and Lewis, J.E. (1998) *Lone Motherhood in Twentieth-Century Britain: From Footnote to Front Page*, Oxford: Oxford University Press.

King, D.S. (1999) *In the Name of Liberalism: Illiberal Social Policy in the USA and Britain*, Oxford: Oxford University Press.

Kintrea, K., St Clair, R. and Houston, M. (2015) 'Shaped by place? Young people's aspirations in disadvantaged neighbourhoods', *Journal of Youth Studies*, 18(5): 666–84.

Knijn, T. and Kremer, M. (1997) 'Gender and the caring dimension of welfare states: toward inclusive citizenship', *Social Politics: International Studies in Gender, State & Society*, 4(3): 328–61.

Knijn, T., Martin, C. and Millar, J. (2007) 'Activation as a common framework for social policies towards lone parents', *Social Policy and Administration*, 41(6): 638–52.

Kraftl, P. and Horton, J. (2007) '"The health event": everyday, affective politics of participation', *Geoforum*, 38(5): 1012–27.

Kupferberg, F. (2012) 'Conclusion: theorising turning points and decoding narratives', in K.B. Hackstaff and F. Kupferberg (eds) *Biography and Turning Points in Europe and America*, Bristol: Policy Press, pp 227–60.

Lamberg, E. (2020) 'Staying in place or moving forward? Young women's imagined futures and aspirations for mobility in care work', *Young*, 28(4): 329–46.

Lambie-Mumford, H. (2017) *Hungry Britain: The Rise of Food Charity*, Bristol: Policy Press.

Lamont, M. (2009) *The Dignity of Working Men: Morality and the Boundaries of Race, Class, and Immigration*, Cambridge, MA: Harvard University Press.

Lamont, M. (2023) *Seeing others: How recognition works—And how it can heal a divided world*, New York: Simon and Schuster.

Lamont, M. and Molnár, V. (2002) 'The study of boundaries in the social sciences', *Annual Review of Sociology*, 28: 167–95.

Larner, W. and Craig, D. (2005) 'After neoliberalism? Community activism and local partnerships in Aotearoa New Zealand', *Antipode*, 37(3): 402–24.

Laurier, E. and Philo, C. (2006) 'Possible geographies: a passing encounter in a café', *Area*, 38(4): 353–63.

Lawler, S. (2015) *Identity: Sociological Perspectives*, Cambridge: Polity Press.

Letablier, M.T., Eydoux, A. and Betzelt, S. (2011) 'Social citizenship and activation in Europe: a gendered perspective', in S. Betzelt and S. Bothfeld (eds) *Activation and Labour Market Reforms in Europe: Challenges to Social Citizenship*, London: Palgrave Macmillan, pp 79–100.

Levitas, R. (2001) 'Against work: a utopian incursion into social policy', *Critical Social Policy*, 21(4): 449–65.

Lewis, J. (1997) *Lone Mothers in European Welfare Regimes*, London: Jessica Kingsley.

Lewis, J. (2005) 'The gender settlement and social provision: the work–welfare relationship at the level of the household', in R. Salais and R. Villeneuve (eds) *Europe and the Politics of Capabilities*, Cambridge: Cambridge University Press, pp 239–55.

Lewis, J. (2010) 'Gender and welfare state change', *European Societies*, 4(4): 331–57.

Lewis, J. and Giullari, S. (2005) 'The adult worker model family, gender equality and care: the search for new policy principles and the possibilities and problems of a capabilities approach', *Economy and Society*, 34(1): 76–104.

Lindsay, C. (2007) 'The United Kingdom's "work first" welfare state and activation regimes in Europe', in A. Serrano Pascual and L. Magnusson (eds) *Reshaping Welfare States and Activation Regimes in Europe*, Brussels: Peter Lang, pp 35–71.

Lindsay, C., McQuaid, R.W. and Dutton, M. (2007) 'New approaches to employability in the UK: combining "human capital development" and "work first" strategies?', *Journal of Social Policy*, 36(4): 539–60.

Linkon, S.L. (2018) *The Half-Life of Deindustrialization: Working-Class Writing about Economic Restructuring*, Ann Arbor: University of Michigan Press.

Lipsky, M. (2010) *Street-Level Bureaucracy: Dilemmas of the Individual in Public Service*, New York: Russell Sage Foundation.

Lister, R. (1990) 'Women, economic dependency and citizenship', *Journal of Social Policy*, 19(4): 445–67.

Lister, R. (2004) 'The third way's social investment state', in J. Lewis and R. Surrender (eds) *Welfare State Change: Towards a Third Way*, Oxford: Oxford University Press, pp 157–81.

Lister, R., Holden, C., Kilkey, M. and Ramia, G. (2011) 'The age of responsibility: social policy and citizenship in the early 21st century', in C. Holden, M. Kilkey and G. Ramia (eds) *Social Policy Review 23*, Bristol: Policy Press, pp 63–84.

Littler, J. (2017) *Against Meritocracy: Culture, Power and Myths of Mobility*, London: Routledge.

Livingston, M., Bailey, N. and Kearns, A. (2008) *The Influence of Neighbourhood Deprivation on People's Attachment to Places*, York: Joseph Rowntree Foundation.

Loney, M. (1983) *Community Against Government: The British Community Development Project 1968–78: A Study of Government Incompetence*, London: Heinemann Educational Books.

Loney, M. and Banting, K. (1979) *Poverty, Politics and Policy: Britain in the 1960s*, London: Macmillan.

Loopstra, R., Reeves, A., McKee, M. and Stuckler, D. (2015) *Do Punitive Approaches to Unemployment Benefit Recipients Increase Welfare Exit and Employment? A Cross-Area Analysis of UK Sanctioning Reforms*, Sociology Working Papers 2015–01, Oxford: University of Oxford.

Luna, Y.M. (2009) 'Single welfare mothers' resistance', *Journal of Poverty*, 13(4): 441–61.

Lynch, K. and Lyons, M. (2016) 'Care-less citizenship? Public devaluation and private validation', in K. Lynch, J. Baker, M. Lyons, M. Feeley, N. Hanlon, J. Walsh et al (eds) *Affective Equality: Love, Care and Injustice*, London: Palgrave Macmillan, pp 78–92.

Lynch, K. and Walsh, J. (2016) 'Love, care and solidarity: what is and is not commodifiable', in K. Lynch, J. Baker, M. Lyons, M. Feeley, N. Hanlon, J. Walsh et al (eds) *Affective Equality: Love, Care and Injustice*, London: Palgrave Macmillan, pp 35–53.

MacDonald, R., Shildrick, T. and Furlong, A. (2014) 'In search of "intergenerational cultures of worklessness": hunting the Yeti and shooting zombie', *Critical Social Policy*, 34(2): 199–220.

MacDonald, R., Shildrick, T., Webster, C. and Simpson, D. (2005) 'Growing up in poor neighbourhoods: the significance of class and place in the extended transitions of "socially excluded" young adults', *Sociology*, 39(5): 873–91.

MacLeavy, J. (2007) Engendering New Labour's workfarist regime: exploring the intersection of welfare state restructuring and labour market policies in the UK', *Gender, Place and Culture*, 14(6): 721–43.

MacLeavy, J. (2011) 'A "new politics" of austerity, workfare and gender? The UK coalition government's welfare reform proposals', *Cambridge Journal of Regions, Economy and Society*, 4(3): 355–67.

Macmillan, L. (2014) 'Intergenerational worklessness in the UK and the role of local labour markets', *Oxford Economic Papers*, 66(3): 871–89.

Mahon, R. (2009) 'The OECD's discourse on the reconciliation of work and family life', *Global Social Policy*, 9(2): 183–204.

Main, G. and Bradshaw, J. (2016) 'Child poverty in the UK: measures, prevalence and intra-household sharing', *Critical Social Policy*, 36(1): 38–61.

Major, L.E. and Machin, S. (2018) *Social Mobility: And Its Enemies*, London: Penguin.

Marmot, M. (2004) 'Status syndrome', *Significance*, 1(4): 150–4.

Martin, D.G., Hanson, S. and Fontaine, D. (2007) 'What counts as activism? The role of individuals in creating change', *Women's Studies Quarterly*, 35(3/4): 78–94.

Massey, D. (1984) *Spatial Divisions of Labour: Social Structures and the Geography of Production*, London: Macmillan.

Massey, D. (1991) 'A global sense of place', *Marxism Today*, 38: 24–9.

Massey, D. (1994) *Space, Place and Gender*, Cambridge: Polity Press.

Massey, D. (2004) 'Geographies of responsibility', *Geografiska Annaler Series B, Human Geography*, 86(1): 5–18.

Massey, D. (2005) *For Space*, Cambridge: Polity Press.

Massey, D. and Wainwright, H. (1985) 'Beyond the Coalfields: the work of the miners support groups', in H. Beynon (ed) *Digging Deeper: Issues in the Miners' Strike*, London: Verso Books, pp 149–68.

Matarese, M.T. and Caswell, D. (2018) '"I'm gonna ask you about yourself, so I can put it on paper": analysing street-level bureaucracy through form-related talk in social work', *British Journal of Social Work*, 48(3): 714–33.

Mau, S. (2004) *The Moral Economy of Welfare States: Britain and Germany Compared*, London: Routledge.

May, V. (2008) 'On being a "good" mother: the moral presentation of self in written life stories' *Sociology*, 42(3): 470–86.

May, V. (2010) 'Lone motherhood as a category of practice', *The Sociological Review*, 58(3): 429–43.

Mayo, M. (2004) 'Exclusion, inclusion and empowerment: community empowerment? Reflecting on the lessons of strategies to promote empowerment', in J. Andersen and B. Siim (eds) *The Politics of Inclusion and Empowerment: Gender, Class and Citizenship*, London: Palgrave Macmillan, pp 139–58.

McAdams, D.P. (2008) 'Personal narratives and the life story', in O.P. John, R.W. Robins and L.A. Pervin (eds) *Handbook of Personality: Theory and Research*, New York: The Guilford Press, pp 242–62.

McCann, P. (2020) Perceptions of regional inequality and the geography of discontent: insights from the UK, *Regional Studies*, 54(2): 256–67.

McCarthy, J.R. and Edwards, R. (2002) 'The individual in public and private: the significance of mothers and children', in A. Carling, S. Duncan and R. Edwards (eds) *Analysing Families: Morality and Rationality in Policy and Practice*, London: Routledge, pp 199–216.

McCollum, D. (2011) '"An acceptance that it's just your lot, I suppose": reflections on turbulent transitions between work and welfare', *People, Place and Policy Online*, 5(3): 149–60.

McCormack, K. (2004) 'Resisting the welfare mother: the power of welfare discourse and tactics of resistance', *Critical Sociology*, 30(2): 355–83.

McDowell, L. (2011) *Redundant Masculinities? Employment Change and White Working Class Youth*, Malden, MA: Blackwell Publishing.

McDowell, L. (2012) 'Post-crisis, post-Ford and post-gender? Youth identities in an era of austerity', *Journal of Youth Studies*, 15(5): 573–90.

McDowell, L. (2017) 'Youth, children and families in austere times: change, politics and a new gender contract', *Area*, 49(3): 311–16.

McDowell, L. and Massey, D. (1984) 'A woman's place?', in D. Massey and J. Allen (eds) *Geography Matters!* Cambridge: Cambridge University Press, pp 128–47.

McGarvey, D. (2017) *Poverty Safari*, Edinburgh: Luath Press.

McKenzie, L. (2012) 'A narrative from the inside, studying St Anns in Nottingham: belonging, continuity and change', *The Sociological Review*, 60(3): 457–75.

McKenzie, L. (2015) *Getting By: Estates, Class and Culture in Austerity Britain*, Bristol: Policy Press.

McNeil, C., Parkes, H., Garthwaite, K. and Patrick, R. (2021) *No Longer 'Managing': The Rise of Working Poverty and Fixing Britain's Broken Social Settlement*, London: Institute for Public Policy Research.

Medvedyuk, S., Govender, P. and Raphael, D. (2021) 'The reemergence of Engels' concept of social murder in response to growing social and health inequalities', *Social Science and Medicine*, 289: article 114377. doi: 10.1016/j.socscimed.2021.114377

Mee, K. and Wright, S. (2009) 'Geographies of belonging', *Environment and Planning A*, 41(4): 772–9.

Mijs, J. J. B. (2018) 'Visualizing Belief in Meritocracy, 1930–2010', *Socius*, 4.

Millar, J. (2006) 'Better-off in work? Work, security and welfare for lone mothers', in C. Glendinning and P. Kemp (eds) *Cash and Care*, Bristol: Policy Press, pp 171–86.

Millar, J. (2008) 'Following families: working lone-mother families and their children', *Social Policy and Administration*, 45(1): 85–97.

Millar, J. (2019) 'Self-responsibility and activation for lone mothers in the United Kingdom', *American Behavioral Scientist*, 63(1): 85–99.

Millar, J. and Bennett, F. (2017) 'Universal Credit: assumptions, contradictions and virtual reality', *Social Policy and Society*, 16(2): 169–82.

Millar, J. and Ridge, T. (2009) 'Relationships of care: working lone mothers, their children and employment sustainability', *Journal of Social Policy*, 38(1): 103–21.

Millar, J. and Ridge, T. (2017) *Work and Relationships over Time in Lone-Mother Families*, York: Joseph Rowntree Foundation.

Millar, J. and Ridge, T. (2020) 'No margin for error: fifteen years in the working lives of lone mothers and their children', *Journal of Social Policy*, 49(1): 1–17.

Millar, K. (2014) 'The precarious present: wageless labour and disrupted life in Rio de Janeiro, Brazil', Cultural Anthropology, 29(1): 32–53.

Mills, C.W. (1940) 'Situated actions and vocabularies of motive', *American Sociological Review*, 5(6): 904–13.

Mills, C.W. (1959) *The Sociological Imagination*, New York: Oxford University Press.

Mitchell, E. (2020) 'Negotiating vulnerability: the experience of long-term social security recipients', *The Sociological Review*, 68(1): 225–41.

Monaghan, M. and Ingold, J. (2019) 'Policy practitioners' accounts of evidence-based policy making: the case of Universal Credit', *Journal of Social Policy*, 48(2): 351–68.

Morris, L. (2019) 'Reconfiguring rights in austerity Britain: boundaries, behaviours and contestable margins', *Journal of Social Policy*, 48(2): 271–91.

Morris, L. (2020) 'Activating the welfare subject: the problem of agency', *Sociology*, 54(2): 275–91.

Morrison, E.W. (2006) 'Doing the job well: an investigation of pro-social rule breaking', *Journal of Management*, 32(1): 5–28.

Muir, J. (2004) 'Public participation in area-based urban regeneration programmes', *Housing Studies*, 19(6): 947–66.

Munch, R. (2012) *Inclusion and Exclusion in the Liberal Competition State: The Cult of the Individual*, London: Routledge.

National Audit Office (2016) *Benefit Sanctions*, HC 628, London: National Audit Office.

Neal, S., Bennett, K., Cochrane, A. and Mohan, G. (2019) 'Community and conviviality? Informal social life in multicultural places', *Sociology*, 53(1): 69–86.

Neale, B. (2021) *The Craft of Qualitative Longitudinal Research*, London: Sage.

Neale, B. and Davies, L. (2016) 'Becoming a young breadwinner? The education, employment and training trajectories of young fathers', *Social Policy and Society*, 15(1): 85–98.

Neitzert, E. (2020) *Spirals of Inequality: How Unpaid Care Is at the Heart of Gender Inequalities*, Commission on a Gender-equal Economy, Women's Budget Group.

Newman, I. (2011) 'Work as a route out of poverty: a critical evaluation of the UK welfare to work policy', *Policy Studies*, 32(2): 91–108.

Newman, J. (2001) *Modernising Governance*, London: Sage.

Newman, J. (2012a) *Working the Spaces of Power: Activism, Neoliberalism and Gendered Labour*, London: Bloomsbury Academic.

Newman, J. (2012b) 'Beyond the deliberative subject? Problems of theory, method and critique in the turn to emotion and affect', *Critical Policy Studies*, 6(4): 465–79.

Nicholls, J., Jupp, E., McDermont, M. and Newman, J. (2025). Beyond resilience? State failure, mutual aid and local action. *Environment and Planning C*, 0(0).

Nicolaisen, H., Kavli, H.C. and Steen Jensen, R. (2019) *Dualisation of Part-Time Work: The Development of Labour Market Insiders and Outsiders*, Bristol: Policy Press.

Nightingale, M. (2020) 'Stepping-stone or dead end: to what extent does part-time employment enable progression out of low pay for male and female employees in the UK?', *Journal of Social Policy*, 49(1): 41–59.

Nothdurfter, U. (2017) 'The street-level delivery of activation policies: constraints and possibilities for a practice of citizenship', in W. Lorenz and I. Shaw (eds) *Private Troubles or Public Issues?* London: Routledge, pp 128–48.

Nussbaum, M.C. (2000) *Women and Human Development: The Capabilities Approach*, Cambridge: Cambridge University Press.

Oakley, A. (1974) *Women's Work: A History of the Housewife*, New York: Pantheon.

O'Brien, M. and Penna, S. (1998) *Theorising Welfare: Enlightenment and Modern Society*, London: Sage.

O'Hara, M. (2014) *Austerity Bites: A Journey to the Sharp End of Cuts in the UK*, Bristol: Policy Press.

O'Hara, M. (2015) 'As a Jobcentre adviser, I got "brownie points" for cruelty', *The Guardian*, 4 February.

O'Hara, M. (2020) *The Shame Game: Overturning the Toxic Poverty Narrative*, Bristol: Policy Press.

O'Neill, M. (2011) 'Restoring the "mam": archives, access and research into women's pasts in Wales', *Public History Review*, 18: 47–64.

Orloff, A.S. (2009) 'Gendering the comparative analysis of welfare states: an unfinished agenda', *Sociological Theory*, 27(3): 317–43.

Orr, S., Brown, G., Smith, S., May, C. and Waters, M. (2006) *When Ends Don't Meet: Assets, Vulnerabilities and Livelihoods: An Analysis of Households in Thornaby-on-Tees*, Manchester: Church Action on Poverty and Oxfam.

Orton, M. (2015) *Something's Not Right: Insecurity and an Anxious Nation*, London: Compass.

Pahl, R. (1984) *Divisions of Labour*, Oxford: Blackwell.

Park, A., Curtice, J., Thomson, K., Phillips, M. Clery, E. and Butt, S. (2010) *British Social Attitudes: The 27th Report. Exploring Labour's Legacy*, London: Sage.

Pascall, G. (2002) *Social Policy: A New Feminist Analysis*, London: Routledge.

Pateman, C. (1989) *The Disorder of Women Democracy, Feminism and Political Theory*, Cambridge: Polity Press.

Pateman, C. (2004) 'Freedom and democratisation: why basic income is to be preferred to basic capital', in K. Dowding, J. DeWispelaere and S. White (eds) *The Ethics of Stakeholding*, London: Palgrave, pp 130–48.

Pateman, C. (2005) Another way forward: welfare, social reproduction, and a basic income', in L. Mead and C. Beem (eds) *Welfare Reform and Political Theory*, New York: Russell Sage Foundation, pp 34–64.

Patrick, R. (2014) 'Working on welfare: findings from a qualitative longitudinal study into the lived experiences of welfare reform in the UK', *Journal of Social Policy*, 43(4): 705–25.

Patrick, R. (2016) 'Living with and responding to the "scrounger" narrative in the UK: exploring everyday strategies of acceptance, resistance and deflection', *Journal of Poverty and Social Justice*, 24(3): 245–59.

Patrick, R. (2017) *For Whose Benefit?* Bristol: Policy Press.

Patrick, R. and Simpson, M. (2020) *Universal Credit Could be a Lifeline in Northern Ireland, but it Must be Designed with People Who Use It*, York: Joseph Rowntree Foundation.

Pattaro, S., Bailey, N., Williams, E., Gibson, M., Wells, V., Tranmer, M. et al (2022) 'The impacts of benefit sanctions: a scoping review of the quantitative research evidence', *Journal of Social Policy*, 51(3): 611–53.

Paz-Fuchs, A. (2008) *Welfare to Work: Conditional Rights in Social Policy*, Oxford: Oxford University Press.

Peacock, L. (2012) 'Profile: Working Links and A4e', *The Telegraph*, 24 May.

Peacock, M., Bissell, P. and Owen, J. (2014) 'Shaming encounters: reflections on contemporary understandings of social inequality and health', *Sociology*, 48(2): 387–402.

Pearce, S., Blakely, H., Frayne, D. and Rees Jones, I. (2021) 'Evaluation in reinforcing and resisting hierarchical relations between state and civil society', *Social Policy and Administration*, 55(5): 891–905.

Pearson, R. and Elson, D. (2015) 'Transcending the impact of the financial crisis in the United Kingdom: towards plan F—a feminist economic strategy', *Feminist Review*, 109(1): 8–30.

Pemberton, S. and Humphris, R. (2018) *Invisible Rules, Social Mobility, Low Income and the Role of Further and Higher Education*, Birmingham: University of Birmingham.

Pemberton, S., Fahmy, E., Sutton, E. and Bell, K. (2017a) 'Endless pressure: life on a low income in austere times', *Social Policy and Administration*, 51(7): 1156–73.

Pemberton, S., Pantazis, C. and Hillyard, P. (2017b) 'Poverty and social harm: challenging discourses of risk, resilience and choice', in G. Bramley and N. Bailey (eds) *Poverty and Social Exclusion in the UK*, Bristol: Policy Press, pp 245–66.

Peterie, M., Ramia, G., Marston, G. and Patulny, R. (2019) 'Emotional compliance and emotion as resistance: shame and anger among the long-term unemployed', *Work, Employment and Society*, 33(5): 794–811.

Petrongolo, B. (2009) 'The long-term effects of job search requirements: evidence from the UK JSA reform', *Journal of Public Economics*, 93(11–12): 1234–53.

Phillips, A. (2022) *Working Together: The Case for Universal Employment Support*, London: Demos.

Phoenix, A. (2013) 'Social constructions of lone motherhood: a case of competing discourses' in E.B. Silva (ed) *Good Enough Mothering? Feminist Perspectives on Lone Motherhood*, London: Routledge, pp 175–90.

Pickerill, J. and Chatterton, P. (2006) 'Notes towards autonomous geographies: creation, resistance and self-management as survival tactics', *Progress in Human Geography*, 30(6): 730–46.

Piven, F. and Cloward, R. (1971) *Regulating the Poor: The Functions of Public Welfare*, New York: Pantheon Books.

Plummer, K. (2019) *Narrative Power: The Struggle for Human Value*, Cambridge: Polity Press.

Pollard, T. and Tjoa, P. (2020) *This Isn't Working: Reimagining Employment Support for People Facing Complex Disadvantage*, London: New Local.

Polletta, F. (2020) *Inventing the ties that bind: Imagined relationships in moral and political life*, University of Chicago Press.

Popple, K. (1996) 'Community work: British models', *Journal of Community Practice*, 3(3–4): 147–80.

Pottinger, L. (2017) 'Planting the seeds of a quiet activism', *Area*, 49(2): 215–22.

Power, A. (2007) *City Survivors: Bringing Up Children in Disadvantaged Neighbourhoods*, Bristol: Policy Press.

Power, A. and Hall, E. (2018) 'Placing care in times of austerity', *Social and Cultural Geography*, 19(3): 303–13.

Probyn, E. (2015) *Outside Belongings*, New York: Routledge.

Pulkingham, J., Fuller, S. and Kershaw, P. (2010) 'Lone motherhood, welfare reform and active citizen subjectivity', *Critical Social Policy*, 30(2): 267–91.

Rabindrakumar, S. (2013) *Paying the Price: Single Parents in the Age of Austerity*, London: Gingerbread.

Rafferty, A. and Wiggan, J. (2011) 'Choice and welfare reform: lone parents' decision making around paid work and family life', *Journal of Social Policy*, 40(2): 275–93.

Rafferty, A. and Wiggan, J. (2017) 'The time-related underemployment of lone parents during welfare reform, recession and austerity: a challenge to in-work conditionality?', *Social Policy and Administration*, 51(3): 511–38.

Ravn, S. (2019) 'Imagining futures, imagining selves: a narrative approach to "risk" in young men's lives', *Current Sociology*, 67(7): 1039–55.

Ravn, S. (2021) 'Reframing immobility: young women aspiring to "good enough" local futures', *Journal of Youth Studies*, 25(9): 1236–50.

Reay, D. (2017) 'The cruelty of social mobility: individual success at the cost of collective failure', in S. Lawler and G. Payne (eds) *Social Mobility for the 21st Century*, London: Routledge, pp 146–57.

Redman, J. and Fletcher, D.R. (2022) 'Violent bureaucracy: a critical analysis of the British public employment service', *Critical Social Policy*, 42(2): 306–26.

Reed, H. and Portes, J. (2018) *The Cumulative Impact on Living Standards of Public Spending Changes*, Manchester: Equality and Human Rights Commission.

Rees, T. (1988) 'Changing patterns of women's work in Wales: some myths explored', *Contemporary Wales*, 2: 119–30.

Rees, T. (1999) *Women and Work: Twenty-Five Years of Gender Equality in Wales*, Cardiff: University of Wales Press.

Rees, G. and Rees, T. (1980) 'Poverty at the periphery: the outline of a perspective of Wales', in G. Rees and T. Rees (eds) *Poverty and Social Inequality in Wales*, London: Routledge, pp 1–16.

Rees, G., Fevre, R., Furlong, J. and Gorard, S. (1997) 'History, place and the learning society: towards a sociology of lifetime learning', *Journal of Education Policy*, 12(6): 485–98.

Reeves, A. and Loopstra, R. (2017) '"Set up to fail"? How welfare conditionality undermines citizenship for vulnerable groups', *Social Policy and Society*, 16(2): 327–38.

Reis, S. (2018) *The Female Face of Poverty: Examining the Cause and Consequences of Economic Deprivation for Women*, London: Women's Budget Group.

Richards-Gray, L. (2020) 'Political discourse and gendered welfare reform: a case study of the UK Coalition government', *Journal of Elections, Public Opinion and Parties*, 32(2): 358–76.

Ricoeur, P. (1980) 'Narrative time', *Critical Inquiry*, 7(1): 169–90.

Ridge, T. and Millar, J. (2011) 'Following families: working lone-mother families and their children', *Social Policy and Administration*, 45(1): 85–97.

Riessman, C.K. (1990) *Divorce Talk: Women and Men Make Sense of Personal Meanings*, New Brunswick: Rutgers University Press.

Riessman, C.K. (2008a) 'Concluding comments', in M. Tamboukou, M. Andrews and C. Squire (eds) *Doing Narrative Research*, London: Sage, pp 265–60.

Riessman, C.K. (2008b) *Narrative Methods for the Human Sciences*, London: Sage.

Rigney, A. (2018) 'Remembering hope: transnational activism beyond the traumatic', *Memory Studies*, 11(3): 368–80.

Roantree, B. and Vira, K. (2018) *The Rise and Rise of Women's Employment in the UK*, Briefing Note BN234, Institute for Fiscal Studies.

Roberts, H., Stuart, S.R., Allan, S. and Gumley, A. (2022) '"It's like the sword of damocles": a trauma-informed framework analysis of individuals' experiences of assessment for the personal independence payment benefit in the UK', *Journal of Social Policy*, 53(4): 997–1015.

Roberts, S. and Evans, S. (2013) '"Aspirations" and imagined futures: the im/possibilities for Britain's young working class', in W. Atkinson, S. Roberts and M. Savage (eds) *Class Inequality in Austerity Britain*, London: Palgrave Macmillan, pp 70–89.

Robertson, D.L., Wright, S.E. and Stewart, A.B. (2020) *How Well is Universal Credit Supporting People in Glasgow?* York: Joseph Rowntree Foundation.

Rodger, J.J. (2003) 'Social solidarity, welfare and post-emotionalism', *Journal of Social Policy*, 32(3): 403–21.

Rogaly, B. and Taylor, B. (2016) *Moving Histories of Class and Community: Identity, Place and Belonging in Contemporary England* (e-book), Basingstoke: Palgrave Macmillan.

Roseneil, S. and Mann, K. (1996) 'Unpalatable choices and inadequate families: lone mothers and the underclass debate', in E.B. Silva (ed) *Good Enough Mothering? Feminist Perspectives on Lone Motherhood*, London: Routledge, pp 191–210.

Rowbotham, S. (2001) *Promise of a Dream: Remembering the Sixties*, London: Verso Books.

Rowbotham, S. (2014) *Women, Resistance and Revolution: A History of Women and Revolution in the Modern World*, London: Verso Books.

Rowbotham, S. and McCrindle, J. (eds) (1979) *Dutiful Daughters: Women Talk about Their Lives*, London: Penguin.

Rowbotham, S., Segal, L. and Wainwright, H. (2013) *Beyond the Fragments: Feminism and the Making of Socialism*, London: Merlin Press.

Rowthorn, R. and Webster, D. (2008) 'Male worklessness and the rise of lone parenthood in Great Britain', *Cambridge Journal of Regions, Economy and Society*, 1(1): 69–88.

Rubery, J. and Rafferty, A. (2013) 'Women and recession revisited', *Work, Employment and Society*, 27(3): 414–32.

Sandel, M.J. (2020) *The Tyranny of Merit: What's Become of the Common Good?* London: Penguin.

Sanders, J. and Munford, R. (2008) 'Losing self to the future? Young women's strategic responses to adulthood transitions', *Journal of Youth Studies*, 11(3): 331–46.

Savage, M. (2015) *Social Class in the Twentieth Century*, London: Pelican.

Sayer, A. (1992) *Method in Social Science: A Realist Approach*, London: Routledge.

Sayer, A. (2000a) *Realism and Social Science*, London: Sage.

Sayer, A. (2000b) 'Moral economy and political economy', *Studies in Political Economy*, 61(1): 79–103.

Sayer, A. (2005) *The Moral Significance of Class*, Cambridge: Cambridge University Press.

Sayer, A. (2011) *Why Things Matter to People: Social Science, Values and Ethical Life*, Cambridge: Cambridge University Press.

Scambler, G. (2018) 'Heaping blame on shame: "weaponising stigma" for neoliberal times', *The Sociological Review*, 66(4): 766–82.

Scott, M.B. and Lyman, S.M. (1968) 'Accounts', *American Sociological Review*, 33(1): 46–62.

Seaman, R., Walsh, D., Beatty, C., McCartney, G. and Dundas, R. (2024) 'Social security cuts and life expectancy: a longitudinal analysis of local authorities in England, Scotland and Wales', *Journal of Epidemiology and Community Health*, 78(2): 82–7.

Sen, A. (1992) *Inequality Re-Examined*, Cambridge: Harvard University Press.

Sen, A. (1999) *Development as Freedom*, New York: Alfred Knopf.

Sennett, R. (2003) *Respect in a World of Inequality*, New York: Norton.

Sennet, R. and Cobb, J. (1972) *The Hidden Injuries of Class*, Cambridge: Cambridge University Press.

Sevenhuijsen, S. (1998) *Citizenship and the Ethics of Care*, London: Routledge.

Sevenhuijsen, S. (2000) 'Caring in the Third Way: the relation between obligation, responsibility and care in Third Way discourse', *Critical Social Policy*, 20(1): 5–37.

Shaw, M. (2011) 'Stuck in the middle? Community development, community engagement and the dangerous business of learning for democracy', *Community Development Journal*, 46(2): 128–46.

Shaw, M. and Martin, I. (2000)' Community work, citizenship and democracy: remaking the connections', *Community Development Journal*, 35(4): 401–13.

Shildrick, T. (2018) *Poverty Propaganda: Exploring the Myths*, Bristol: Policy Press.

Shildrick, T. and MacDonald, R. (2012) *Poverty and Insecurity: Life in Low-Pay, No-Pay Britain*, Bristol: Policy Press.

Shildrick, T. and MacDonald, R. (2013) 'Poverty talk: how people experiencing poverty deny their poverty and why they blame "the poor"', *The Sociological Review*, 61(2): 285–303.

Shildrick, T., MacDonald, R., Webster, C. and Garthwaite, K. (2010) *The Low-Pay, No-Pay Cycle*, York: Joseph Rowntree Foundation.

Shildrick, T.A., MacDonald, R., Furlong, A., Rodan, J. and Crow, R. (2012) *Are 'Cultures of Worklessness' Passed Down the Generations?* York: Joseph Rowntree Foundation.

Shipler, D.K. (2005) *The Working Poor: Invisible in America*, New York: Vintage.

Sidel, R. (2006) *Unsung Heroines: Single Mothers and the American Dream*, Berkeley: University of California Press.

Skeggs, B. (1997) *Formations of Class and Gender: Becoming Respectable*, London: Sage.

Skeggs, B. (2004) *Class, Self, Culture*, London: Routledge.

Skeggs, B. (2014) 'Values beyond value? Is anything beyond the logic of capital?', *The British Journal of Sociology*, 65(1): 1–20.

Skeggs, B. and Wood, H. (2008) 'The labour of transformation and circuits of value "around" reality television', *Continuum*, 22(4): 559–72.

Smart, C. (2007) *Personal Life*, Cambridge: Polity Press.

Smith, A. and McBride, J. (2021) '"Working to live, not living to work": low-paid multiple employment and work–life articulation', *Work, Employment and Society*, 35(2): 256–76.

Smith, D.E. (2005) *Institutional Ethnography: A Sociology for People*, Oxford: Rowman Altamira.

Smith, F., Barker, J., Wainwright, E., Marandet, E. and Buckingham, S. (2008) 'A new deal for lone parents? Training lone parents for work in West London', *Area*, 40(2): 237–44.

Smith, N. (2024) 'History in the pub: the historiography of J.D. Wetherspoon', *Endeavour*, 48(1): article 100889. doi: 10.1016/j.endeavour.2023.100889

Smith, S.J. (2005) 'States, markets and an ethic of care', *Political Geography*, 24(1): 1–20.

Soss, J., Fording, R.C. and Schram, S. (2011) *Disciplining the Poor: Neoliberal Paternalism and the Persistent Power of Race*, Chicago: University of Chicago Press.

Spence, J. and Stephenson, C. (2007) 'Female involvement in the miners' strike 1984–1985: trajectories of activism', *Sociological Research Online*, 12(1): 1–11.

Spencer, L. and Pahl, R. (2007) *Rethinking Friendship: Hidden Solidarities Today*, Princeton, NJ: Princeton University Press.

Squire, V. (2018) 'Mobile solidarities and precariousness at City Plaza: beyond vulnerable and disposable lives', *Studies in Social Justice*, 12(1): 111–32.

Srnicek, N. and Williams, A. (2015) *Inventing the Future: Postcapitalism and a World Without Work*, London: Verso Books.

Staeheli, L.A. (2003) 'Cities and citizenship', *Urban Geography*, 24(2): 97–102.

Staeheli, L.A. (2011) 'Political geography: where's citizenship?', *Progress in Human Geography*, 35(3): 393–400.

Staeheli, L.A., Ehrkamp, P., Leitner, H. and Nagel, C.R. (2012) 'Dreaming the ordinary: daily life and the complex geographies of citizenship', *Progress in Human Geography*, 36(5): 628–44.

Steedman, C. (1987) *Landscape for a Good Woman: A Story of Two Lives*, New Brunswick: Rutgers University Press.

Steedman, C. (2000) 'Enforced narratives: stories of another self', in T. Coslett, C. Lury and P. Summerfield (eds) *Feminism and Autobiography: Texts, Theories, Methods*, London: Routledge, pp 25–39.

Steedman, C. (2013) *An Everyday Life of the English Working Class: Work, Self and Sociability in the Early Nineteenth Century*, Cambridge: Cambridge University Press.

Steedman, C., Urwin, C. and Walkerdine, V. (2016) *Routledge Revivals: Language, Gender and Childhood*, Abingdon: Routledge.

Stevens, A. (2011) 'Telling policy stories: an ethnographic study of the use of evidence in policy-making in the UK', *Journal of Social Policy*, 40(2): 237–55.

Stinson, H. (2019) 'Supporting people? Universal Credit, conditionality and the recalibration of vulnerability', in P. Dwyer (ed) *Dealing with Welfare Conditionality*, Bristol: Policy Press, pp 15–40.

Stone, D.A. (1989) 'Causal stories and the formation of policy agendas', *Political Science Quarterly*, 104(2): 281–300.

Stratford, E. (2009) 'Belonging as a resource: the case of Ralphs Bay, Tasmania, and the local politics of place', *Environment and Planning A*, 41(4): 796–810.

Strauss, A., Fagerhaugh, S., Suczek, B. and Wiener, C. (1982) 'Sentimental work in the technologized hospital', *Sociology of Health and Illness*, 4(3): 254–78.

Studdert, D. and Walkerdine, V. (2016) *Rethinking Community Research: Inter-Relationality, Communal Being and Commonality*, London: Palgrave Macmillan.

Sturge, G. (2024) 'Insight 2024 general election: turnout', *House of Commons Library*, 5 September.

Sussman, M. (1976) 'The family life of old people', *Handbook of Aging and the Social Sciences*, New York: Van Nostrand, pp 218–43.

Symonds, A. and Kelly, A. (2005) *A Childcare Revolution in Wales: Summary and Action*, Merthyr Tydfil: The Bevan Foundation.

Tannock, S., Burgess, S. and Moles, K. (2013) *Military Recruitment, Work and Culture in the South Wales Valleys: A Local Geography of Contemporary British Militarism*, WISERD Working Paper Series/009, Cardiff: WISERD.

Tarkiainen, L. (2017) 'Long-term unemployed Finnish interviewees address deservingness: separating, declining and enriching as means of resisting', *Journal of Poverty and Social Justice*, 25(3): 219–31.

Taylor, D. (1998) 'Social identity and social policy: engagements with postmodern theory', *Journal of Social Policy*, 27(3): 329–50.

Taylor, M. (2011) *Public Policy in the Community*, London: Bloomsbury Publishing.

Taylor-Gooby, P. (2013) *The Double Crisis of the Welfare State and What We Can Do about It*, Basingstoke: Palgrave Macmillan.

Tebbit, N. (1981) 'Speech at Conservative Party Conference, 15th October', *Daily Telegraph*, 16 October.

Thane, P. and Evans, T. (2012) *Sinners? Scroungers? Saints? Unmarried Motherhood in Twentieth-Century England*, Oxford: Oxford University Press.

Thompson, G. (2024) General Election 2024 analysis: low turnout and rise of Reform, *South Wales Argus*, 5 July.

Thompson, S. (2015) *The Low-Pay, No-Pay Cycle*, York: Joseph Rowntree Trust.

Tirado, L. (2014) *Hand to Mouth: The Truth about Being Poor in a Wealthy World*, London: Virago Press.

Titmuss, R. (1967/2000) 'Universalism versus selection', in C. Pierson and F.G. Castles (eds) *The Welfare State Reader*, Cambridge: Polity Press, pp 40–48.

Todd, S. (2004) 'Poverty and aspiration: young women's entry to employment in inter-war England', *Twentieth Century British History*, 15(2): 119–42.

Todd, S. (2005) *Young Women, Work, and Family in England 1918–1950*, Oxford: Oxford University Press.

Treanor, M.C. (2020) *Child Poverty: Aspiring to Survive*, Bristol: Policy Press.

Trickey, H. and Walker, R. (2001) 'Steps to compulsion within British labour market policies', in I. Lødemel and H. Trickey (eds) *'An Offer You Can't Refuse': Workfare in International Perspective*, Bristol: Policy Press, pp 181–214.

Tronto, J.C. (1993) *Moral Boundaries: A Political Argument for an Ethic of Care*, New York: Routledge.

Tronto, J.C. (1995) 'Women and caring: what can feminists learn about morality from caring?', in V. Held (ed) *Justice and Care: Essential Readings in Feminist Ethics*, Boulder, CO: Westview Press.

Tronto, J.C. (2015) *Who Cares? How to Reshape a Democratic Politics*, Ithaca, NY: Cornell University Press.

Turner, V.W. (1969) *The Ritual Process: Structure and Anti-Structure*, London: Routledge and Kegan Paul.

Tyler, I. (2008) '"Chav mum chav scum": class disgust in contemporary Britain', *Feminist Media Studies*, 8(1): 17–34.

Tyler, I. (2013) *Revolting Subjects: Social Abjection and Resistance in Neoliberal Britain*, London: Bloomsbury Publishing.

Tyler, I. (2020) *Stigma: The Machinery of Inequality*, London: Zed Books.

Ungerson, C. (1999) 'Personal assistants and disabled people: an examination of a hybrid form of work and care', *Work, Employment and Society*, 13(4): 583–600.

Ungerson, C. and Yeandle, S. (eds) (2007) *Cash for Care in Developed Welfare States*, Basingstoke: Palgrave.

United Nations Development Programme (1997) *Human Development Report 1997: Human Development to Eradicate Poverty*, New York: Oxford University Press.

Uphoff, N. and Krishna, A. (2004) 'Civil society and public sector institutions: more than a zero-sum relationship', *Public Administration and Development: The International Journal of Management Research and Practice*, 24(4): 357–72.

Vacchelli, E., Kathrecha, P. and Gyte, N. (2015) 'Is it really just the cuts? Neo-liberal tales from the women's voluntary and community sector in London', *Feminist Review*, 109(1): 180–9.

van Berkel, R. (2020) 'Making welfare conditional: a street-level perspective', *Social Policy and Administration*, 54(2): 191–204.

van Berkel, R., Larsen, F. and Caswell, D. (2017) 'Introduction: frontline delivery of welfare-to-work in different European contexts', *International Social Security Review*, 71(4): 3–11.

van den Berg, G.J. and Vikström, J. (2014) 'Monitoring job offer decisions, punishments, exit to work, and job quality', *The Scandinavian Journal of Economics*, 116(2): 284–334.

Veitch, J. and Bennett, F. (2010) *A Gender Perspective on 21st Century Welfare Reform*, Oxfam.

Viney, M. (2014) 'Work Programme adviser: "almost every day one of my clients mentioned feeling suicidal"', *The Guardian*, 5 November.

Wacquant, L. (1998) 'Sacrifice', in G. Early (ed) *Body Language: Writers on Sport*, Saint Paul: Graywolf Press, pp 47–60.

Wacquant, L. (2002) 'Scrutinising the street: poverty, morality, and the pitfalls of urban ethnography', *American Journal of Sociology*, 107(6): 1468–532.
Wacquant, L. (2008) *Urban Outcasts*, Cambridge: Polity Press.
Wacquant, L. (2009) *Punishing the Poor: The Neoliberal Government of Social Insecurity*, London: Duke University Press.
Wacquant, L. (2010) 'Crafting the neoliberal state: workfare, prisonfare, and social insecurity', *Sociological Forum*, 25(2): 197–220.
Wacquant, L., Slater, T. and Pereira, V.B. (2014) 'Territorial stigmatization in action', *Environment and Planning A*, 46(6): 1270–80.
Walby, S., Armstrong, J. and Strid, S. (2012) 'Intersectionality: multiple inequalities in social theory', *Sociology*, 46(2): 224–40.
Walker, A. (2021) '"Everyone always did the same": constructing legacies of collective industrial pasts in ex-mining communities in the South Wales Valleys', Emotion, Space *and Society*, 41: article 100834. doi: 10.1016/j.emospa.2021.100834
Walker, R. and Bantebya-Kyomuhendo, G. (2014) *The Shame of Poverty*, Oxford: Oxford University Press.
Walker, R. and Chase, E. (2013) 'Separating the sheep from the goats: tackling poverty in Britain for over four centuries', in E.K. Gubrium, S. Pellissery and I. Lødemel (eds) The Shame of It, Bristol: Policy Press, pp 133–6.
Walkerdine, V. and Jimenez, L. (2012) *Gender, Work and Community after De-Industrialisation: A Psychosocial Approach to Affect*, Basingstoke: Palgrave Macmillan.
Walter, E.V. (1977) 'Dreadful enclosures: detoxifying an urban myth', *European Journal of Sociology/Archives Européennes de Sociologie*, 18(1): 150–9.
Ward, S. (2016) *Unemployment and the State in Britain*, Manchester: Manchester University Press.
Warhurst, C. (2016) 'Accidental tourists: Brexit and its toxic employment underpinnings', *Socio-Economic Review*, 14(4): 819–25.
Warwick, D. and Littlejohn, G. (1992) *Coal, Capital and Culture: A Sociological Analysis of Mining Communities in West Yorkshire*, London: Routledge.
Watkins-Hayes, C. (2009) *The New Welfare Bureaucrats: Entanglements of Race, Class and Policy Reform*, Chicago: Chicago University Press.
Watts, B. and Fitzpatrick, S. (2018) *Welfare Conditionality*, London: Routledge.
Watts, B., Fitzpatrick, S., Bramley, G. and Watkins, D. (2014) *Welfare Sanctions and Conditionality in the UK*, York: Joseph Rowntree Foundation.
Webster, D. (2016) *Explaining the Rise and Fall of JSA and ESA Sanctions 2010–16. Briefing: The DWP's JSA/ESA Sanctions Statistics Release*, Glasgow: University of Glasgow.
Wellman, B. and Wortley, S. (1990) 'Different strokes from different folks: community ties and social support', *American Journal of Sociology*, 96(3): 558–88.

Welsh Assembly Government (2001) *Communities First Consultation Paper*, Cardiff: National Assembly for Wales.

Welsh Assembly Government (2007) *Communities First Guidance*, Cardiff: National Assembly for Wales.

Wetherspoon (2024) 'Pub histories', www.jdwetherspoon.com/pub-histories

Wharton, A.S. (2009) 'The sociology of emotional labor', *Annual Review of Sociology*, 35: 147–65.

Wheatley, D., Lawton, C. and Hardill, I. (2018) 'Gender differences in paid and unpaid work', in V. Caven and S. Nachmias (eds) *Hidden Inequalities in the Workplace: Palgrave Explorations in Workplace Stigma*, Cham: Palgrave Macmillan, pp 181–214.

White, R.J. (2009) 'Explaining why the non-commodified sphere of mutual aid is so pervasive in the advanced economies: some case study evidence from an English city', *International Journal of Sociology and Social Policy*, 29(9/10): 457–72.

Whitworth, A. (2013) *Tailor-Made? Single Parents' Experiences of Employment Support from Jobcentre Plus and the Work Programme*, London: Gingerbread.

Whitworth, A. and Griggs, J. (2013) 'Lone parents and welfare-to-work conditionality: necessary, just, effective?', *Ethics and Social Welfare*, 7(2): 124–40.

Wickham, S., Bentley, L., Rose, T., Whitehead, M., Taylor-Robinson, D. and Barr, B. (2020) 'Effects on mental health of a UK welfare reform, Universal Credit: a longitudinal controlled study', *The Lancet Public Health*, 5(3): e157–e164.

Wiggan, J. (2012) 'Telling stories of 21st century welfare: the UK Coalition government and the neo-liberal discourse of worklessness and dependency', *Critical Social Policy*, 32(3): 383–405.

Wiggan, J. (2024) *The Politics of Unemployment Policy in Britain: Class Struggle, Labour Market Restructuring and Welfare Reform*, Bristol: Policy Press.

Wilkinson, R. and Pickett, K. (2010) *The Spirit Level: Why Equality is Better for Everyone*, London: Penguin.

Williams, F. (2001) 'In and beyond New Labour: towards a new political ethics of care', *Critical Social Policy*, 21(4): 467–93.

Williams, F. (2021) *Social Policy: A Critical and Intersectional Analysis*, Cambridge: Polity Press.

Williams, R. (1965) *The Long Revolution*, Harmondsworth: Pelican Books.

Williams, R. (1989) *Resources of Hope. Culture, Democracy, Socialism*, London: Verso Books.

Williams, R. (2013) '"Lying thieving b******s": BBC documentary lifts the lid on offensive code used to describe disabled and jobless', *The Independent*, 28 January.

Willis, P. (1978) *Learning to Labour: How Working Class Kids Get Working Class Jobs*, London: Routledge.

Wills, J. (2012) 'The geography of community and political organisation in London today', *Political Geography*, 31(2): 114–26.

Wills, J. (2016) '(Re)locating community in relationships: questions for public policy', *The Sociological Review*, 64(4): 639–56.

Wood, N. and Waite, L. (2011) 'Scales of belonging', *Emotion, Space and Society*, 4(4): 201–2.

Work and Pensions Committee (2018) *Benefit Sanctions: Government Response to the Committee's Nineteenth Report of Session 2017–19*, London: House of Commons.

Worth, N. (2009) 'Understanding youth transition as "becoming": identity, time and futurity', *Geoforum*, 40(6): 1050–60.

Wright, S. (2003) 'The street level implementation of unemployment policy', in J. Millar (ed) *Understanding Social Security: Issues for Policy and Practice*, Bristol: Policy Press, pp 235–53.

Wright, S. (2011) 'Relinquishing rights? The impact of activation on citizenship for lone parents in the UK', in S. Betzelt and S. Bothfeld (eds) *Activation and Labour Market Reforms in Europe: Challenges to Social Citizenship*, London: Palgrave Macmillan, pp 59–78.

Wright, S. (2012) 'Welfare-to-work, agency and personal responsibility', *Journal of Social Policy*, 41(2): 309–28.

Wright, S. (2016) 'Conceptualising the active welfare subject: welfare reform in discourse, policy and lived experience', *Policy and Politics*, 44(2): 235–52.

Wright, S. (2023) *Women and Welfare Conditionality: Lived Experiences of Benefit Sanctions, Work and Welfare*, Bristol: Policy Press.

Wright, S. and Dwyer, P. (2022) 'In-work Universal Credit: claimant experiences of conditionality mismatches and counterproductive benefit sanctions', *Journal of Social Policy*, 51(1): 20–38.

Wright, S. and Patrick, R. (2019) 'Welfare conditionality in lived experience: aggregating qualitative longitudinal research', *Social Policy and Society*, 18(4): 597–613.

Wright, S., Fletcher, D.R. and Stewart, A.B. (2020) 'Punitive benefit sanctions, welfare conditionality, and the social abuse of unemployed people in Britain: transforming claimants into offenders?', *Social Policy and Administration*, 54(2): 278–94.

Wright, S., Dwyer, P., Jones, K., McNeill, J., Scullion, L. and Stewart, A.B. (2018) *Final Findings: Universal Credit*, Welfare Conditionality project report, www.welfareconditionality.ac.uk/wp-content/uploads/2018/05/40414-Universal-Credit-web.pdf

Young, I.M. (1995) 'Mothers, citizenship, and independence: a critique of pure family values', *Ethics*, 105(3): 535–56.

Zacka, B. (2017) *When the State Meets the Street: Public Service and Moral Agency*, Cambridge, MA: Harvard University Press.

Zadoroznyj, M. (2009) 'Professionals, carers or "strangers"? Liminality and the typification of postnatal home care workers', *Sociology*, 43(2): 268–85.

Zartler, U. (2014) 'How to deal with moral tales: constructions and strategies of single-parent families', *Journal of Marriage and Family*, 76(3): 604–19.

Index

A

Aberfan disaster 39
activism 9, 40–8, 48–51, 73, 120
   implicit activism 93
   working activists 79–83, 83–90, 121
Adamson, David 21
agency and choice 24
Alston, Philip 119
Army recruitment 34
Askins, K. 94
austerity 3, 5, 16, 23, 31, 121

B

belonging, sense of 37, 41, 94, 101, 102
benefits 8, 52
   effects of cuts 31
   eligibility 2, 9, 13, 65–71, 71–8
   incapacity premise 12
   'moving people off' 3, 76
   and poverty 5, 55, 55–7, 114
   sanctions 15, 22, 65, 66, 70–2, 75, 77–8
Berlant, Lauren 115
biographies 52, 125
   childhoods, traumatic 61–2
'broken' families 16

C

care, ethic of 123
care work (paid) 112
   health and care work 33
   work routines 25–6
caring roles 11
   conferring dignity 60
   recognition of 15, 22, 122
   seen as 'workless' 13
   women as carers 4
   for working-class women 44–5
   as 'worklessness' 2
   see also women
Cheryl 66, 73–4
childcare 42, 44, 109, 120
   and employment 60
   lack of 14, 15, 31
   and Lifeline 1, 45–6
children
   age thresholds 14, 15, 65
   attachment to 59
   child maintenance 58
   older children 110–11
   prioritising their needs 56–7
   traumatic childhoods 61–2, 71
   and working mothers 111
   see also childcare
choice, illusion of 24, 107, 116
Churchill, Winston 9, 38–9
citizenship 2, 3, 11, 123
   everyday practices 103
   'good' citizens 2, 11, 22, 112
   a valuable citizen 69
civil society
   see communities
class 9, 54, 107
   class-based struggle 93
   working-class life 16, 27–8, 35, 44–5, 57–9, 116
coal/steel 26–7, 30
   contraction of 28
   miners' strikes 29, 38–9
collective memories 38–9, 121
college courses 46–8, 54, 82, 105, 111, 113
communities 32–7, 38–9
   Communities First 18–20
   community projects 17–21, 41, 94
   and de-industrialisation 31, 118–19
   shared experiences 27–8
   see also activism; Lifeline project
Conservative Party/governments 5, 20, 22, 29, 70
   Welfare Reform and Work Act 2016 14
counselling 107
COVID-19 25, 112, 113

D

debt 57, 59, 62, 71, 85
de-industrialisation 5, 20–1, 31, 38, 118–19
dependency 15–16, 22
deserving/undeserving poor 11, 23, 35
Diana 41, 43, 44–8, 80, 88–9
domestic abuse 15, 58, 72, 90, 97, 119
Dudley, Kathryn 119

E

education 46–7, 54, 63, 81, 82, 90, 95–6
   moving into 6, 106–11, 114, 120
eligibility interviews 9, 13, 65–71, 71–8
employment 4, 33, 120
   availability for work 15
   care work 25–6, 33, 112
   'employability' 43, 48
   'job clubs' 34
   lack of jobs 31, 74
   low-paid work 4, 14, 31, 33, 42, 60, 69, 78
   male/female roles 30–1
   moving into work 109–14

NHS 26, 33–4, 67, 111
shift work 67
unemployment 12, 28, 33, 38
women and poor quality work 4
work in heavy industries 27–8
in-work poverty 4
see also childcare
Engels, F. 4
EQUAL Community Initiative 18–19
estate, the 8, 32–7, 40–1
  depictions of estates 35
ethnographic research 6–7
European Social Fund 18–19
everyday lives 2, 5, 24, 35, 41, 102
  acts of care 100
  biographies 52, 61–2, 125
  complexities of 122
  everyday politics 5–6
  and individual responsibilities 49
  and meritocracy 115
  in NW England 94
  and symbolic violence 54
  see also 'stories'
extractive industries 26, 27–8, 38

F

fathers 57–9
feminism 50, 122
financial sanctions 15, 22, 65, 66, 70–2, 75, 77–8
  appeals 73–4
food banks 3, 84, 119
Fraser, Nancy 123
funding 41, 45, 49
futures 104, 106, 107, 108, 114
  and optimism 115–16

G

gender 9, 35, 107
  and caring roles 44–5
  stereotypes 97
'girls' of Lifeline project 1, 52–63, 63–4
  view of themselves 9, 53
government policy 1
  'hostile' environment 70
  and the welfare state 11–17, 18–24
  see also Conservative Party/governments;
    Labour Party/government; welfare state
graduation ceremony 6–7, 47, 53

H

Hall, S.M. 94
Hanisch, Carole 5, 125
Hanley, Lynsey 6, 32
hardship and stigma 1, 48, 55, 98, 115, 118
health 31, 33, 77
  COVID-19 25, 112, 113

death rates 33
healthy living 42
ill-health 15, 90, 110
life expectancy 119
homelessness 62, 85, 119
Hoovers 28
Horton, J. 94
housing 32
  depictions of estates 35

I

individual responsibility 15, 124
Industrial Revolution 26–7
industry 38
  miners' strike 1984–85 29
  of South Wales 26–8
  see also de-industrialisation
inequalities 15, 23, 118, 124
  entrenched 122
  health 25
  in localities 3, 11
  and place-based policies 17–18
institutional settings 124
interviews, research 6–7
isolation 62–3, 94–5

J

Jimenez, L. 30
Jobcentres 8, 60, 64, 66, 71, 73, 77, 122
  conflict with education 113
  dehumanising systems 71–2
  eligibility interviews 9, 13, 65–71, 71–8
  online vacancy portal 70
  view of officials 74–6, 120
job searching 14, 15, 70, 74
Jobseeker's Allowance 13

K

Kraftl, P. 94

L

labour market 1, 2, 22
  see also employment
Labour Party/government 22, 42, 65
  and lone parent policy 5, 13–14
language/vocabulary 8, 70, 79, 107
  ideas of 'community' 18, 21
life histories 52, 61–2, 106
  'good' work ethic 113
  'stories' 66–8
  see also everyday lives
Lifeline project 5, 18, 41, 44–51, 78, 103, 121
  about the 'girls' 9, 52–63, 63–4
  Diana 41, 43, 44–8, 80, 88–9
  and future hope 115–16
  graduation ceremony 6–7, 47, 53
  impact of changes 114–15
  recruitment of staff 81, 88

a second chance 64, 113
'site of contestation' 8, 40
sociable atmosphere 94–5
study of 2–10
support workers 9, 79–83, 83–90, 91–2, 120
see also education; employment
listened to, being 86, 88, 92, 97
literacy 73–4
lone mothers 3, 4, 8, 42, 52, 110
  age thresholds of children 14–15, 65
  and Lifeline 44
  myths and moral panics 16
  New Deal for Lone Parents 5, 14
  and paid work 13
  recognition as caregivers 12
  seen as 'workless' 22
  see also Lifeline project; women
low esteem 62, 92, 104

M

male/female roles 30–1, 96
marginalisation 53–4, 97
marital status 2, 13
masculine pride 27, 30
Massey, Doreen 37
McKenzie, Lisa 6, 37, 63
men 30
  as breadwinners 2
  and dependent wives 12
  as fathers 57–9
  'macho' culture 34, 58
  male/female roles 30–1
  masculine pride 27
  working away from home 34
  work in heavy industries 26–7
  young men and work 30–1
meritocracy 15, 23, 107, 115
Millar, Jane 110
morality 7, 15–17, 49, 67, 76, 77
  double standard 58
Morris, L. 24, 64

N

Nadine 66, 75–6
National Assistance Act 1948 12
National Insurance Act 1946 12
Neale, Bren 6
neoliberalism 3
Neville, Angela 76–7
New Deal for Lone Parents 13
NHS 26, 33–4, 67, 111
Nicole 66, 71–2, 77
Nussbaum, Martha 69

P

paid work
  see employment

parenting, good 16
Pateman, Carole 12
patriarchal system 2, 12, 34
personal as political 5, 125
personal deficiency 22, 23
personal development 48, 106, 107, 109, 115, 126
places and prosperity 3, 31, 37, 39, 118–19
  marginalised places 17–18
  representations of deprived areas 23
Polletta, Francesca 124
post-industrial localities
  see de-industrialisation
post-war settlement 2, 9, 12, 15, 118
poverty 8, 15, 23, 124
  deserving/undeserving poor 11, 23, 35
  hunger marches 28
  as individual failing 22, 23, 24
  lives of Lifeline girls 55–7
  and miners' strike 30
  and the pandemic 25
  poverty porn 35–7
  in-work poverty 4, 31
pride 27, 30, 37, 38, 101, 112
professional workers, view of 54
psychological referrals 14
pub gathering 25
Public and Commercial Services Union 66
public issues and personal troubles 5
public services 3, 16, 31

Q

qualifications 33, 42, 43, 47, 48, 63, 90, 108, 111
quality of life 33, 113

R

Ravn, Signe 114
reading and writing 73–4
refugees in NE England 94
reinvention 104, 105
relationships 59, 102
  of care 99–101, 120
  close family relationships 60–1
  with support workers 85–7
  through Lifeline 1
representations
  of deprived areas 23
  of housing estates 35–7
  of poor/unemployed 16, 23
  of young people 41
research 6–7
resilience 82–3, 91
resistance 37, 66, 69, 70, 92, 94, 119
respect 69, 85, 86, 117
  culture of 80
reunion 7

Ridge, Teresa 110
right-wing views 124

S

Sarah 66, 67–8, 70, 77
Sayer, Andrew 70
second chance 64, 113
Sennett, Richard 69
sexual abuse/violence 58, 61
shame 23, 70, 74
  and employment 30
shared experiences 90, 96–8, 102
shared values and beliefs 79, 93
Skeggs, B. 116
Smart, Carol 6
social attitudes 124
socialism 27–8
social security
  see benefits
societal injustice 24
solidarities 27–8, 93, 98, 102, 120, 125
South Wales Valleys 1, 8
  and community projects 18–19
  de-industrialisation 20, 24, 31
  deprived communities in 18
  economic cycles 38
  financial sanctions in 72
  industry of 26–8
  living in 118–19
  male/female roles in 27, 29–31
  miners' strike 29–30
  solidarity and socialism 27–8
special occasions 56
St Ann's, Nottingham 37
state, the
  a common enemy 39
  state dependency 14
Steedman, Carolyn 118
stigma 11, 15, 36–7, 48, 70, 98
  of housing estates 35
'stories' 66–8, 77, 98, 99
  of the Job centre interviews 67–9, 71–3
  of reinvention 105, 106
street-level provisioning 5, 17
street-level workers 76, 77
  officials under pressure 74–5
support 9, 40, 48, 100–1, 103, 121
  from family 60–1, 110
support workers 79–83, 83–90, 92, 94–5, 120
surveillance 15, 16, 54, 70

T

talk, opportunity to 97–8, 125
Tebbit, Norman 29
teenagers, pregnant 16
television depictions of estate 35

Tirado, Linda 6
trade unions 27, 75, 76, 124
training, compulsory 14
trajectories 104, 107, 110
  moving into education/work 109–14
trust, cultivating 80, 90, 99
Tyler, Imogen 4, 11, 70

U

unemployment
  see employment
Unite Community 66, 73
United Nations 119
Universal Credit 14
university 6, 47, 108, 110, 111

V

values 11, 15, 24, 38, 52, 79, 89, 109

W

Welfare Reform and Work Act 2016 14
welfare state 1, 2, 3, 43, 118
  in alternative places 4–5
  contracted-out services 17
  failing to support 77
  restructuring of the 11–17, 18–24, 123–4
  welfare conditionality 3, 5, 14, 22, 65–6, 70, 72, 77–8, 122
welfare resettlement 8, 9, 15, 21
Welsh Government Communities First 18–20
Wetherspoons 25, 26
widows 2, 12
Williams, Raymond 39
Willis, P. 116
Wire, Nicky 63
women
  bringing together 125
  caring and working 4
  and caring roles 22, 27, 29, 44–5
  changing their lives 119–20
  and community projects 41
  economic dependence on men 12
  effect of cuts on 3–4
  'getting by' 55, 114
  'holding family together' 34
  of the Lifeline project 5, 52–63, 63–4
  and low-paid work 77–8
  male/female roles 2, 27, 29, 30–1
  personal development 48
  and policy environment 122
  and strike activism 29
  and welfare conditionality 65–6, 70, 72, 77–8
  working women 33
  see also education; employment; support workers

Index

Workers' Educational association (WEA) 46–7
working-class life 63, 116
  and caring 44–5
  communities 27–8
  depictions of estates 35
  fathers 57–9
Working Links 17
Work Programme 14
Wright, Sharon 72, 122

www.ingramcontent.com/pod-product-compliance
Lightning Source LLC
Chambersburg PA
CBHW071709020426
42333CB00017B/2196